Identity Capitalists

IDENTITY CAPITALISTS

*The Powerful Insiders Who Exploit
Diversity to Maintain Inequality*

Nancy Leong

STANFORD UNIVERSITY PRESS
Stanford, California

STANFORD UNIVERSITY PRESS
Stanford, California

Printed in the United States of America on acid-free, archival-quality paper

Library of Congress Cataloging-in-Publication Data
Names: Leong, Nancy, author.
Title: Identity capitalists : the powerful insiders who exploit diversity to maintain
    inequality / Nancy Leong.
Description: Stanford, California : Stanford University Press, 2021. |
    Includes bibliographical references and index.
Identifiers: LCCN 2020020328 (print) | LCCN 2020020329 (ebook) |
    ISBN 9781503610132 (cloth) | ISBN 9781503614277 (epub)
Subjects: LCSH: Group identity—United States. | Cultural pluralism—
    United States. | Exploitation—Social aspects—United States. | Exploitation—
    Economic aspects—United States. | Minorities—United States—
    Social conditions. | Discrimination—Law and legislation—United States.
Classification: LCC HN59.2 .L466 2021 (print) | LCC HN59.2 (ebook) |
    DDC 305.800973—dc23
LC record available at https://lccn.loc.gov/2020020328
LC ebook record available at https://lccn.loc.gov/2020020329

Cover design: Rob Ehle

Cover background: iStockphoto

Text design: Kevin Barrett Kane

Typeset at Stanford University Press in 11/15 Adobe Garamond Pro

To Scott

Contents

Identity Capitalists

Introduction

GETTING USED

THE ENVELOPE IN MY MAILBOX, lettered in delicate callig-
raphy, was a surprise. A decade had passed since my college friend
and I had been close. Our communications in recent years had
mostly taken the form of brief messages on social media. Still, I've learned
that people do funny things when they're getting married. I marked off "will
attend" on the little card and found myself a date and a dress.

It was a beautiful ceremony and reception; indeed, with only sixty people
or so in attendance, I was both surprised and honored to be included at a
relatively intimate event. Late in the day—after we'd heard toasts, after we'd
eaten cake, after she'd downed several glasses of champagne—my friend
threw her arms around me. "I am so glad that you could come tonight,"
she said, glowing with happiness. And then: "I mean, if you hadn't been
here"—she lowered her voice a little and gestured around the room with a
self-deprecating laugh—"everyone here would have been *white*." And then

she waved the photographer over to take a picture of us together. A few days later she posted it on Facebook.

I have a copy of that picture. We're smiling like any two longtime friends at a celebration. But the photo also captures a moment when something changed. At the time, I didn't tell my friend that I found her comment off-putting. I couldn't bring myself to cast the slightest shadow on her wedding day. At the same time, I was no longer nearly so surprised, nor nearly so honored, to have been included in the guest list. I realized that I was not at the wedding solely in my capacity as an old friend. I realized that my friend valued my presence for other reasons. I realized that I was part of the color scheme, just like the bridesmaids' dresses and the flowers on the tables. I realized that when my friend thought of me, she saw a particular kind of opportunity—and she capitalized on it.

The drive back to my hotel that night marked the moment that I first named identity capitalism to myself. I had noticed this sort of behavior before: the way someone accused of sexism would immediately talk about his devotion to his daughters, or the way a college's website inevitably features a lot of photos of people of color, or the way a company sued for sex discrimination would point to its female executives. But that night was the first time that I saw these disconnected observations as pieces of a puzzle that, when put together, formed a larger picture.

When I looked at the big picture, I saw people of one identity group trying to benefit from the identity of another group. White people trying to benefit from people of color. Men trying to benefit from women. The beneficiaries were generally the ingroup—the group that controlled power and resources.[1] And the source of the benefit was always the outgroup—the group, often a numerical minority, without access to the ingroup's power and resources.

Ingroup members already get a lot of benefit from their own identities. A brief in the famous Supreme Court case *Plessy v. Ferguson*, which upheld state-sanctioned racial segregation, argued that whiteness was "the most valuable sort of property."[2] Today, the benefits of whiteness remain. White people are less likely to be the victims of unjustified force by police officers. They are treated better at places of business and receive better prices while doing business. People with white-identified names receive better mentorship in school and more job opportunities after school. Society perceives white people as more intelligent, more competent, more reliable, and more attractive.

Whiteness provides countless advantages, and, perhaps unsurprisingly, it turns out that one is the opportunity to benefit from nonwhite people. Having a nonwhite person around can, for example, enhance a white person's social status. Many white people want to seem cosmopolitan and most very much want to avoid seeming racist. Having a nonwhite friend is one solution. Although I doubt she spelled it out to herself quite so explicitly—at least not until after the champagne—I am sure this is at least part of the reason my long-ago friend wanted me at her wedding.

This behavior isn't limited to race. It might also extend to gender, sexual orientation, disability status, or other identity categories. In each case, the identity ingroup—men, straight people, the non-disabled—can benefit in certain ways from those outside their identity group, who are often members of historically disempowered groups. These benefits can take many forms: economic, social, political, or even simply psychological. Sometimes an ingroup member wants to achieve social status, like my friend at her wedding. Other times the ingroup member wants to refute a claim of bigotry: "I can't be racist (or sexist, or homophobic) if I have a friend who is Latino (or a woman, or gay)."

And the effort to benefit from outgroups is not limited to individual behavior. Institutions controlled by an ingroup also benefit from individuals not part of the ingroup. Colleges and universities enhance their appeal to prospective students by featuring members of outgroups in their promotional materials. Businesses hoping to attract clients or customers showcase outgroup employees on their websites or outgroup models in their pitches. Politicians attempting to broaden their appeal seek outgroup surrogates or feature outgroup members in their advertisements.

These efforts by ingroup members to benefit from outgroup members are examples of what I call *identity capitalism*, and ingroup members who profit from outgroup identity are *identity capitalists*. This book takes a hard look at identity capitalists. It examines the motivations and tracks the consequences of identity capitalism: for identity capitalists themselves, for other ingroup members, for members of outgroups, for institutions, and for society as a whole.

Identity capitalists are everywhere. Some are ordinary people going about their daily lives. Others are famous politicians, entertainers, CEOs, and public intellectuals. One prominent identity capitalist is Donald Trump, the forty-fifth president of the United States. Trump is a consummate ingroup member: a heterosexual white man born into great wealth and social status. Even among politicians—many of whom are notable identity capitalists—Trump's behavior stands out. In 2015, then-presidential candidate Trump addressed a black man in the audience by saying, "Look at my African-American over here." He then told a story designed to demonstrate that he had substantial support among black people. His message was clear: black people support me, check it out, there's even one right here at my rally. Yet Trump's disapproval ratings among black people typically hover in the 80 percent range, and only 6 percent of black voters cast a ballot for Trump in the 2016 presidential election.[3] This disapproval reflects Trump's statements and policies as president. On issues ranging from his fondness for Confederate monuments, to his disapproval of black football players kneeling to protest police violence, to his insistence that white supremacists in Charlottesville are "very fine people," his administration has offered virtually no concrete support for issues important to a large percentage of black people.

Lest anyone think that identity capitalism is reserved for right-wing politicians, I give you Bernie Sanders, independent member of Congress from Vermont for nearly three decades and runner up in the 2016 Democratic presidential primary. Sanders has trumpeted his civil-rights-era affiliations: he (and two hundred and fifty thousand other people) participated the 1963 March on Washington, where Martin Luther King Jr. gave his "I Have a Dream" speech; later, Sanders was arrested during a demonstration against public school segregation in Chicago. By emphasizing these affiliations repeatedly, Sanders' message is clear: I'm with the black people. Yet Sanders has accomplished little of racial substance in the intervening fifty years leading up to the 2016 presidential contest, thirty-five of which he spent in elected office. As a senator, he sponsored only three bills that were signed into law, two of which were about naming post offices. He appears acutely uncomfortable when the topic of race arises, usually turning the conversation back to economic, rather than explicitly racial, justice. In a typical pivot, he cited Martin Luther King Jr.: "We have got to look at the candidates . . . not by the color of their skin, not by their sexual orientation or their gender and not by their age. I mean, I think we have got to try to move us toward a nondiscriminatory society, which looks at people based on their abilities."[4] In polls, a substantial majority of black people are skeptical of Sanders, and that skepticism emerges in traditional and social media. During one rally, the hashtag #BernieSoBlack trended, including sarcastic comments such as "#BernieSoBlack he wrote MLK's 'I have a dream' speech," "#BernieSoBlack He founded Wakanda," and "#BernieSoBlack that if elected, he will be our first black president." Bernie's attempt to capitalize on his civil rights affiliations from half a century ago does not equate to tangible racial progress now. And racial skepticism of Sanders emerged throughout the 2016 presidential primary: Sanders won only 14 percent of the black vote in South Carolina, 14 percent in Georgia, 11 percent in Mississippi, and a pitiful 6 percent in Alabama.[5]

Like Trump and Sanders, identity capitalists are doing nothing of substance by showcasing their affiliations with members of racial outgroups. A superficial affiliation with a member of an outgroup means nothing on its own. Strategically taking a photo with a person of color to post on social media doesn't mean you have a deep and honest friendship with them that transcends racial barriers. Casting a person of color for a few speaking lines in an otherwise all-white sitcom doesn't signify real progress toward racial equality in the entertainment industry. And hiring a woman at an all-male startup is not in itself a noteworthy contribution to gender equality. But identity capitalists act like these superficial gestures ought to earn them all the credit in the world.

Really, though, what's so wrong with identity capitalism? Occasionally interacting with people with something other than true, pure affection or appreciation is just part of life. Everyone has an identity. Don't we inherently gain value from one another's identities as part of our relationships with them? One could argue that outgroup members are simply laboring under the same rules as all of us are—just, in some cases, for different reasons.

I disagree. Identity capitalism harms both individual members of out-groups and society as a whole in ways significant and serious. Outgroups suffer under the pressure to be who the ingroup wants them to be. A company may wish to hire more women, but only those women who dress in conventionally feminine ways, wear makeup, smile tolerantly at sexist jokes, and don't mind organizing the annual holiday party in their free time. Women who don't want to do those things—or perhaps *can't* do those things—face an unattractive choice: either forfeit professional and personal opportunities, or else set aside the way they would prefer to act and perform the way the company wants them to perform. Allowing ingroups to set the agenda for how outgroup members should act is deeply harmful to the outgroup.

Identity capitalism also harms society as a whole. At a time when America is deeply divided, identity capitalism fuels racial resentment. Nobody wants to feel as though someone is their friend only for the purpose of posting photos on social media or dabbling in an unfamiliar culture. Nobody wants to feel as though a school admitted them or a company hired them purely to show off their identity. When such incidents are common, outgroup members view even sincere expressions of appreciation as dubious. Identity capitalism stands in the way of deeper and more authentic relationships among members of different groups.

Perpetrating or tolerating identity capitalism gives the impression that everything is fine when it's not, and that all of us are treated equally when we're not. Identity capitalism distracts from and displaces real substantive reform. This leads to misconceptions: more than half of white Americans believe that discrimination against them is as big a problem as discrimination against any other race, notwithstanding that a mountain of social science evidence begs to differ.[6] Identity capitalism promotes the dangerous myth that black people and other outgroups are getting all the advantages while white people and other ingroups are the real victims. Worse, to embrace identity capitalism uncritically is to endorse fake diversity at the expense of real progress. Real progress would give outgroups substantive power in arenas ranging from home to school to work to politics to business to sports to entertainment. Identity capitalism just approximates the appearance of progress.

Identity capitalism is not about promoting tolerance, diversity, inclusion, or equality. It's about self-interest and power. Self-interest, because individuals and institutions use identity capitalism to make themselves look good. Power, because in order to attempt identity capitalism in the first place, an individual or an institution has to belong to an ingroup in some way.[7] Identity capitalism is an effort to gain the social status associated with diversity without doing any of the difficult work to make substantive racial progress a reality.

What about the targets of identity capitalism? Although identity capitalism is driven by ingroups, members of outgroups are not necessarily oblivious or involuntary participants. Some outgroup members are conscripted into the process of identity capitalism without their consent, or in some instances, without even their knowledge. The black man Trump called out at his rally, Gregory Cheadle, later told reporters that he was not a Trump supporter and that it was "surreal" to be addressed by Trump. While Trump tried to use Cheadle's identity to insinuate that his campaign had support among black people, Cheadle hadn't approved of the message in advance: it was an identity capitalism stealth attack.

But not every target of identity capitalism is as surprised as Cheadle. Media personalities Diamond and Silk—legally named Lynnette Hardaway and Rochelle Richardson—are self-described "biological sisters" who have made a career out of being black women who are willing to vouch for the Republican Party and, more specifically, for Donald Trump. The duo campaigned for Trump in several states, were pulled onstage by him in Raleigh to (in his words) "do a little routine" that echoed his talking points, and during his presidency have remained frequent guests on Fox News and other conservative media.[8] They started a "Ditch and Switch" initiative to encourage people to leave the Democratic Party and register as Republicans. They were featured in a documentary called *Dummycrats*, which disparaged the Democratic Party. They characterize themselves as "President Trump's most Outspoken and Loyal Supporters."

Diamond and Silk are what I call *identity entrepreneurs*. Rather than unknowingly or passively getting pulled into identity capitalism, the sisters actively leveraged their identity as black women and used it to their advantage. They made their race and gender salient to Trump, the Republican Party, and the public at large. Unlike many black women in politics or entertainment who tailor their behavior to mainstream cultural norms driven by white men, Diamond and Silk unabashedly embody stereotypes about black women to a level that many black people see as caricature. Black activist Bree Newsome has called them "a modern day minstrel show."[9] The two use traditionally black dialect and mannerisms to spout Trump talking points. They embody the sassy black woman that many Trump supporters want to befriend to prove they aren't racist, with the crucial distinction that Diamond and Silk also say things that Trump supporters want to hear. After 94 percent of black women voters cast ballots against Donald Trump,[10] Diamond and Silk are a rare commodity, and as entrepreneurs they know that this inflates their value.

Diamond and Silk have profited from their identity entrepreneurship. Riding the wave of Trump's success, they went from obscure vloggers to national fame almost overnight, and they run a lucrative business ranging from their various media activities to the merchandise they sell on their website. (Sample item: coffee mug bearing the slogan "Trump's Yo President," $25.) They went on a speaking tour that offered fans the chance to see them live for $50 a ticket, or $150 for VIP access including a reception and photo. They have over a million Twitter followers and more than two hundred thousand YouTube subscribers.

Diamond and Silk's efforts demonstrate both the benefits and limits of identity entrepreneurship. For an entrepreneur to leverage her identity successfully, her identity must be visible to the ingroup yet must also take a form of which the ingroup approves. Diamond and Silk are successful identity entrepreneurs precisely because their appearance and demeanor are both unmistakably black and entirely unthreatening to members of the ingroup. They offer an opportunity for Republicans, and particularly Trump and his supporters, to defend their political party against accusations of racism and misogyny—without actually doing the hard work of examining whether their party or its leaders say racist and misogynistic things.

Diamond, Silk, and other identity entrepreneurs play a high-stakes game. Their willing participation in identity capitalism can yield considerable social and economic advantages. But they also run the risk that their value to the ingroup will expire, and they limit what they can say and do while still accessing these advantages. If Diamond and Silk suddenly announced their vehement support for the Black Lives Matter movement, no doubt the many benefits bestowed by the Republican Party would be swiftly withdrawn. As political commentator Keith Boykin explains, "If these two women, the way they speak, the way they talk and act and behave, were saying anything that was contradictory to Trump, the Trump supporters who defend them would be the first to attack them."[11]

Identity entrepreneurship also has serious and far-ranging consequences beyond the individual entrepreneur. Commentators express concern about the way that Diamond and Silk reinforce stereotypes that are superficially harmless but in fact damaging to a group's equal status in society. Newsome suggests that the duo's performance is targeted at "white conservatives who want to believe Trump can't be racist or they themselves can't be racist because there are these two black women named Diamond and Silk who are constantly rooting for Trump." In the long run, identity entrepreneurs may damage the interests of their own outgroup while yielding rewards for a few privileged outgroup members. Diamond and Silk are making money, visiting the Oval Office, and starring in their own movie. But meanwhile, according to the Institute for Women's Policy Research, the median black woman in the United States makes $33,600—only 64.6 percent of the earnings of the median white man—and black women over age sixty-five are more than twice as likely to live in poverty as white women in the same age group.[12] Identity entrepreneurship helps *individual members* of outgroups, but it rarely helps the outgroup as a whole.

Identity capitalism is intricately intertwined with law. Four decades ago, in 1978, the Supreme Court endorsed diversity as a rationale for affirmative action in *Regents of the University of California v. Bakke*.[13] In his opinion, Justice Lewis Powell declared, "[T]he attainment of a diverse student body . . . clearly is a constitutionally permissible goal for an institution of higher education."[14] Powell's solo-authored opinion brought diversity mainstream. Thanks to him, diversity became *the* way to justify affirmative action, and this legal preoccupation with diversity both reflects and reinforces identity capitalism.

This is not to say that affirmative action jurisprudence invented identity capitalism. Identity capitalism has been part of American history from the beginning and, as a result of the incentives and pressures created by identity capitalism, so has identity entrepreneurship. Nor was the *Bakke* opinion's reliance on diversity what brought diversity to the forefront of our culture. Indeed, "diversity" was part of our lexicon decades before *Bakke*.

Still, *Bakke* helped bring diversity to the legal foreground. As a result of the legal significance of diversity, the Supreme Court has come to rely increasingly on the importance of diversity and, therefore, so have litigators, policymakers, and the general public. Indeed, an entire industry has emerged around diversity. Today, "diversity consultant" is a profession. Companies have diversity officers. Schools have deans or entire offices dedicated to diversity. Publications, movies, political movements, sports teams, businesses, and other organizations are evaluated on whether they are diverse. They are praised when they are and criticized when they are not.

There is nothing wrong with diversity—indeed, quite the opposite. Research has shown that diversity improves outcomes in many areas of human endeavor.[15] In a Credit Suisse study of two thousand global companies, those with at least one woman on their board had higher returns on equity, lower debt ratios, and better average growth. A Gallup survey found that hospitality businesses with significant diversity have 19 percent greater profits than those that are not diverse.[16] Research has shown that diverse groups make better decisions and exhibit more creativity.[17] In educational settings, researchers have found that racial diversity improves critical thinking, particularly among members of ingroups.[18]

But one result of the emphasis on diversity—or, at least, the appearance of diversity—is an enhanced incentive for identity capitalism. Ingroup individuals and institutions want the social and legal credit associated with diversity. So they engage in practices that seem to display diversity to get the credit, but without undertaking the work that makes the credit deserved. Again, identity capitalism is not new. But the explosion of the diversity industry has led to an unprecedented explosion in the incidence of identity capitalism.

Beyond affirmative action, other areas of the law reward identity capitalism. Laws prohibiting discrimination in schools, workplaces, and housing encourage those sued for discrimination to showcase members of outgroups as a defense. Other areas of the law, ranging from criminal justice to intellectual property to tort to contract, provide similar incentives. The American legal system is rife with identity capitalism.

As a lawyer and law professor, I find myself simultaneously fascinated and repelled by identity capitalism precisely because of the way it infects our legal system. But this explanation for my preoccupation with identity capitalism is incomplete. As a woman of color who grew up in a predominantly white suburb, who attended a predominantly white college and then a predominantly white law school, who pursued a profession that remains predominantly white and predominantly male, I have often found myself the target of identity capitalism. My photo has been on the websites. My friendship has been the defense against racism and sexism. My name has been added to conference lineups so that that the conference wouldn't (as the organizers realize late in the game) end up being all white, or all male, because that would "look bad." And, yes, my presence has been the bulwark against the dreaded all-white wedding. I hope to convince you that we are all participants in identity capitalism, willing or not, witting or not—me included.

My primary purpose in this book is not to vilify identity capitalists or people who participate in identity capitalism, although many do have troubling motivations and cause great harm. Rather, I'm hoping not only to describe a problem but also to propose some ways of solving it. I will explore how the law reflects and encourages identity capitalism. And I will explain several legal reforms that could remove incentives for identity capitalism and substitute incentives for real, substantive reform.

But the law alone cannot complete such reforms. We also need better policies. We need leadership from the public and private sectors. We need investment from corporations and universities. And we—as individuals, with our colleagues, with our friends—need to do the hard work of searching our own minds and hearts for the truth about the way we relate to one another and our reasons for doing so.

Mitigating the harmful effects of identity capitalism will not be easy. But it will be worth the struggle. Improving relationships among different identity groups in America requires a painfully honest reckoning with our current system of identity exploitation and a sincere, collective resolve to do better.

1

FAKE DIVERSITY

DIALLO SHABAZZ was a student at the University of Wisconsin when he caught sight of the school's admissions booklet. The photograph should have been unremarkable: a group of Wisconsin-clad students cheering at a football game. But what Shabazz saw caused him to do a double take. It was his own face. But he had never been to a Wisconsin football game.

The image on the left in Figure 1.1 is the original photograph. The image on the right appeared on the cover of the University of Wisconsin's admissions brochure in 2001. At a quick glance they might appear identical, but upon closer inspection we see that Shabazz was added behind the right shoulder of the woman in the white sweatshirt. As Shabazz put it, "I saw my head cut off and kind of pasted onto the front cover of the admissions booklet."[1] Over one hundred thousand copies of the brochure went out to prospective students.

FIGURE 1.1. A photograph of students at a University of Wisconsin football game (left) and an altered version of the photograph as it appeared on the cover of the 2001 University of Wisconsin admissions brochure (right).

Why did the admissions office alter the photo this way? Investigation by Shabazz and others revealed that, when presented with a staff selection for the initial photo of the brochure, Wisconsin's admissions office found the choice lacking. "Find something more diverse," admissions staffers were told. The result was the photoshopped insertion of Shabazz.

The school officials responsible for the photoshopping decision apologized to Shabazz and to the broader community, and the school's application materials were reprinted at a cost of about $64,000. But this was not enough for Shabazz. He sent the university a letter indicating his intent to sue. The university eventually settled with Shabazz. He sought and received a "budgetary apology" in the form of $10 million earmarked for recruitment of minority students and diversity initiatives within the University of Wisconsin system. Yet even after the University of Wisconsin was roundly shamed, and even after its settlement with Shabazz, the school continued to defend its actions. "Our intentions were good" even if "our methods were bad," explained the director of university publications. The director of undergraduate admissions agreed, contending that the photoshop incident "was not an attempt—ever— to mislead, but to show the diversity that exists on campus."[2]

While Shabazz objected strongly to his manufactured appearance in the University of Wisconsin's admissions brochure, not everyone recruited into a misleading promotional campaign feels the same way. In 2008, presidential candidate John McCain chose Sarah Palin as his running mate. When McCain selected Palin, she was a little-known governor from Alaska, and his choice sent shock waves through the election cycle.

Comments from Republican Party insiders indicate that Palin's selection was partly—perhaps mostly—an effort to win over women voters disappointed that Hillary Clinton was not the Democratic Party's nominee for president, and that Barack Obama had not chosen Clinton as his running mate. Former Arkansas governor Mike Huckabee voiced the sentiments of the party when he stated, "Governor Palin . . . will remind women that if they are not welcome on the Democrat's ticket, they have a place with Republicans."[3] Commentator Jim Geraghty characterized Palin as "probably the only pick McCain could make who could simultaneously appeal to Hillary supporters who think sexism cost her the nomination, *and* consolidate large swaths of the conservative base."[4]

The strategy had mixed results. One in three white women said that they were more likely to vote for McCain after he selected Palin, although many also saw the selection primarily as political calculation—59 percent took this view, according to one poll, including an even higher percentage of women who identify as independent.[5] But other women found the choice off-putting. "You think I'm stupid," commentator Kaili Joy Gray accused McCain. "You think I will forget every single one of my personal and political values just because there's a vagina on your pro-war, anti-woman, anti-science ticket." McCain and Palin lost the election—although it is an unanswerable question whether McCain would have done better if he had selected a man as his running mate.

Diallo Shabazz and Sarah Palin may seem like an odd pairing. And there are obvious differences between the two—for example, Palin was brought onto the national stage with her knowledge and consent. Still, certain similarities in their treatment deserve reflection. In each instance, an institution—the University of Wisconsin, the Republican Party—found value in presenting an outsider as one of its own.

Shabazz and Palin illustrate the phenomenon of *identity capitalism*. Identity capitalism is a process in which an ingroup benefits from outgroup identity. In America today, the ingroup is usually white, male, heterosexual, and wealthy. These characteristics describe ingroups in most workplaces and institutions of higher education. It's true of ingroups in Hollywood and in Congress. It's true of America as a whole.

Both individuals and institutions—which, after all, are just collections of individuals—can be identity capitalists. Individual members of ingroups can benefit from associations with outgroup members, such as friends, romantic partners, or colleagues. Institutions that are dominated by members of one or more ingroups—schools, workplaces, political parties, retailers— can similarly benefit from associations with outgroup members—students, workers, viewers, consumers. Ingroup individuals and institutions both benefit from outgroups. Some potential benefits are economic, such as increased revenue, new business relationships, or broader marketing appeal. Other benefits are noneconomic, such as social status, moral authority, or credibility with outgroup members.

To be clear, diversity is not a bad thing. Research has demonstrated that diversity has many benefits. And showcasing diversity is not necessarily a bad thing either. It communicates that diversity is important to the institution doing the showcasing—a message important to many stakeholders, ranging from prospective students to prospective donors. Most of us have been identity capitalists at one time or another, and our behavior is not always harmful. The problem arises, however, when displays of diversity misrepresent the reality of diversity and mislead the viewer, in the process using a member of an outgroup as a prop—as was the case with both the University of Wisconsin and the Republican Party.

The University of Wisconsin's racial photoshopping adventure was an attempt to gain both economic and noneconomic benefits. In 2000, the school was predominantly white: at the time Shabazz was enrolled, only 2 percent of the undergraduate student population was black. The school sought to benefit economically by photoshopping Diallo Shabazz into its brochure. Diversity is a selling point in higher education. Showcasing racial diversity in an admissions brochure is an appeal to tuition-paying students—white students who value diversity as well as nonwhite students who wish to attend a school where they will not be racially isolated. Likewise, the University of Wisconsin hoped to attract donations from alumni who care about diversity. But the school also hoped for noneconomic benefits. By displaying a racially diverse group of students on its cover, the school sought to communicate a positive message about the current state of race relations on its campus. The school tried to gain the social status associated with diversity and racial harmony. In its attempt to derive value from Shabazz's racial identity, the University of Wisconsin became an identity capitalist.

By selecting Sarah Palin as the vice-presidential nominee, John McCain and the Republican Party attempted a similar move. More men identify as Republican than women, and the Republican Party's lack of enthusiasm for issues many people see issues of particular interest to women—parental leave, pay equality, and reproductive health—has damaged the party's image with many women voters. The party hoped to appeal to precisely those voters with the choice of Palin. Like the University of Wisconsin, the Republican Party sought both economic and noneconomic benefits. By signaling to women that the Republican Party cared about women, the party hoped to gain political advantage—and, ultimately, votes. And by putting McCain and Palin in power, the party hoped to implement a policy agenda that would benefit its wealthy supporters by lowering taxes, cutting social programs, and appointing conservative judges.

Identity capitalism is common and pervasive. A mostly white law firm that plasters its website with photos of people of color is an identity capitalist. A politician accused of homophobia who indignantly invokes his many gay friends is an identity capitalist. A corporation sued for sex discrimination that refers reporters to its percentage of women employees is an identity capitalist. A television producer who belatedly includes one black character in an otherwise all-white cast is an identity capitalist. Anyone who has ever said they can't be racist because they have a black friend, or that they can't be misogynist because they coach a girls' basketball team, is an identity capitalist.

Once we start paying attention to identity capitalism, we see that it's everywhere. It's at school and at work. It's in politics and in entertainment. It's in every branch of government, in policy papers and in judicial decisions, in history and in current events. It's woven into the laws that govern our society. Identity capitalism is a part of American society itself.

Look at All My Black Friends, Part I

"I've always had a great relationship with the blacks," then presidential hopeful Donald Trump said in 2011.[6] His words were received with considerable skepticism. After all, way back in 1973, the Nixon administration sued the Trump Management Corporation for violating the Fair Housing Act by refusing to rent to black applicants. In 1989, Trump stirred racist sentiments by taking out newspaper ads against the Central Park Five—four black teenagers and one Latino—accused of raping a jogger in New York City; he later refused to acknowledge that the five were innocent, even after their convictions were vacated and the city paid $41 million to them in a settlement. And he spent years spreading the unfounded conspiracy theory that President Barack Obama was not born in the United States, even sending his own investigators to Obama's birthplace in Hawaii.

Identity capitalism has long been a favored tool for politicians accused of racial insensitivity. After Hurricane Katrina in 2005, Kanye West made headlines when he stated on live television: "George Bush doesn't care about black people." West's impromptu remarks reflected the devastation of black communities in New Orleans—partly the result of flooding in disproportionately black areas affected by poorly built levees, and partly the federal government's inadequate response to those horrific conditions. Bush later called West's criticism "an all-time low" in his presidency. But at the time, he immediately turned to identity capitalism. He accepted an invitation to speak to the NAACP after declining to do so for several years in a row. During the speech, he name-dropped many black people with whom he'd worked or socialized: Bruce Gordon, Donna Brazile, "Condi" Rice, and others.[7] He explicitly referred to some as his "friends": Tony Evans, a well-known Dallas pastor, and Bob Johnson, the founder of Black Entertainment Television. Bush's identity capitalist message was that if specific black individuals liked him, then it refuted Kanye's charge that he didn't care about black *people*.

Ironically, Kanye West—the impetus for President Bush's identity capitalism—a dozen years later became the target of identity capitalism by Donald Trump. At Trump's invitation, West attended a highly photographed lunch in the White House wearing a "Make America Great Again" hat. Parallel to Bush's speech, the message was that West's supposed affection for Trump overrode Trump's long history of racial insensitivity and over-whelming unpopularity with black people. West is far from the only target of Trump's identity capitalism relating to black people. Trump's Twit-ter feed showcases the small number of black people who support him in some capacity: Clarence Thomas, one of the most conservative justices on the Supreme Court. Ben Carson, a one-time presidential candidate turned Trump cabinet member as Secretary of Housing and Urban Development. Candace Owen, a conservative media figure. And of course, Diamond and Silk—who, as noted in the Introduction, describe themselves as "President Trump's most Outspoken and Loyal Supporters."

David Duke—former "Grand Wizard" of the Ku Klux Klan and mem-ber of the Louisiana legislature—is also an identity capitalist. Duke claims that he "got into the racial thing through the rational arguments I saw in science," a racial "awakening" that led him to join the Ku Klux Klan in his senior year of high school. He also says, "I had a lot of black friends at the time. It was difficult to shed my emotional commitment to the equality of blacks. I had a lot of guilt feelings. But I couldn't deny the facts."[8] Duke's faceless posse of alleged black friends serves a particular rhetorical purpose: the subtext is that he was predisposed to reject the science given his warm feelings for his friends, and yet by approaching the topic rationally he was still convinced. The theme continued during college, where, Duke claimed, "Even the blacks and Jews respected me"—even though he was perhaps best known for wearing a Nazi uniform with a swastika armband.

In politics, the I-have-black-friends-therefore-I'm-not-racist message is sel-dom subtle. It also isn't particularly logical. Even if a politician has a few black friends and associates, it doesn't mean that politician's platform is good for most black people. It doesn't mean that black people support the politician. It doesn't even mean the politician *likes* black people. Loathing for a group does not preclude affection for a few select members of that group. (Even Hitler had a few Jewish friends—he personally intervened to spare Ernst Hess, his Jewish former company commander from World War I, from the concen-tration camps, and he declared his Jewish friend and chauffeur Emil Maurice an "Honorary Aryan" and allowed him to serve in the German military.[9])

The lack of subtlety and logic is actually the point. If identity capital-ists were masters of racial sensitivity and nuance, they likely wouldn't be in the position of playing defense in the first place. Actions speak louder than words, and a politician whose track record is one of dedication to racial equality seldom needs to resort to listing their black friends to prove his or her racial bona fides. The same stunted racial understanding that leads identity capitalists to parade their black friends is often the root cause of the behavior for which they need to parade their friends as a defense.

Look at All the Women I Didn't Sexually Assault

"I have always had a lot of close female friends," Brett Kavanaugh said.[10] To many, his remark reveals a strategy a long time in the making. Even before he was accused of sexual assault by his high school acquaintance Christine Blasey Ford and college dorm-mate Deborah Ramirez, a lot of women didn't want Kavanaugh on the Supreme Court. Many women's rights groups opposed Kavanaugh's appointment from the time of his nomination, expressing particular concern for his views on reproductive rights and other issues affecting women's equality. During his confirmation hearings, women protested both outside and inside the Senate building, some dressed in white hoods and crimson robes evoking the subordinate status of women in the dystopian novel and television show *The Handmaid's Tale*. Throughout the hearing women protesters intermittently yelled out their objections before they were removed by security guards.

In response, Kavanaugh brought forward a parade of women. He was introduced by Condoleezza Rice, the former secretary of state, and Lisa Blatt, a self-described "liberal feminist lawyer" and partner at large law firm Arnold & Porter. The women testifying for him at his initial Senate confirmation hearing included a former student, two former law clerks, a former deputy solicitor general, and a real estate agent and long-time friend. A bus carrying female supporters, decorated with the slogan "Women for Kavanaugh" and a large image of the nominee's face, toured states represented by key senators, including Florida, Missouri, Indiana, West Virginia, and North Dakota. Kavanaugh brought the girls' basketball team that he coaches to sit behind him during part of the hearing. He touted his long record of hiring female clerks. (A cynic might wonder whether Kavanaugh, who has reportedly held Supreme Court ambitions for a long time, may have focused on hiring female clerks precisely so that they would be able to defend him in a possible future Supreme Court battle.)

While identity capitalism surfaced throughout the Kavanaugh confirmation hearings, it increased by an order of magnitude after Christine Blasey Ford and Deborah Ramirez accused Kavanaugh of sexually assaulting them. The additional Senate Judiciary Committee hearing at which both Ford and Kavanaugh testified was a pageant of identity capitalism. With a row of female supporters seated behind him, Kavanaugh spent almost one-third of his forty-five-minute opening statement listing women who like and respect him. He read aloud statements from (mostly anonymous) female friends who had contacted him in support, including one friend whom he pointedly characterized as "a self-described liberal and feminist." He noted that in his professional life he had "devoted huge efforts to encouraging and promoting the careers of women." He emphasized that he had provisionally hired four female clerks to staff his chambers should he be confirmed: "I'll be the first Justice in the history of the Supreme Court to have a group of all-women law clerks." (Again, the cynic might wonder whether Kavanaugh truly finalized his list of potential clerks before or after the sexual assault allegations emerged.) And he referred repeatedly to a letter authored by sixty-five women who knew Kavanaugh in high school who had stated that Kavanaugh "has always been a good person."

The vaunted letter from high school friends reveals that identity capitalism is about show rather than substance. A woman named Renate Dolphin was among the sixty-five women who signed the letter. After Ford and Ramirez's allegations, journalists examined Kavanaugh's yearbook and found many references to Renate as a teenage girl. A group of nine football players, including Kavanaugh, appeared in a photo labeled "Renate Alumni," and Kavanaugh also listed himself as "Renate Alumnius [sic]" on his personal yearbook page. One of Kavanaugh's classmates said that Kavanaugh and he teammates "were very disrespectful, at least verbally, with Renate." Another remembers Kavanaugh singing a song with the lyrics, "Renate, Renate, if you want a date, can't get one until late, and you wanna get laid, you can make it with Renate." Dolphin did not know about the yearbook comments and other behavior until after she signed the letter, when she learned of it from the media. She told reporters, "I don't know what 'Renate Alumnus' actually means. I can't begin to comprehend what goes through the minds of 17-year-old boys who write such things, but the insinuation is horrible, hurtful and simply untrue. I pray their daughters are never treated this way." She added that she was "profoundly hurt" and that "[t]here is nothing affectionate or respectful in bragging about making sexual conquests that never happened. . . . It is heartbreaking if these guys who acted like my friends in high school were saying these nasty false things about me behind my back."[11] Dolphin asked that her name be removed from the list of sixty-five women who signed the letter.

Kavanaugh's response did not suggest that he cared very much about Renate Dolphin. At the Senate Judiciary Committee hearing, he continued to refer to the letter signed by "sixty-five" women, despite Dolphin's request that her name be removed. Senate Judiciary Committee chair Chuck Grassley also referred to the letter from Kavanaugh's "sixty-five" acquaintances, also without correction from Kavanaugh. Kavanaugh responded angrily to questions about Renate from senators, claiming that the reference was meant to "show affection, and that she was one of us" and that "It was not related to sex." Kavanaugh erased Dolphin's desire not to be included in the letter as well as her own understanding of the yearbook comments. He also inadvertently revealed that his empathy for the women in his life does not run very deep. A man who actually cared about Renate Dolphin as an individual would have apologized for a teenage stunt. For Kavanaugh, an adult identity capitalist, it was enough to include Dolphin's name among a list of women supporters.

Nonetheless, many advocates touted Kavanaugh's parade of women as conclusive proof that he should be confirmed to the Supreme Court despite Ford's and Ramirez's allegations. The argument, apparently, is that because a lot of women like and respect Kavanaugh, he could not have sexually assaulted a few specific women. Kavanaugh's identity capitalism suffers from the same logical flaws as the "black friends" defense. Whether Kavanaugh has helped women's careers, or whether he has female friends, is irrelevant to whether he sexually assaulted anyone. Most rapists have female friends and can point to several women whom they definitely didn't rape.

Kavanaugh's identity capitalism contains more nuance than that of the crudest identity capitalists. He has undoubtedly advanced women's well-being in some instances through certain actions, like hiring women as his clerks. Yet Kavanaugh is still an identity capitalist even if his behavior sometimes helps women too: Kavanaugh benefited from hiring women, just as women benefited from his hiring them. This complexity also reveals another incentive for identity capitalism. Investing resources in outgroup members can pay off down the line. Hiring women can pay dividends for a man later accused of indifference to women's rights, and this is precisely how Kavanaugh benefited. One might think of identity capitalism as an investment that, when undertaken judiciously, appreciates and becomes more valuable in the future.

Look at All the Diversity on Our Website

"As a global company, UPS' values are rooted in the diversity and inclusion that thrives inside and outside our walls."[12]

"At Walmart, we believe [in] understanding, respecting, and valuing diversity . . . while being inclusive of all people."[13]

"At Nike, we believe that diversity fosters creativity and accelerates innovation. . . . [W]e are committed to a workplace that is increasingly diverse and inclusive."[14]

What do all of the companies above have in common? An obvious answer is that each company expresses a strong commitment to diversity on its website. An equally accurate answer is that each of these companies has been recently sued for either race or gender discrimination.[15] The sweeping language of diversity and inclusion on the companies' websites provides a stark contrast to the language of the plaintiffs in the lawsuits. In the 2018 gender discrimination lawsuit against Nike, the two lead plaintiffs described the company hierarchy as "an unclimbable pyramid—the more senior the job title, the smaller the percentage of women."[16]

Identity capitalism is a business strategy. Professing the value of diversity—as UPS, Nike, and Walmart have done on their websites—helps to rehabilitate a company's image at a time of negative publicity—the kind that often results when a company is sued. When accused of discrimination, a company generally turns to its professed values and existing numerical diversity as a way of defending itself in the media and in the marketplace.

Identity capitalism also makes strategic business sense apart from litigation. Many companies emphasize that their workforce includes diverse employees to attract both clients and employees. Virtually every large business has a section of its website devoted to its commitment to diversity. And industry rankings solidify the importance of broadcasting diversity. In the legal sector, *The American Lawyer* releases an annual "Diversity Scorecard," which evaluates the largest law firms to determine their percentage of nonwhite lawyers and partners. White & Case, the top-ranked law firm for several years running, devotes a page of its website to the achievement. My point is not that the firm does not deserve praise for its commendable record of diversity—33 percent of lawyers and 21 percent of partners are nonwhite—but rather that White & Case benefits from touting this record, and other firms would like to benefit similarly.

Some clients demand diversity. Recent interactions between law firms—historically, one of the least diverse employment sectors—and their clients provide a prime example. In 2018, Facebook announced an initiative requiring that one-third of any law firm's team working for them must be composed of women and racial minorities and has also instructed its law firms to show that they proactively create leadership opportunities for historically underrepresented groups.[17] Similarly, Hewlett Packard (HP) issued a "diversity holdback" mandate, stating that it will withhold up to 10 percent of amounts invoiced by law firms that do not field either a relationship partner who is "diverse" or else at least one woman and one racial minority who performs or manages at least 10 percent of the billable hours worked on HP matters. According to HP, a "diverse" lawyer is "limited to race/ethnicity, gender, LGBT status, and disability status."[18] And MetLife required its outside law firms to submit formal plans demonstrating how they will advance and retain a diverse cohort of lawyers. Law firms that want to retain these important corporate clients have little choice but to comply.[19] Leveraging outgroup identity within the firm is not only good for business—in some instances it is *necessary* for business.

Mandates to diversify—whether formal or informal—unquestionably have value. And companies' expressed commitments to diversity aren't a bad thing. It's beneficial at a symbolic level to attest to the value of diversity, and proactive efforts to diversify lead to opportunities for outgroup members. Yet mandates from corporations also create incentives for an identity capitalist to game the system rather than actually make substantive changes such as hiring more outgroup members or creating the conditions that organically attract a diverse work force. One such tactic is what law professors Patrick Shin and Mitu Gulati have called "showcasing," in which companies place outgroup members in prominent positions in order to signal desirability to potential business associates.[20] But this practice does not inherently signify any particular commitment either to outgroup representation or to the quality of experience for outgroup members. Identity capitalism via showcasing is selling an image of a corporation—not an authentic product.

Beyond showcasing, even a sincere diversity statement is not a panacea. No matter how committed to diversity a company is, problems arise when that company unjustifiably treats its diversity issues as resolved. This can happen when a company thinks it has achieved some minimal acceptable level of diversity and stops making efforts to address diversity proactively, such as by seeking diversity in hiring or by holding and improving regular training on bias and discrimination. Relatedly, a company may achieve numerical diversity without actually creating a company culture that is congenial to members of outgroups: a company can have a lot of women working there without having a culture that is actually good for women. And a company can achieve numerical diversity at one level without diversifying its entire chain of command—at Nike, for example, perhaps the sales associates include near-equal numbers of men and women, but this does not mean the same is true at the executive level.

The better diversity statement is an honest one: touting the company's accomplishments but explaining that there is more work to do both within and beyond the company itself. Imagine if companies said: "We're proud that over 30 percent of our executives are women. But we won't be satisfied until the composition of our executives matches the composition of our society." Such a statement would both broadcast the company's accomplishments and signal its commitment to continuing progress with a list of concrete policies and programs the company intends to implement to make diversity a reality.

Look at All the Diversity in Our Brochures

At the 2016 Film Independent Spirit Awards, comedian Kumail Nanjiani joked, "Tonight's nominees are more diverse than the cover of a brochure for a liberal arts college, while the Oscar nominees are as diverse as the actual student body at a liberal arts college." The audience laughed uncomfortably. They recognized the pattern Nanjiani was invoking. Photos in college and university promotional materials are always diverse, even when the campus isn't.

As a professor, I see a lot of performative diversity in the world of higher education. It's a way of virtue signaling, and photoshopping Diallo Shabazz is an extreme example but by no means an isolated one. Prominently displaying nonwhite and nonmale students is a way both of recruiting other students and of appeasing stakeholders who care about diversity, such as trustees, alumni, and donors. Indeed, the influential rankings giant *U.S. News and World Report* maintains a separate ranking system based on its "diversity index," and schools that score well on that metric often publicize their status.

At first glance, the photo in Figure 1.2 appears to be of four happy and racially diverse friends, all of whom are very pleased to attend the University of Texas at Arlington. A slightly closer inspection, however, reveals that the black woman on the right side of the photo does not seem to be standing in the same light as the three white women, and we can see several odd white dots against the brick wall along the side of her head.

Nobody knows exactly how common racial photoshopping is. But while preparing to write this book I had the chance to speak with several photographers who work for institutions of higher education. Nearly all of them said they had been asked to edit a photo to make it appear more diverse— sometimes by photoshopping the photo, other times by subtly altering the hue of someone's skin. And they generally agreed with the observation that schools overrepresent the diversity in their student bodies.

It's easy to laugh at crude racial photoshop jobs like those I've mentioned here. But even when photos promoting institutions of higher education are

FIGURE 1.2. The University of Texas at Arlington promotes the diversity of its student body.

not photoshopped, they're often still designed to overrepresent both numerical diversity and interracial interaction. One study examined the promotional materials of 371 colleges and universities and found that nonwhite students were significantly overrepresented in photographs.[21] Asian American students made up 3.3 percent of students enrolled at the sampled schools but were 5.1 percent of students portrayed in promotional materials; similarly, black students were 7.9 percent of enrolled students but were 12.4 percent of portrayed students. And the overrepresentation wasn't limited to a few egregious offenders. Rather, researchers found that most schools overrepresented their diversity, with 75 percent of the schools they studied choosing photos that significantly overrepresented the racial diversity present in their student bodies.

During conversations with administrators, professors, students, and alums, I've found that anecdotal evidence bears out the trends documented in quantitative research. A black male student at a law school associated with a university—one of only three black men in his class—described to me how a photo that just happened to include both him and one of the other two black men in the class was featured on the law school's website for months. This was not surprising or unusual. What made the story notable was that he later found that the same photo had been used on the website for the university's *business* school. (When he pointed it out, the school removed the photo.) An undergraduate student, who identifies as Latina, wryly showed me a university website featuring a photograph that had been taken while she visited the school as a prospective student. The catch: she ended up enrolling at a different school, meaning that the school was advertising itself by using an image of a student who'd chosen not to buy the product.

Schools often overrepresent diversity not only in the selection of photographs for viewbooks but also in the very creation. One of my Asian American students described to me how a photographer approached her in the hallway to ask whether he could take her photo, which soon led to him staging a photograph in the office of a professor of color whose class my student had never actually taken. A colleague who is a woman of color told me that her school's communications department once interrupted a meeting with her research assistant—also a person of color—to ask if they could take photos. The impromptu photo shoot ended up lasting so long that they had to schedule another meeting to talk about the actual research. Another colleague, also a woman of color, described how, while visiting a friend at another school, she was asked to participate in a photo for her friend's department. (She declined.)

One of the most remarkable stories about diversity inflation I've ever heard came courtesy of an acquaintance. Participants in a prestigious summer educational program were asked to take a group photo (Figure 1.3).

FIGURE 1.3. A prestigious summer educational program values its lone black participant so much they included him twice. Source: Sam Denlinger.

Midway through the photo shoot the one black student in the group was asked to move from one end of the back row to the other. At the time the students were puzzled about what was going on. Maybe their colleague had to move so that there would be an even number of people in the back row? But all became clear when the photo was released and it consisted of a single photo, spliced together to make it seem as though there were *two* black students in the program—identically dressed, but hopefully people wouldn't notice—rather than just one.

Perhaps due to the high value placed on diversity at many colleges and universities, identity capitalism is alive and well within institutions of higher learning and other educational programs. Ironically, clumsy efforts to attract and broadcast diversity are frequently off-putting to outgroup members already present at the school.

Look at All the Diversity in Our Stock Photos

"Republicans Are People Too," proclaimed a 2014 ad campaign designed to bolster the image of the Republican Party. The short-lived campaign ads featured photos of people along with slogans such as "Republicans Have Tattoos and Beards," "Republicans Read the *New York Times*," and "Republicans Assemble IKEA Furniture," casually mixed together with identity-based claims: "Republicans Are Women," "Republicans Are Black," "Republicans Are Asian," and "Republicans Are Hispanic."[22] The creator of the ads, Republican strategist Vinny Manchillo, claimed that the campaign was simply an antidote to the fact that "discourse is so nasty and mean. . . . People say things about Republicans that they would say about a terrorist or thug."

Yet beyond aspirations of civility, the ad campaign was also a strategic effort. It seems designed to address the concern that Republicans are often stereotyped as old white men, and, perhaps unspoken, that there is some truth to the stereotype. As of 2016, Pew research found that 87 percent of black voters identify with the Democratic Party, as well as 63 percent of Hispanic voters and 66 percent of Asian American voters; relatedly, men are more likely to identify as Republican than are women, 51 percent to 41 percent.[23] And, among white men, 61 percent identify with the Republican Party, compared with only 32 percent who identify with the Democratic Party.

The ad campaign leveraged outgroup identity to make people feel better about being Republicans. Current Republicans could point to the ads as evidence that their party is not really so demographically homogenous. Potential Republicans could cross homogeneity off their list of concerns. Racially anxious white people—a sizable portion of the Republican base—had a response, both to themselves and to others, to the claim that Republicans are mostly old white men who long for the days when they got to run literally everything, unimpeded by women and people of color.

The irony is that an ad purporting to reveal the real Republican Party relied on fake content (Figure 1.4). The black woman featured in the ad may or may not have been a Republican—but she was definitely a model in a stock photo. Her photo appeared in the "Republicans Are Black" campaign.

The same photo appeared in a number of other Internet locations, ranging from the website for the Georgia Association of Black Women Attorneys to advertisements for a payday loan company and a digital assistant (Figure 1.5).

The ad-makers' decision to use a stock photo reveals something important about identity capitalism. It wouldn't have been that hard to get a photo of a real black Republican woman—they do exist! (My guess is that Diamond and Silk would have been thrilled to oblige.) But the stock photo demonstrates that the point of the ad wasn't to showcase a real black

FIGURE 1.4. The Republican Party's black friend. Source: istockphoto.com.

WELCOME TO THE GABWA WEBSITE

"My car broke down. I needed cash for emergency repairs. QuickPaydayNow.com was fast and easy."

Virtual Clone
Your Virtual Office Assistant!

"I am a fashion designer and wanted to start an online store of my designer wear but didn't had time to manage it. I hired Virtual Office Assistant, and they are doing a fabulous job"

FIGURE 1.5. The Republican Party's black friend having a busy day. Source: istockphoto.com

Republican woman. The point was to extract the value associated with a black Republican woman's identity. For the identity capitalists behind the ad, a stock photo worked just fine for that purpose.

Look at Our Edgy Marketing Campaign

In 2016, San Francisco 49ers quarterback Colin Kaepernick began kneeling during the national anthem before each game to draw attention to police violence against black people. Kaepernick's actions were closely tied to his identity as a young black man, and he explicitly aligned himself with the "Black Lives Matter" movement. Many believe that Kaepernick's political gesture made him toxic to NFL teams: he became a free agent in 2017, was not signed by any team, and has not played since. Nonetheless, in September 2018, Nike launched an ad campaign featuring Kaepernick. "Believe in something, even if it means sacrificing everything," reads the text superimposed over Kaepernick's face. And then, at the bottom of the ad: the Nike swoosh and the words "Just Do It."

Nike's ad campaign featuring Kaepernick is an act of identity capitalism. The campaign is calculated to reach the millions of Americans—young men of color, as well as those who sympathize with them—who are inspired by Kaepernick's protest and horrified by the police brutality that his symbolic gesture highlights. Nike profits directly from Kaepernick's identity as a young black man who has chosen to draw attention to the issues facing his community. And for this, Nike has attracted both praise and criticism. But the move paid off: less than a month after the campaign launched, Nike's stock closed at an all-time high.

We should not necessarily equate Nike's marketing move to alignment with Kaepernick's political views. Nike's co-founder and major shareholder, Phil Knight, gave nearly $2 million to Republican candidates during the 2018 campaign cycle,[24] while Nike's political action committee gave roughly equal amounts of money to Republican and Democratic candidates and causes.[25] This means that a portion of the revenue Nike generated from Colin Kaepernick went directly to politicians who oppose the policing reforms for which he protested and, many believe, lost his job. For example, Knight donated to North Carolina Republican senator Thom Tillis, who falsely claimed, while advocating for an anticrime bill, that 2016 was "one of the deadliest years ever for law enforcement officers."[26]

Identity capitalism in marketing sometimes comes in subtler forms—for example, in the form of five attractive, stylish, and charismatic gay men in an SUV. Like many people, I have often taken refuge in the popular television show *Queer Eye* (as well as its previous incarnation, *Queer Eye for the Straight Guy*) and been charmed by the gentle interventions of the "Fab Five," who administer life makeovers to select recipients. Harder hearts than mine have been melted by the sight of fashion expert Tan France helping some hapless man pick out a shirt that actually fits, or grooming guru Jonathan Van Ness earnestly explaining to him why he should not shampoo every day, or culture specialist Karamo Brown encouraging him to talk about feelings for the first time. The Fab Five are incredibly *kind*, and many viewers are captivated by men who are unafraid to show affection to each other and everyone around them. As Laurie Penny has written, "[I]n each new installment . . . queerness is gently suggested as an antidote to the hot mess of toxic masculinity under late-stage capitalism." *Queer Eye* beguiles its fans with a sharp contrast to the violence and masculine anger that not only permeates television and other entertainment but also contributes to the polarization and misogyny of society at large.

None of this, of course, changes the fact that *Queer Eye* is also a show that allows heterosexual people to make a lot of money from gay male identity. *Queer Eye* allows entertainment and commercial interests to reach new markets. One market is the audience for the show, which generates revenue via Netflix's subscriber base. Although LGBTQ people have become increasingly prominent in many facets of American life, from entertainment to politics, many Americans still have relatively little firsthand exposure to LGBTQ people. Some of these viewers would really like to feel like they know some LGBTQ people—women, in particular, are often so explicit in their longing for a sassy gay best friend that their desire has become a cultural trope.[27] Other viewers watch because they have internalized stereotypes about the entertaining stylishness of gay men and want to see their preconceptions portrayed on the small screen. Still others—members of the LGBTQ community—may simply wish to see queer people like them represented on television.

Beyond attracting paying viewers to the show itself, *Queer Eye* capital-
izes on stereotypes about the stylishness of gay men to generate publicity
and revenue for the products that appear on the show. In one episode,
members of the Fab Five take Bobby Camp, an overworked father of
six, and his family to Target for a shopping excursion. "Stores like this,
they're designed for the Bobby Camps of the world," Fab Five member
Antoni Porowski announces in the episode. Other *Queer Eye* "brand in-
tegrations" have been wildly successful for the companies featured—for
example, a $1,500 pink cashmere Ralph Lauren jacket featured on an early
show sold out the next day. (As I'll discuss later in the book, the Fab Five
benefit too: for example, Jonathan Van Ness has a lucrative marketing
deal with Target.)

Queer Eye offers multifaceted opportunities for identity capitalism. The
mostly heterosexual entertainment executives who make a lot of money
from gay male identity are identity capitalists.[28] The mostly heterosexual
fashion executives behind the brands featured on the show are also identity
capitalists.[29] The viewers who brag about watching the show to gain the social cache associated with tolerance and open-mindedness are also identity
capitalists. The viewers who watch the show because they really wish they
had a gay friend or two are *aspiring* identity capitalists.

Perhaps most intriguingly, *Queer Eye* is also a way of selling capitalism
itself through gay identity—which implicates all of us as identity capitalists.
As Penny puts it, "Money is the silent sixth member of the rescue squad.
The services that the Fab Five are offering are worth more than most of
these men could possibly afford—there are thousands of dollars of new
clothes and furniture on offer here, and frankly, that's no shabby way to
advertise tolerance." The show suggests that part of individual growth is
buying things—new throw pillows, new polo shirts, new skin products.
The show's backers use the Fab Five to strengthen the precise capitalistic
structures that make the show popular in the first place. Reinforcing these
materialistic impulses will continue to generate revenue for the show—and
its identity capitalist backers—in the future.

None of this, of course, is to suggest that *Queer Eye* is *bad*. In fact, I
think quite the opposite. At the same time, we should grapple with the
way that queer identity—not to mention actual queer human beings who

have struggled against discrimination their entire lives—is used to make a lot of money for heterosexual people who have never experienced such a struggle.

Look at All My Black Friends, Part II

Artist and author damali ayo has some advice for white people: "Relax. Now that you're dating a black person, you're obviously not racist."[30] As ayo's sarcasm underscores, Americans' understanding of racism is often unsophisticated and incomplete. People know racism is socially unacceptable, but many people think of racism only as *overt* racism—racial epithets and blatant discrimination. Cognitive psychology research reveals that much racism actually takes place at a subconscious level. For example, research shows that many people unthinkingly prefer white-identified names to other names—both socially or in more structured contexts, such as the workplace.[31] Research also shows that people frequently employ racial stereotypes in making decisions, albeit often unintentionally. But this subtlety continues to escape many people.

As a result, identity capitalists desire a relationship with a black person—or, more generally, any nonwhite person—as a defense against any possible charge of racism. After all, many white people believe that "racist" is literally the worst name one can be called.[32] But having a racially diverse group of friends signals more than merely an absence of racism. It also signals characteristics of cosmopolitanism, tolerance, cultural literacy, and in some cases outright *coolness*.[33] The popular blog-turned-book *Stuff White People Like* includes entries such as "Having Black Friends," "Being the Only White Person Around," and, most generically, "Diversity."

The identity capitalist desire for nonwhite friendship surfaces not just anecdotally but systematically. In his seminal work *Racism Without Racists*, sociologist Eduardo Bonilla-Silva interviewed hundreds of white people, finding that white people tend to inflate both the number and closeness of their nonwhite friends.[34] Bonilla-Silva also examines the stories that white people tell about race. He separates these narratives into "story lines"—impersonal, generic claims about race—and "testimonies"—narratives in which the speaker is an integral part of the story. A common storyline involves "a positive incident or relationship with a black person as a way to signify the narrator's good relationships with or views toward blacks." Such storylines were common: about a third of the participants in Bonilla-Silva's research told them. Mary, a college student, offered the following narrative:

> My floor actually, the year I had a black roommate, happened to be predominantly African American and so those became some of my best friends, the people I was around. And we would actually sit around and talk about stereotypes and prejudices and I learned so much just about the hair texture, you know? What it means for a black person to get a perm versus me, you know. I learned a lot. And it really, I think, for me, broke down a lot of barriers and ended a lot of stereotypes I may still have had. Because like I said, I mean, those really became some of my best friends. And even still we don't really keep in touch, but if I see any of 'em on campus, still, you know, we always talk with each other and everything.[35]

Bonilla-Silva says that "Mary's story rings of self-presentation from start to finish." It also rings of identity capitalism. While engaged in an activity that many white people find difficult and anxiety-producing—talking about race—Mary copes by adopting common tropes of identity capitalism. She has black friends. She was open-minded. She learned so much! She even still talks to "those people" if she sees them around campus! The self-centered and congratulatory tone of Mary's comments unintentionally reveals that she was most interested in her African American floormates because they provided her with a specific type of social status.

A more quantitative analysis examined data gathered from students at Harvard and the University of Michigan and likewise found that white people tend to exaggerate their relationships with nonwhite people. Of white students, 92.4 percent reported having three or more close friends of other races, as compared to only 37.3 percent of black students, 29 percent of Latino/a students, and 53.4 percent of Asian American students. Further analysis revealed that if everyone was telling the truth, then every student of color reporting three or more cross-racial friendships must have had more than *nineteen* close friendships with white students. The result seems, to say the least, rather unlikely.[36] A more likely explanation is that some white students were inflating their tally of nonwhite friends. The pervasive inclination for white people to exaggerate the number and closeness of their friendships with nonwhite people is a testament to the power of identity capitalist impulses.

Everyone wants a nonwhite friend, from college freshmen to American presidents. Examples arise on the daily news and in federal court cases.[37] The impulse animating this common form of identity capitalism is quite similar: no one wants to look racist, and everyone wants to look tolerant. Claiming a relationship with a nonwhite person is a virtually nonexistent step toward racial progress. Such inauthenticity might even be viewed as a step backward. But quantitative and anecdotal evidence suggest that this behavior is so common that some people must find it convincing.

Look at All the Fake Social Progress
We could fill an old-fashioned set of encyclopedias with instances of identity capitalism. From Donald Trump to Nike, identity capitalists are legion, and their motivations for identity capitalism are varied and often overlapping. When Walmart boasts about diversity on its website, the company may be simultaneously playing defense in the face of imminent litigation, marketing itself to prospective customers or business partners, and virtue-signaling to bolster its reputation. The multiple benefits from any given instance of identity capitalism create an extra incentive for companies to engage in identity capitalistic activity.

Identity capitalism happens a lot and involves both public figures and private individuals. It's a part of day-to-day life in America: all of us have seen it or done it or had it done to us or—perhaps most likely—all of the above. And, when identity capitalism happens, ingroups often benefit in ways both overt and subtle, significant and trivial, tangible and intangible. Identity capitalism is a way for ingroups to benefit from outgroup identity.

Identity capitalism is harmful. At the individual level, it often presents an difficult dilemma. A target of identity capitalism must either go along with what the ingroup wants or else face negative consequences. This is true even when the demand in question is relatively minor. As one woman of color—a junior faculty member at a predominantly white school—told me, administrators asked her "to pose in staged candid pictures for a department

I have nothing to do with." She complied because "I felt vulnerable enough that I couldn't refuse to do it. I was young and too inexperienced to raise a fuss and they took advantage of that." By coercing outgroup participation, identity capitalism places outgroup members on unequal footing with their ingroup peers.

Similarly, identity capitalism gives ingroup members a stake in outgroup identity, and the ingroup prefers some expressions of identity over others. Netflix would cancel *Queer Eye* if the Fab Five suddenly started dressing in gym shorts, just as Nike would likely want little to do with Colin Kaepernick if he suddenly started wearing a MAGA hat. On a less public scale, ingroup preferences influence the way women, people of color, and LGBTQ people present themselves at work and at school. Outgroups are usually not literally compelled to present themselves in the way ingroups would like, but they experience pressure to do so, ranging from subtle to coercive.

This is not to say that there are no benefits to identity capitalism for outgroup individuals. Many reap benefits from identity capitalism—as I mentioned in the Introduction, those who leverage outgroup identity for personal gain are *identity entrepreneurs*, and some of them benefit substantially. This is true of some of the outgroup members I've mentioned: Colin Kaepernick, the Fab Five, Diamond and Silk, and Brett Kavanaugh's female clerks are all getting certain benefits. Identity capitalism creates an environment in which identity entrepreneurs often win advantages for themselves—and, as I'll explain a bit later, we shouldn't necessarily condemn them for it. But this does not mean that identity capitalism is good for outgroup members overall: on balance, it's not.

Identity capitalism also harms society as a whole by fostering resentment among outgroup members. One professor, a woman of color at a predominantly white school, told me that she had to ask the photographers at her school to stop following her around school events—first nicely, then not so nicely. One photographer apologetically told her that he was following orders that came straight from her dean, leaving her with few options. And a student of color at a predominantly white school told me that she was asked to pose for viewbook photos with a handful of other students. "I was flattered at the time," she recalled, but after realizing that the catalog photos were blatantly more diverse than the actual university campus, "I felt a bit used."

Members of outgroups are not oblivious to identity capitalism. And while identity capitalism sometimes makes for good comedic material, the harm it causes to human relationships is anything but funny. It cheapens interactions between members of ingroups and outgroups while vexing attempts at mutual understanding. A society awash in identity capitalism encourages ingroups to think of outgroup members in terms of their instrumental value. At the same time, identity capitalism fosters an understandable cynicism among members of outgroups. This cynical view warns—not without justification—that every member of an ingroup must be viewed as an identity capitalist trying to diversify their friend group or populate their website until proven otherwise. Such interactions are damaging even if an outgroup member acquiesces in identity capitalism, like the vulnerable faculty member I mentioned in the previous paragraph. Outgroup members may view such demands as the price of attendance at a school or employment at a company and go along with them. Nonetheless, identity capitalism causes outgroup members to feel objectified and alienated. Identity capitalism worsens relationships in a diverse society.

Perhaps most problematically, identity capitalism implies that social problems are easy to solve or have been solved already, yet in reality they offer only a superficial gesture toward a solution. The satirical website Rent-A-Minority mockingly advertises "a revolutionary new service designed for those oh-shit moments where you've realized your award show, corporate brochure, or conference panel is entirely composed of white men."[38] Like much satire, the website contains an uncomfortable truth. By focusing on aesthetic or numerical diversity, identity capitalism diverts attention and resources away from tangible substantive improvements to race relations.

Individuals and institutions engage in identity capitalism at the expense of substantive reform. Particularly troubling is that substantive reform is badly needed. In the workplace, research shows that outgroup members often struggle to thrive. Currently, more than half of law students are women, and this has been the case for over a decade, yet at the large law firms discussed earlier in the chapter, the number of women partners has stagnated at 20 percent.[39] Research suggests that this long-standing disparity is due in part to macho institutional culture, lack of mentoring, and the intransigence of old-boy networks—factors that are within the power of law firms to change. Instead, by pouring energy into glossy brochures, slick websites, and carefully crafted marketing pitches, companies are putting the focus on appearance rather than experience. They are putting a great deal of effort into claiming that the problem is solved rather than actually trying to solve it.

Looking at Identity Capitalism in Context

Why is identity capitalism so common right now? Identity capitalism is not new, but in recent years it has become more frequent and less subtle. Outgroups have made enormous strides in the past few decades, and as these outgroups make legal, social, political, and economic gains, identity capitalism becomes more common. Why? Because identity capitalism promotes the status quo. It's a way of maintaining the existing social hierarchy for those who benefit from it. Identity capitalism is an assertion of power—an effort at outgroup control premised on inequality. And as we're about to see, the troubling history of identity capitalism offers important insights for today.

2

ALL-AMERICAN EXPLOITATION

"AMERICA" is the title of a drawing by Edward William Clay published in *Harper's* magazine in 1841 (Figure 2.1). The drawing depicts a slaveowner, who has politely removed his hat in the presence of an elderly black man he has enslaved, engaged in a discussion with the old man about his well-being. The enslaved man is seated on a comfortable bench and holds onto a sturdy cane. In the background, other enslaved people, clean and neatly dressed, are smiling and dancing. The text accompanying the drawing summarizes the supposed perspective of the slaveowner: "These poor creatures are a sacred legacy from my ancestors and while a dollar is left me, nothing shall be spared to increase their comfort and happiness." Not content with that invention, Clay then purports to channel the sentiments of the slaves: "God bless you massa! You feed and clothe us. When we are sick you nurse us, and when too old to work, you provide for us!"

FIGURE 2.1. "America," by Edward William Clay. Source: *Harper's*, 1841.

Clay's intended audience was white Northerners concerned about the plight of slaves in the South. His drawing attempts to communicate that enslaved people were treated well by literally putting words in their mouths—regardless of whether any enslaved person actually held the views he attributed to them. Pretending to channel the sentiments of enslaved people, rather than merely describing slaveowners' perspectives, is an act of identity capitalism.

American history is drenched in identity capitalism.[1] Throughout our history, powerful ingroup members—primarily wealthy white men—used outgroup identity to benefit themselves and their social class. We see this pattern repeated over and over for more than two centuries, in circumstances both significant and trivial, involving matters relating to law, politics, society, work, education, entertainment, and day-to-day life. While not intended as anything like a comprehensive review, this chapter highlights instances of identity capitalism in slavery, suffrage, and segregation.

The Lies of Slaveholders

Advocates of slavery resorting to identity capitalism to justify themselves is hardly the worst criticism one could mount about the evils of slavery. It's not even a strong contender for the top ten. Still, examining the way that pro-slavery discourse relied on identity capitalism reveals the way that identity capitalism helped defend the institution of slavery. It also demonstrates that identity capitalism is not a new or unique phenomenon—rather, it's as much a part of American history as slavery itself.

In 1840, Reverend Leander Ker authored an influential book, *Slavery Consistent with Christianity*.[2] He argued forcefully that Christianity didn't just permit slavery, it actually *required* slavery. Abolition, he contended, "would be an act of positive inhumanity to the negroes, for there is no class of beings on earth so incompetent to provide for, and take care of, themselves, as the slaves of the south." Ker went on, "To turn [slaves] loose with no more experience than they have, would be like a parent turning his helpless children out on the world to get along as well as they could."

The claim that enslaved people enjoyed slavery or that slavery was good for them was a lie from its very inception before the Civil War and is a lie today. But in the years leading up to the Civil War, white slaveowners often made the case for slavery by using precisely this argument—that slavery was good for enslaved people or, at the very least, better than any of the alternatives. In other words, they turned to identity capitalism to validate slavery.

Prominent pro-slavery intellectual George Fitzhugh vocalized the views of the South for a broad audience, gaining both fame and infamy in the process. He published a series of pro-slavery books and pamphlets, and in 1850 he argued that slavery was affirmatively good for enslaved people:

> The negro slaves of the South are the happiest, and, in some sense, the
> freest people in the world. The children and the aged and infirm work
> not at all, and yet have all the comforts and necessities of life provided
> for them. They enjoy liberty, because they are oppressed neither by care
> nor labor. . . . The balance of their time is spent in perfect abandon.[3]

While Fitzhugh did not explicitly attribute these views to slaves, he bol-
stered his pro-slavery narrative by implying that the slaves themselves enjoyed a high quality of life. He leveraged insight into the supposed thinking
of the slaves, explaining that their life was "happiness in itself—and results
from contentment with the present, and confident assurance of the future."
A few years later, in 1854, he wrote that his primary concern was for the
slaves themselves: "But the chief and far most important enquiry is, how
does slavery affect the condition of the slave?" The answer, he concluded
happily, was "very positively." Fitzhugh explained that a slave "is as happy
as a human being can be."[4] The slave lifestyle was quite comfortable according to Fitzhugh: "[S]laves are all well fed, well clad, have plenty of fuel, and
are happy. They have no dread of the future nor fear of want." The idea
of the devoted slave was apparently particularly persuasive to him, as he
repeated it in many other writings. "Virginia negroes have become moral
and intelligent," he wrote in 1857, as the Civil War drew closer. "They love
their master and his family, and the attachment is reciprocated."[5]

At best these passages show that Fitzhugh was wildly deluded about
the conditions of slavery. More likely is that Fitzhugh was an intentional
identity capitalist. He understood the brutal reality of slavery, but instead
chose to engage in an extended testimony to the well-being of enslaved black
people, part of which purported to channel the opinions of those enslaved
black people themselves. To the atrocity of literal capitalism built on the
labor of commodified black bodies, Fitzhugh added the injury of a false
account of slave well-being and a fake rendition of slaves' own views. I am
not arguing that identity capitalism was as bad as slavery. Rather, identity
capitalism was used to obscure the horrors of slavery and to translate the
practice into something palatable, or even preferred.

Other advocates of slavery adopted similar rhetorical tactics. John
Caldwell Calhoun—the seventh vice president of the United States, and

later a senator—was another notable pro-slavery identity capitalist. Calhoun was personally invested in slavery: he owned a plantation of over one thousand acres and as many as eighty enslaved people. He devoted much of his career to protecting the southern states' interest in maintaining slavery.

From the United States Senate floor, Calhoun publicly aired the argument that slavery was good for slaves. Like Fitzhugh, he argued that slavery was good for slaves: "[W]here two races" coexist, "the relation now existing in the slaveholding States between the two, is, instead of an evil, a good—a positive good."[6] He elaborated, "Never before has the black race of Central Africa, from the dawn of history to the present day, attained a condition so civilized and so improved, not only physically but morally and intellectually." And he favorably compared the condition of black slaves in America with those of other countries: "[L]ook at the sick, and the old and infirm slave, on one hand, in the midst of his family and friends, under the kind superintending care of his master and mistress, and compare it with the forlorn and wretched condition of the pauper in the poorhouse." Calhoun invokes the well-being of black people to argue in favor of an institution from which he benefitted, and they suffered.

Calhoun's writing inspired others, including those in government leading into the Civil War. After reading Calhoun's works, Joel H. Berry argued at Mississippi's Secession Convention for a "special additional tax on negroes" on the ground that "African slavery, as it exists in the South, is a blessing to both the white and black races. In no other country, nor in any other age of the world, so far as their history is known, have the African race attained so high an elevation, or enjoyed so much happiness, as they have in a state of servitude in the South."[7] In a similar vein, Texas' Articles of Secession from the Federal Union state, "That in this free government all white men are and of right ought to be entitled to equal civil and political rights; that the servitude of the African race, as existing in these States, is mutually beneficial to both bond and free."[8] By declaring that slavery was also for the good of the slaves themselves, wealthy white men used identity capitalism to advocate for perpetuating slavery.

Particularly telling is the failure of these prominent defenders of slavery to engage the arguments of actual formerly enslaved people. There was no shortage of such accounts. Frederick Douglass' letter to his former master,

Thomas Auld, appeared in 1848 in Douglass' newspaper, *The North Star*. Douglass wrote: "I am myself; you are yourself; we are two distinct persons, equal persons. What you are, I am. You are a man, and so am I. God created both, and made us separate beings."[9] William Brown Wells' autobiography testified to a routine of whippings and other cruelty imposed upon enslaved people, and emphasized that "[t]he slave is brought up to look upon every white man as an enemy to him and his race."[10] Unsurprisingly, prominent defenders of slavery opted not to engage with these wrenching accounts from actual black intellectuals, preferring to articulate the fictional views of supposedly happy slaves in the South.

That slavery was good for slaves and that slaves themselves liked it were not the only arguments well-respected men made in favor of slavery. But such arguments gained particular traction during the last few decades of legal slavery precisely *because* they claimed to represent the perspectives of the slaves themselves and expressed the view that the slaves liked slavery. The men who promoted these arguments were identity capitalists: they derived value from the identities of the black people whose bodies they and their peers literally owned.

Convenient Anti-Suffragists

Not all women wanted to vote. The anti-suffragists—white, wealthy, and members of elite social groups—feared that suffrage would undermine their privileged status. According to one scholar, "[C]onservative women believed that the traditional virtues of true womanhood—the ideological apparatus justifying their entire way of life and form of civic membership—were under threat."[11] The anti-suffragists were concerned that, were women given the vote, they would be lumped together with common women; moreover, their ability to exert nonpartisan influence in charitable enterprises would collapse. Anti-suffragists were numerous—the exact number remains a subject of dispute, but one prominent organization, the National Association Opposed to Woman Suffrage, claimed seven hundred thousand members at its apex.[12] The anti-suffragists publicized their views by making speeches, writing letters to politicians and local papers, organizing events, and publishing pamphlets and newsletters.

While anti-suffragist women sincerely believed the arguments they advanced, they also provided men who opposed suffrage with a strategic opportunity. During the sixty-year march toward women's suffrage, anti-suffrage men often engaged in identity capitalism. In particular, they used the words, arguments, and identities of women who opposed suffrage to bolster the case against giving women the vote.

One such strategist was William Croswell Doane, the Bishop of Albany. In an article titled "Why Women Do Not Want the Ballot," he ostentatiously deferred to women's views: "Let a woman tell the facts," he exhorted the reader near the beginning of his essay.[13] He then quoted at length from "Mrs. Schuyler Van Rensselaer's admirable papers," which expressed the many perceived advantages enjoyed by "all the women of New York." Doane concluded that "[t]here is no freer human being on earth today, thank God, than the American woman." Doane framed his argument against women's suffrage as an "appeal . . . rightly made, first, in behalf of the women of America who are earnestly opposed to the imposition upon them of a burden which, from their point of view, not only is *not* a duty, but *is* an evil; not only not a right, but actually a wrong." He concluded by exhorting women to rally against the franchise:

> I cannot but feel, that, however the other women may shrink from the publicity, it is their bounden duty by influence, by argument, by petition, to "fight fire with fire"; to see to it that, in the approaching elections for the Senate and Assembly of the State of New York, men shall be chosen who will defend them from this wrong; and when the elections are completed, to let it be known and felt in Albany that what some women claim as a political right, they consider a personal grievance and a public harm.[14]

This is textbook identity capitalism. After professing his admiration for a woman's thinking that fortuitously happens to align with his own, Doane frames his anti-suffrage arguments as merely bolstering those of women themselves.

The rhetoric used by Doane and other anti-suffrage men like him was put into practice by William C. Coffey, an assemblyman in New York's state legislature who vocally opposed women's suffrage.[15] To demonstrate that women did not want the right to vote, Coffey—seemingly oblivious to irony—held a referendum on the issue open only to the women of his district. The referendum yielded 230 votes against women suffrage out of 360 cast, or about 64 percent. Coffey broadcast the result of the poll to support his anti-suffrage views. Other politicians likewise adopted this strategy: as Eleanor Flexner and Ellen Fitzpatrick put it, "[T]he antis' appearance at hearings and in print, through a flood of pamphlets and letters to the newspapers . . . furnish[ed] legislators with the excuse that a body of respectable women did not want the vote."[16] Such tactics foreshadow the way that other men, such as Brett Kavanaugh a century later, point to the views of a subset of women to support their own self-interest.

Some notable publishers also adopted identity capitalist tactics in advocating against women's suffrage. Anti-suffrage essayist Ernest Bernbaum compiled an entire "little book" consisting of "anti-suffrage essays by Massachusetts women," explaining in the introduction that a suffrage amendment failed in Massachusetts because men "discovered that nine women out of ten did not want to vote."[17] Lyman Abbott, the editor-in-chief of popular *Outlook* magazine, wrote more than two dozen pieces opposing suffrage for women and put the magazine on record as "opposed to woman suffrage primarily because it is an advocate of woman's rights."[18] That is, Abbott framed concern for women as a reason to prevent women from voting. Edward Bok—publisher of *Ladies' Home Journal*—engaged in similar tactics, personally writing more than twenty articles arguing against suffrage. The men behind certain publications professed concern for their primarily female readership in order to advance their own political views.

Many anti-suffrage men had wives and daughters who were active in the anti-suffrage movement, which facilitated identity capitalism.[19] Perhaps the most brazen example involved anti-suffrage biologist William T. Sedgwick, who historians believe ghost-wrote an article arguing against women's suffrage from a scientific standpoint that was published in *Gunton's Magazine* under the name of his wife, Mary T. Sedgwick.[20] Sedgwick probably thought that arguments about women's biological unfitness to vote sounded better coming from a woman. In general, the men and women who opposed suffrage ran in the same elite circles. They had many opportunities for social interaction and long-standing family ties. These relationships gave rise to identity capitalism.

Why was identity capitalism appealing to men who opposed women's suffrage? Pointing to women as the chief opponents of suffrage allowed many men in elite circles to remain somewhat removed from the political fray: rather than "suffer the indignities of public political activism," these high-status men "preferred to assist behind the scenes through donations and the distribution of circulars to other men of their social circle."[21] These men derived value simply by letting women do the dirty work for them. And men from all walks of life saw both a rhetorical and a social advantage to invoking the views of anti-suffrage women. Rhetorical, because they could simply present their argument as that of women themselves. And social because many of the suffragists were also from elite circles: men who wanted to oppose suffrage without suffering repercussions for their views could try to have their cake and eat it too by presenting their views as not really *theirs*, but simply an effort to support the *real* views of the women in their milieu.

Anonymous Eminent Negro Scholars

Black people generally supported desegregation. Many black people protested segregation, and some risked or even gave their lives to integrate their communities. Tragically, this goal remains elusive today, as schools in many cities have become *more* segregated since the 1990s and the school-to-prison pipeline disproportionately affects predominantly black schools.[22] Just as black people fight for civil rights today, they fought for civil rights during segregation.

During the Jim Crow era and its aftermath, some prominent black intellectuals expressed sentiments that might be described as concerns about integration. Zora Neal Hurston, for example, wrote that she regarded *Brown v. Board of Education*, the famous case ordering desegregation of schools nationwide, "as insulting rather than honoring my race."[23] She wrote, "[I]f there are adequate Negro schools and prepared instructors and instructions, then there is nothing different except the presence of white people." Hurston's perspective was actually a deeply nuanced one shared by a number of other black intellectuals: they worried that integration would come at the expense of black cultural traditions, or that the need for integration would itself come to signify black inferiority.[24] This does not mean that they opposed desegregation. Rather, they worried about possible unintended consequences for their communities.

Other black people, generally members of the working class, had reservations about the practical effect of desegregation on their lives. Some black teachers expressed concern for their jobs if schools were desegregated. Others worried about the safety of their children in desegregated schools—a reasonable concern given the frequency of lynchings like the one that took the life of fourteen-year-old Emmett Till in 1955—or the possibility of retaliation from white people who would otherwise leave them alone. But these concerns did not mean these black people opposed desegregation and access to truly equalized educational opportunities. Rather, they had concerns about how desegregation would be implemented—entirely reasonable ones, as subsequent racist harassment in schools and white flight to the suburbs bore out.

Despite what black people actually said and did and believed about desegregation, white people who opposed integration often distorted and selectively repurposed these sentiments to serve their own interests. White segregationists often robbed these sentiments of nuance or left out important context. These white segregationists were identity capitalists, and their identity capitalism was a symptom of changes to society that they feared.

Author Robert Penn Warren, Kentucky-born and Oxford-educated, viewed the Jim Crow South "not [as] a dungeon of dehumanization and repression so much as a hub of slow-paced, leisurely living."[25] In his widely read 1956 monograph, *Segregation: The Inner Conflict*, he suggested that both black and white cultures were worthy, and that at some point—not yet, and certainly not due to governmental force—these cultures would naturally intertwine. But his writings profoundly understate the way that black people suffered under Jim Crow. He penned the remarkable statement that "the races had made out pretty well in the south," and that members of different races related to one another with "some sort of human decency and charity."[26]

Warren simply ignored historical events demonstrating great racial unrest in the South as well as events demonstrating a powerful desire for desegregation among black people. He did not mention *Irene Morgan v. Virginia*, in which the Supreme Court took up the case of a young mother of two in

Virginia who refused to yield her seat on a Greyhound bus and held that segregation in interstate travel is unconstitutional. He did not mention the Freedom Riders, who sought to force Southern states to enforce the holding of *Irene Morgan* on the ground. He did not mention Emmett Till. He did not mention Rosa Parks or the Montgomery bus boycott.

But when it came to identity capitalism, Warren was prolific. As Anders Walker puts it, "To shore up his point that no one in the South really wanted to integrate, Warren included a string of black voices who expressed doubts about *Brown*."[27] Warren interviewed an (unnamed) black individual who stated that the move to integrate immediately was "absurd," and that it was "foolish thinking for people to believe you can get the South to do in four or five years what the North has been doing for a hundred years." The anonymous black interviewee further observed that "the ultimate goal" of black people in the South was more than "just to go to white schools and travel with white people on conveyances over the country"; rather, blacks were "a growing people" and would "strive for all the equalities belonging to any American citizen."

Warren particularly emphasized the views of those who did not see desegregation as a prerequisite to black advancement. He cited another individual—also anonymous, although Warren described him as an "eminent Negro scholar"—who did not see integration as the goal of black people in the South: "It's not so much what the Negro wants as what he doesn't. He does not want to be denied human dignity." Likewise, he referenced a black "school inspector for country schools" who expressed misgivings about integration: "We don't want to socialize. That's not what we want. But I don't want to be insulted." The issue, according to Warren, was not segregation per se; it was respect. The inspector further stated: "We do everything the white folks do already, even if we don't spend as much money doing it. And we have more fun." Another anonymous interviewee told Warren, "My boy is happy in the Negro school where he goes. I don't want him to go to the white school and sit by your boy's side." And an anonymous black college student stated that "the Negro doesn't want social equality. My wife is my color. I'm above wanting to mix things up. That's low class. Low class of both races."[28]

Warren's work was not a balanced ethnography: we don't even know for sure that his many anonymous sources were real, or if they were, we don't know that he quoted them accurately. Rather, as Walker observes, Warren "foregrounded black speakers who seemed to collectively argue that interracial respect, economic opportunity, and an end to white-on-black violence were paramount, creating the overall impression that integration by itself was not an urgent priority, even among African Americans."[29] And perhaps as notable as what Warren included is what he did not: he failed to include an interview with even one black person who supported the integration imperative of *Brown v. Board of Education*.

What Warren's work does suggest to us today, however, is that white people were ready and willing to advance their views using claims supposedly made by black people. Warren's approach was generally laudatory of black people—at least of those holding a certain set of views—and was unabashedly complimentary toward black culture. But his strategy was still fundamentally to buttress his arguments against desegregation by suggesting that black people agreed with them. This tactic served two purposes. First, it insulated Warren from charges of racism by suggesting that black people agreed with his views; indeed, he was so thoroughly not racist that he spoke with several black people for his book. Second, it provided credence to his broader claim that black people and white people wanted similar things, and that perhaps integration would come—at some point well in the future—but was not a priority now.

Lessons from History

History teaches that identity capitalism is an ingroup's response to a perceived loss of power. As outgroups gain power or seem poised to do so, ingroups engage in identity capitalism. When white people saw a threat to legal slavery, they responded with false claims that black slaves supported slavery and the confederacy. When men saw a threat to their control of the franchise, they relied on the statements of anti-suffragist women. When white people feared desegregation, they referenced (anonymous and possibly imaginary) black people and attributed to them dubious claims that they also opposed integration.

In each of these historical examples, identity capitalism is an assertion of power. The ingroup is not only expressing support of the status quo, but also purporting to show that the outgroup, too, supports the status quo. In some instances—slavery, for example—the ingroup's behavior amounts to an attempt to control the outgroup's ability to communicate its own experience. Here, white slaveowners assert their power to use outgroup identity to buttress ingroup control. The assertion of power is real, even if the views imputed to slaves are as fake as the photo of Diallo Shabazz at the Wisconsin football game.

At other times, identity capitalists assert power by communicating approval of outgroup statements with which they agree or by inventing outgroup views to serve their purposes. Incorporating outgroup statements in order to buttress one's own argument is an expression of power: the power to use other's ideas and words as one chooses. It's also an assertion of the power to police the outgroup. Anti-suffrage men expressed approval of anti-suffrage women and disapproval of suffragist women, providing the former with social benefits withheld from the latter. Again, it's not just that the ingroup agrees with one segment of the outgroup and not the other: it's that the ingroup uses its power to confer benefits on favored members of the outgroup and impose negative consequences on disfavored members of the outgroup.

A particularly popular way for identity capitalists to assert power occurs when the ingroup turns an outgroup member's narrative to its own ends. This is one lesson of the supposed black opponents to desegregation: while their positions were often nuanced and sophisticated—for example, some highly respected black intellectuals did not actually oppose desegregation, they simply saw it as less of a priority and wanted thoughtful implementation so that desegregation did not come at the expense of black dignity—white people who opposed desegregation took such arguments, stripped them of context, and twisted them to fit their own ends. Appropriating and misconstruing the outgroup's message is a deliberate demonstration of ingroup power.

Identity capitalism is also an expression of ingroup anxiety about the loss of power. Throughout history, ingroup members have turned to identity capitalism when they feared loss of control over outgroup members. Identity capitalism is a means of maintaining such control. While these impulses have long existed, they were magnified and accelerated by a critical Supreme Court decision about affirmative action.

Affirmative Action

The term "affirmative action" appeared in government documents for the first time in 1963, when President John F. Kennedy issued an order establishing the President's Committee on Equal Employment Opportunity. The order stated simply that all government contractors "will take affirmative action to ensure that applicants are employed, and that employees are treated during employment, without regard to their race, creed, color, or national origin." The language is arguably ambiguous. It might be interpreted to mean something like the modern concept of colorblindness. Alternatively, the idea of *affirmative* action to ensure treatment without regard to race might be interpreted as remedial—that is, requiring some sort of remedy for past wrongs that were responsible for creating inequality between racial groups in society.

When the first affirmative action programs emerged in workplaces during the 1960s, their justification was explicitly remedial.[30] Courts accepted remedial justifications as constitutional.[31] And the U.S. government explicitly stated that the purpose of affirmative action was remedial: in 1977 the U.S. Commission on Civil Rights defined affirmative action as an effort "beyond simple termination of a discriminatory practice, adopted to correct or compensate for past or present discrimination or to prevent discrimination from recurring in the future."

The understanding of affirmative action as a remedial measure changed in 1978 in the Supreme Court's decision in *Bakke v. Regents of the University of California*. There, the opinion of a single member of the Supreme Court, Justice Lewis Powell, became the controlling opinion because the remainder of the justices were evenly divided 4-4. Justice Powell rejected several possible rationales for an affirmative action program at a college or university, including the remedial rationale—that is, the argument that affirmative action was constitutional because it helped to remedy past wrongs. Perhaps without realizing the enormous consequences, he accepted just one rationale for affirmative action: diversity. Justice Powell declared that "the attainment of a diverse student body . . . clearly is a constitutionally permissible goal for an institution of higher education." He linked diversity to academic freedom:

"[U]niversities must be accorded the right to select those students who will contribute most to the 'robust exchange of ideas.'" In short, "our tradition and experience lend support to the view that the contribution of diversity is substantial."[32]

Diversity thus became the primary focus of civil rights advocates, policy-makers, colleges, universities, employers, and the U.S. government. The Supreme Court's emphasis on diversity both reflected and reinforced schools' own behavior:[33] schools already valued diversity, but now that diversity was the *only* legal justification for affirmative action, it became exponentially more important. At the same time, diversity also became the target of those who wanted to do away with affirmative action altogether: if they could show that diversity is not that valuable, or if it is achievable by means other than affirmative action, then this provides a pathway for doing away with affirmative action altogether. And while *Bakke* only dealt with race in higher education, advocates quickly extrapolated the emphasis it placed on diversity to other arenas and other identities. For example, the emphasis on diversity spread to workplaces, politics, and entertainment, and included not only race but also sex, gender, and eventually disability, sexual orientation, class, and other categories.

Gradually, diversity discussions began to overtake conversations about social problems such as discrimination and social ideals such as equality. In some cases, diversity became what people talked about *instead of* discrimination or equality—that is, diversity became a way of avoiding more difficult topics. A google analysis of term frequency in books—a source of insight into Americans' collective preoccupations—reveals that the term "diversity" began to trend upward in the 1940s, climbed more steeply around the time of the *Bakke* decision in the 1970s and 1980s, and increased almost exponentially during the 1990s (Figure 2.2). During the meteoric rise of the term "diversity," the word surpassed both "discrimination" and "equality" in its frequency (Figure 2.3).

The new era of diversity also ushered in a new era in the age of identity capitalism. The Supreme Court had communicated that diversity was important. As a result, schools and workplaces sprang into action to trumpet the diversity of their campuses as a way of communicating their alignment with the educational ideals the Supreme Court had endorsed.

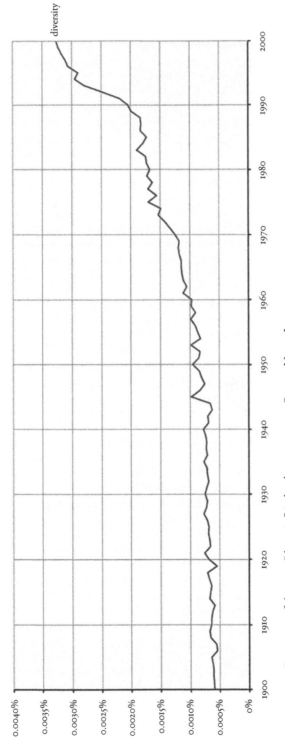

FIGURE 2.2. Frequency of the term "diversity" in books, 1900–2000. Source: Nancy Leong.

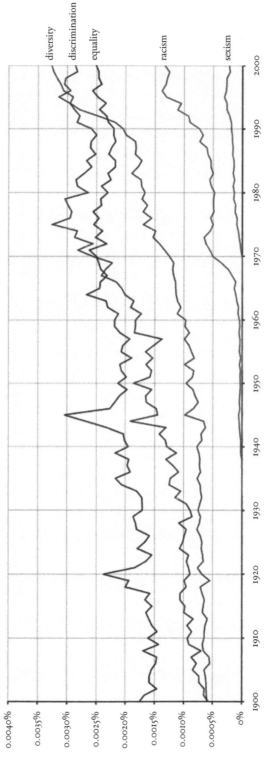

FIGURE 2.3. Frequency of the term "diversity" in books, 1900–2000, as compared to the terms "discrimination," "equality," "racism," and "sexism." Source: Nancy Leong.

At the same time, those who did not support affirmative action—and those who were relatively indifferent—still got the message that diversity was something that other people valued even if they didn't. Schools with all-white student bodies became increasingly anxious about being known as schools with all-white student bodies. All-white workplaces became anxious about being seen as all-white workplaces. These institutions began to undertake measures to avoid such embarrassment, without necessarily addressing concerns of workplace equality that led to all-white work environments in the first place.

The emphasis on diversity spread beyond schools and workplaces to other forums. Politicians began to talk about the diversity of their support or to highlight their identity as a way of demonstrating that they would bring a different perspective to elected office. Entertainment picked up on the importance of diversity in programming, leading to television shows such as the *The Cosby Show* and *A Different World*. These early efforts reveal the spread of diversity thinking throughout American society—and while certainly not all the consequences were negative, many of them involved crude attempts at identity capitalism.

More recent Supreme Court decisions have not exactly been enthusiastic about affirmative action or the diversity rationale for it.[34] In 2003 the Court upheld an affirmative action program at the University of Michigan School of Law in *Grutter v. Bollinger*. Writing for the majority, Justice Sandra Day O'Connor stated, with odd specificity, that affirmative action programs should come to an end within the next twenty-five years. Still, O'Connor formed part of a five-justice majority that validated the program as constitutional. Affirmative action has been tested again since then, every few years, and each time, racial justice advocates braced themselves for its demise. So far, it has survived, but no one knows for how much longer.

Yet even if the Supreme Court narrows the permissible scope of affirmative action programs or invalidates them wholesale, the cultural change that the diversity rationale has brought about will not disappear overnight. What legal scholar Camille Gear Rich calls "diversity talk" has permeated our culture, even as many people—particularly white people—have become hesitant to talk about race, other than to assert, with great conviction, that they are not racist.[35] Sociologist Robin DiAngelo attributes this reluctance to what she calls "white fragility," a reluctance to discuss race implicitly undergirded by the idea that "if we pretend not to notice race, there can be no racism."[36] Identity capitalism serves the goal of avoiding hard conversations about race and identity more generally. Constructing diverse photos is relatively easy; determining why women and people of color are less frequently recognized than their white male peers at school and at work is painful. And actually improving the situation is difficult and unforgiving work.

The Age of Trump

Some heralded the two-term presidency of Barack Obama as a sign that America was finally over race. Identity capitalists pointed to Obama as evidence that the country had paid off its racial debts. See? A black man could do anything in America—even become president. Never mind the four-hundred-year history of slavery—for which America has never formally apologized—Jim Crow, redlining, de facto segregation, discriminatory implementation of the GI bill, hate crimes, and ongoing evidence of implicit and explicit racial bias: America is finally post-racial!

Ominous signs belied this rosy narrative. One was birtherism, a conspiracy theory that Barack Obama was not born in the United States, which was promoted by Donald Trump, among others.[37] Hate crimes, particularly those targeting Muslims, rose in 2015.[38] White supremacist activity increased.[39] Racism was accompanied by misogyny. Researchers documented a depressing drumbeat of hatred directed at women online.[40] Aided by technology, nonconsensual pornography increased, victimizing both female celebrities and the nonfamous.[41] Fox News maintained its popularity—leading all news channels in 2015[42]—and grew increasingly polarized. White people, especially straight white men who felt that they no longer recognized America, responded eagerly to the racist dog whistles of many Fox network personalities: "The America we know and love doesn't exist anymore," Laura Ingraham said, and "Latin American countries are changing election outcomes here by forcing demographic change on this country, at a rate that American voters say they don't want," commented Tucker Carlson.[43]

History teaches that ingroups tend to engage in identity capitalism when they perceive their status to be threatened in some way, and the time prior to and during the Trump presidency presents precisely this sort of status threat. Eight percent of people in a 2015 Gallup poll were unwilling to vote for a woman for president and were willing to say so to a pollster.[44] This is not an overwhelming number, but in a close election, it might well determine the outcome. Perhaps it was unsurprising that so many people refused to vote for Hillary Clinton for ill-defined reasons. Following the 2016 election, Donald J. Trump's presidency is a testament to an ongoing perceived threat to status. Many Trump voters, research shows, were reacting to social changes that, in their view, diminished their social standing. One study found that a majority of white people—Trump's base—believe that discrimination against white people is as serious a problem as discrimination against black people and other minorities.[45] Other recent threats to status range from legalization of same-sex marriage to the unexpected death of staunchly conservative Supreme Court justice Antonin Scalia. Trump's 2016 campaign slogan—"Make America Great Again"—was thinly disguised code for making America the way it was before all these undesirable changes began to diminish the relative status of people who are white, male, straight, wealthy, or all of the above.

During the Trump presidency, identity politics have become more salient than ever before. Ta-Nehisi Coates describes Trump as the "first white president"—meaning that, for the first time, a president ran on a platform of "whiteness as his sole attribute" and "the very core of his power."[46] Part of the power of whiteness is power *over* people who are not white, as well as other outgroup members—the power to control people who are not white men, straight, and wealthy.

The Trump presidency creates a hospitable environment for identity capitalism. Trump himself frequently nods to white supremacy, misogyny, and other types of bigotry that maintain the unequal status of outgroups. But these gestures to the ingroup are not enough: Trump does not merely want to disparage the outgroup, he wants to control it. Identity capitalism provides just such a technique of control. By pointing out the relatively small number of racial minorities, women, and other outgroup members who support him, Trump renders invisible the much larger proportion of outgroup members who actively oppose him and his policies. For Trump, identity capitalism is a way to trivialize the concerns of vast swaths of people who are not fortunate enough to be part of the ingroup. "Kanye West likes me," he all but says out loud. "What's wrong with the rest of you black people?"

Identity capitalism under Trump echoes the techniques of many identity capitalists throughout history. Trump benefits from the identities of a few outgroup members to deny the narratives of many others. Moreover, he uses select outgroup members in a way that changes the meaning of their experiences for his benefit and distorts reality for everyone.

Identity capitalists during the age of Trump are more crass than those in recent memory. Rather than the superficially polite writings of the anti-suffragist men, chivalrously acknowledging the arguments of their female counterparts, we now have political organizers handing out "WOMEN 4 TRUMP" signs at political rallies and calling it a day. In a photo gleefully publicized by many of his supporters, a middle-aged woman at a Trump rally wears a shirt stating "Trump can grab my" followed by an arrow pointing straight down (Figure 2.4). Trump is not a subtle identity capitalist, and his followers take a cue from him.

Other political figures have also engaged in crude Trump-style identity capitalism. Republican congressman French Hill ran a remarkable ad on radio stations targeted to the black community in support of his 2018 reelection

FIGURE 2.4. See, women support Donald Trump. Source: *The Guardian*, Ben Jacobs.

campaign. The ad features a conversation between women speaking in a stereotypical black dialect and discussing Brett Kavanaugh's Supreme Court nomination. The two women deliver lines such as "Our Congressman French Hill and the Republicans know that it's dangerous to change the presumption of innocence to a presumption of guilt, especially for black men," and "Girl, white democrats will be lynching black folks again!" The ad was paid for by "Black Americans for the President's Agenda," a group that seems to involve very few black people.[47] While the president of the organization appears to be black, nearly all of its individual contributors appear to be white. The lead photo on the group's Facebook page includes—in a montage of black faces— a photo of rapper Eazy-E, whose relationship with the Republican Party was dubious at best and who—perhaps more importantly—died in 1995.

The ad in support of Hill entails—in painfully obvious ways—an ingroup member using outgroup identity for his benefit. And the timing and targeting of the ad aptly illustrate the idea that identity capitalism is often a tactic that comes into use when the identity capitalist is threatened with loss of status: polls in October 2018 showed incumbent Hill within five points of a Democratic challenger in a district that Donald Trump won by twelve points. After the ad attracted public outcry, Hill distanced himself from it—but only after it had played on local radio stations for a week. One might reasonably question whether it would be possible for such a striking ad to escape the attention of him *and* all his staff members for a whole week less than a month before the election.

Identity capitalism helps to explain the way that ingroups and outgroups have interacted throughout American history. Examining moments of progress toward equality reveals that identity capitalism often surfaces in such moments as a mechanism for the ingroup to preserve its status and reassert its power. And focusing on identity capitalism offers a substantial payoff. Drawing from these historical lessons allows us to better understand identity capitalists' determination to use outgroup members to benefit themselves. With this history as a point of departure, the next chapter delves further into the psyches of the identity capitalists, exploring their beliefs, motivations, and anxieties.

3

ANXIETY AND ABSOLUTION

Writing for the satirical publication *McSweeney's*, author Mia Mercado envisions a dialogue she titles "White Friend Confessional."[1] It begins with the following:

WHITE FRIEND: Forgive me, Designated Friend of Color, for I have sinned. It has been two Macklemore singles since my last white confession.

FRIEND OF COLOR: Go on.

WHITE FRIEND: I maybe did a racist thing.

FRIEND OF COLOR: Did you say the n-word during karaoke again?

WHITE FRIEND: No! I was definitely tempted to do "Formation" by Beyonce but did "Single Ladies" instead.

As it turns out, White Friend has a few things weighing on her mind. She mixed up two Asian women; she spelled Frederick Douglass' name wrong and couldn't remember what he actually did, and she even forgot that the Friend of Color is Filipino, not "Half-Mexican." Friend of Color is patient, alternating between asking pointed questions ("You had to google [Frederick Douglass], didn't you?"), assigning White Friend racial awareness tasks ("Your penance will be to read something by or about Frederick Douglass."), and nudging the friend toward substantive action ("You can donate to the ACLU as an act of contrition.")

While "White Friend Confessional" is a work of fiction, it deftly captures the identity capitalist mindset. At its core, identity capitalism is motivated by ingroup members' concern that others might perceive them as bigoted. As it turns out, the smiling diverse photo spreads and the testaments to diverse friendship mask a tangle of human defensiveness and insecurity. Understanding identity capitalism requires dissecting these feelings and the behavior they motivate.

"White Friend Confessional" also holds another important lesson. Identity capitalism is often partially an ingroup member's quest for absolution. The imagined dialogue concludes as follows:

WHITE FRIEND: I'm so glad I can come to you for this kind of stuff.

FRIEND OF COLOR: I mean, I'm not an expert on all non-white people, but no problem.

WHITE FRIEND: Right, of course. It's still such a relief to know I'm not racist.

FRIEND OF COLOR: You know I can't actually absolve you of that, right?

WHITE FRIEND: You just did. See you next week!

As we'll see, White Friend and other ingroup members seeking absolution from bigotry are everywhere. Let's take a backstage look at the complex pageant playing at a school or workplace very near you—and just about everywhere else—to uncover the why and the how of identity capitalism. Join me as we peer inside the mind of an identity capitalist.

Status Anxiety

Everyone worries about their status in society. The writer Alain de Botton describes status anxiety as "worry, so pernicious as to be capable of ruining extended stretches of our lives, that we are in danger of failing to conform to the ideals of success laid down by our society and that we may as a result be stripped of dignity or respect."[2] Status is fluid: historically, a person's status might have been affected by how many wives he had or how many slaves he owned. Today the stakes are quite different. De Botton observes, "As the determinants of high status keep shifting, so, too, naturally, will the triggers of status anxiety be altered."[3]

In America today, some status anxiety results from ingroup members' concerns about their relationship with the outgroup. Many white people are deeply anxious about their interactions with those who are not white. Among white people, "racial anxiety is experienced as the concern that they will behave in ways that will be evaluated as racist by a person of color."[4] Racial anxiety is severe: white people experience criticism of their racial views as accusations of racism. In turn, white people experience an accusation of racism as an attack on their moral character. Often, the result is reflexive outrage at the idea that they might harbor prejudice, however unconscious.

Status anxiety related to race translates to a powerful desire to prove that one is not racist. Such anxiety sows the seeds for identity capitalism. Racially anxious white people want to demonstrate their nonracism, and identity capitalism seemingly provides one possibility for doing so. Anxiety is the motivation that ultimately leads to identity capitalism.

Research indicates that this motivation is particularly powerful for people who score high on measures of racial bias. White people who are more racially biased are *more* friendly in interracial interactions than people who are low in bias. The research suggests that the most biased people are also the most highly motivated to demonstrate that they aren't racist.

For those of you who thought you were home free, not so fast: racially egalitarian beliefs don't exempt people from racial anxiety. Many well-intentioned people, and the institutions they inhabit, also experience acute status anxiety. Sometimes racially egalitarian beliefs are actually correlated with *more* problematic behavior: for example, people with racially egalitarian views tend to simplify their vocabulary or "talk down" to black people, while the same is not true of people with less racially egalitarian views.[5] Robin DiAngelo writes that "white progressives cause the most daily damage to people of color," noting, "To the degree that white progressives think we have arrived, we will put our energy into making sure that others see us as having arrived."[6] As we'll see, this type of performative arrival *also* frequently involves identity capitalism.

Researchers have found ingroup status anxiety that goes beyond race. In a clever study, researchers paired a male subject with a female confederate—someone who was secretly collaborating with the researchers, unbeknownst to the subject of the study.[7] They assigned the pairs to read a series of ethical dilemmas and discuss how to address them, including a situation in which a nurse discovers that a hospital patient has been given tainted blood. During the interaction, the female confederate either confronted her male partner for sexism because he assumed the nurse in the dilemma was female (every male in the study appeared to do this—a telling finding in itself, although one for a different book) or else confronted him about something gender-neutral such as how to resolve a particular dilemma. Men reacted more strongly to a confrontation about sexism than to a gender-neutral confrontation: they smiled and laughed more, appeared more surprised, gestured more often and more energetically, and were more likely to try to justify or apologize for their remark. The men did not, however, react with more hostility or anger; they reported liking the female confederate in each condition; they liked her equally well whether she confronted them about sexism or about something gender-neutral; and their behavior was cordial overall. Men who had been accused of sexism were then significantly nicer and more agreeable to their female partner while discussing a second set of dilemmas—they even smiled at her more—than the men who had simply been told they were wrong.

The study indicates that—similar to white people's anxiety about appearing racist—men are often anxious about appearing sexist. Upon being accused of sexism, men will often respond by performing antisexist behavior. Being extra nice to their female partners and reporting that they liked them were typical responses to that anxiety. The results of the study might not translate precisely to the real world—for example, the study placed participants in equal roles, so it did not account for power differentials, such as confronting a boss—but it revealed anxiety about sexism, concern about being perceived as sexist, and efforts to compensate by performing antisexism.

Even when individuals were actively engaged in behavior that could be viewed as antiracist or antisexist, they still experienced status anxiety. After the 2008 Democratic presidential primary, which pitted Barack Obama against Hillary Clinton, researchers found evidence of what they called "compensatory egalitarianism" among white voters. Those who held egalitarian views—that is, those who did not want to be seen as either racist or sexist—were more likely to begin their explanation of their candidate choice by condemning prejudice against the outgroup they didn't choose. In other words, those who voted for Obama began by condemning sexism, and those who voted for Clinton began by condemning racism. Researchers interpreted these statements as intended to alleviate anxiety about being labeled either racist or sexist.[8]

Individuals who are anxious that others will perceive them as either racist or sexist often take measures to alleviate that anxiety. This effort to quiet outgroup-related status anxiety is an effort to acquire social capital.

The Quest for Social Capital

In one episode of *Seinfeld*, George Costanza's boss accuses him of racism, and George desperately wants to prove him wrong. "You know what'd be great? If he could see me with some of my black friends," George muses. "Yeah, except you don't really have any black friends," Jerry observes. George eventually pays Jerry's pest exterminator—the only black person he knows—to go to lunch with him in the presence of his boss. The plan backfires and George's boss uncovers the scheme; George's boss tells him that he has "sunk to a new low."[9]

George's efforts can be understood using the lens of social capital. The sociologist Nan Lin describes "social capital" as an "investment in social relations with expected returns in the marketplace."[10] Lin specifies that the "market chosen for analysis may be economic, political, labor, or community." Lin's research speaks to identity capitalism in two important ways. First, his work speaks to identity: ingroup members invest in relationships with outgroup members because they expect returns. Second, he demonstrates that relationships with outgroup members are valuable in all kinds of settings, from the workplace to the university to the big screen to the campaign platform.

Social capital influences "exchange"—a sociological term referring to an interaction involving a transaction of resources. Exchange has both a social component—the exchange requires a relationship between the actors—and a market component—the transaction of resources. The transaction of resources may be economic or noneconomic: it might involve a transfer of money, commodities, power, opportunity, status, or any of the other benefits I've discussed.

The desire for social capital neatly explains George's behavior and its underlying motivation. George has made an investment in social relations, albeit a rather small one: he has taken Jerry's black pest exterminator to lunch. In return, George expects returns in a market of sorts: he expects his standing to improve in his work environment. The "exchange" in question is straightforward: George buys the pest exterminator lunch; the pest exterminator appears with him in public and implies, via his presence, that George isn't racist. While of course the story is fictional, it replicates the real dynamic that appears in countless social interactions, including many in this book.

Social capital can also elevate groups. *Seinfeld*'s foray into the "black friends" defense involves identity capitalism both *within* the show—George's attempt to showcase a black friend—and *by* the show—a sitcom with an all-white starring cast attempting to get credit for racial awareness by presenting a humorous take on a common racial phenomenon. As a result, the show and the people associated with it—actors, producers, entertainment executives—also gained social capital. In Lin's terminology, the show acquired social capital by investing in social relations with an expectation of gains in the marketplace. Again, the "exchange" is straightforward: the show recruits a black actor, Ellis Williams, willing to perform the specific scripted role to generate benefits for the show; the actor takes home his paycheck. The transaction occurs without any substantive commitment such as giving the black pest exterminator a larger role—or even an occasionally recurring one.

These simple examples lead us to a broader understanding of social capital. Sociologists often focus on the value contained in social networks.

By adding outgroup members to their social networks, ingroup members increase the value of their social networks as well as their social capital.[11] Relationships provide value, and relationships with outgroup members have unique benefits for the ingroup. The process can involve individuals, organizations, or frequently both.[12]

The quest for social capital explains why identity capitalists pursue the appearance of diversity through relationships and other affiliations. It also explains why diversity is particularly desirable to market participants seeking either to distinguish themselves favorably from other participants or to avoid distinguishing themselves unfavorably.

When Status Leaks

Social capital isn't just out there free for the taking. Researchers have documented the many ways outgroup members lack social capital in comparison to ingroup members. Women tend to have less social capital in areas relating to their careers than do men.[13] Similarly, nonwhite people tend to have less social capital in workplace environments,[14] and they are therefore more likely to be negatively affected by layoffs.[15] Outgroup members are more likely than ingroup members to approach workplace interactions from a social capital deficit.

Sociologist Joel Podolny explains that status—defined as someone's position in a hierarchy—similarly explains behavior in market settings and in social settings.[16] Our desire for status and our position in the hierarchy influence our willingness to form relationships and affiliate with other people. A high-status person is unlikely to affiliate with a low-status person unless the latter has something the former wants, and people are always looking to trade up. As Groucho Marx famously said, "I don't want to belong to any club that will accept people like me as a member."[17]

Podolny and others demonstrate that status "leaks": when two people associate with one another, the higher-status person tends to lose status while the lower-status person tends to gain status. (Remember when Britney Spears married Kevin Federline? He temporarily became kind of famous; meanwhile tabloids ran headlines about her fall from grace.[18]) Such relationships are common: the odd couple whose friends and family question their attraction is a staple of cinematic romantic comedy.

But the idea of status leaks extends beyond pop stars and romcoms to all sorts of institutions. In the investment banking industry, for instance, individual investment banks hesitate to enter exchanges with lower-status banks. Similarly, wineries sometimes hesitate to list the appellation of lower-status regions on their labels—and may even hesitate to create objectively higher-quality products if that would involve associating themselves with a region with subjectively lower status. The desire for status influences the exchanges that generate social capital. It partially determines which exchanges actors will undertake, and why.

The same principles influence less overtly economic markets, too. America today has a status market in what I'll call "nonracism." Within this market, white people and predominantly white institutions tend to have relatively low status. This might result from an institution's particular history, such as resisting integration. It might result from ongoing practices, such as displaying Confederate monuments around a college campus. It might simply be that historically nonwhite institutions, such as HBCUs, or institutions that lack a majority racial group, like many community colleges, benefit from a presumption that they will be less racist and more inclusive than their predominantly white counterparts.

Whatever the specific reason, when a white person or a predominantly white institution affiliates with a nonwhite person, the result is a status leak. The nonwhite person loses some amount of status, and the white person absorbs some of the status that the nonwhite person has lost. The white person or predominantly white institution has increased its status within the "nonracism" market by demonstrating an affiliation or relationship with a nonwhite person. Meanwhile, the nonwhite person's status is often diminished within that same market because they've chosen to affiliate with a white individual or predominantly white institution.

Randall Kennedy has chronicled how black people often experience diminished status, particularly those who seek out "elite, predominantly white settings," when other black people perceive that they have "sold out" to the expectations of white society.[19] His observation holds true on the ground. Black people have lost credibility on racial matters by affiliating with Donald Trump. Of Clarence Thomas—whose estrangement from many blacks did not begin with Trump, but who did not help matters by posing with Trump for a photo in the Oval Office—the rapper KRS-One says, "The White man ain't the Devil I promise / You want to see the Devil take a look at Clarence Thomas."[20] Of Omarosa, writer Earl Ofari Hutchinson offers this assessment: "Her tell-all mea culpa won't win her any brownie points with most blacks. . . . Their loathing of Omarosa is virtually frozen in stone. She's still roundly lambasted as a two-bit opportunist, a racial sellout and an ego-driven hustler."[21] Of Kanye West, following a bizarre meeting with Trump in the Oval Office, former DNC chair Donna Brazile stated that West "has set us back 155 years"—apparently referring, roughly, to the time the South surrendered in the Civil War.[22] Without question, whatever racial credibility Donald Trump's outgroup supporters and surrogates had before they encountered him, that credibility has been sorely diminished with their affiliation.

The status analysis applies to other identity markets. Consider Brett Kavanaugh's parade of women supporters, from his former clerks to his high school friends to the infamous "carpool mom."[23] One particularly outspoken supporter was Lisa Blatt, the head of the appellate and Supreme Court practice at large law firm Arnold and Porter. Blatt wrote an op-ed praising Kavanaugh's qualifications, in which she twice identified herself as a "liberal feminist Democrat" and then introduced him on the Senate floor.[24] Blatt's op-ed reveals significant blind spots. She emphasized in particular her concern about *Roe v. Wade*, citing her own teenage daughter—ignoring, perhaps intentionally, that wealthy women, such as women who are partners at major law firms and their daughters, will always be able to obtain abortions, by traveling to other countries if necessary.

The affiliation between Blatt and Kavanaugh also led to a status leak. Kavanaugh increased his status as a result of Blatt's op-ed and willingness to put her reputation behind him. Likely some people found Blatt's defense of Kavanaugh at least somewhat persuasive, and his credibility increased as a result. At the same time, the affiliation diminished Blatt's credibility on women's issues. Many women's groups view Kavanaugh's views on reproductive rights as well outside the mainstream of American legal thought.[25] The accusations of sexual assault against him—and, even more so, his angry frat boy defense before the Senate Judiciary Committee—disgusted and repulsed millions nationwide. Blatt's decision to support Kavanaugh despite these issues will, for many people, forever diminish her credibility on issues relating to the well-being of women.

Why would Blatt willingly sacrifice her own credibility to support Kavanaugh? One possible answer is a straightforward one: at the time of his confirmation she was the head of the appellate and Supreme Court practice at Arnold and Porter; she has since moved to a similar position at Williams and Connolly. As journalist Mark Joseph Stern explains, any large law firm "will always, *always*, value capital over justice. The needs of its paying clients will take priority . . . every single time. That is the cardinal rule of Big Law, and it should come as no surprise that Blatt is playing this nomination by the books."[26] The narrow market in which Blatt's outgroup identity as a woman is valuable to Kavanaugh is far outweighed by the larger social context in which Kavanaugh now has lifetime access to massive judicial power. Blatt's worst-case scenario was that Kavanaugh would not be confirmed and she would merely have an excellent relationship with a judge on the D.C. Circuit. Kavanaugh's elevation to the Supreme Court was a coup for both of them.

Lisa Blatt is not a low-status person. She's a well-known and powerful lawyer. But a Supreme Court justice such as Brett Kavanaugh unquestionably holds more power—some of it affecting Blatt herself and her career. The status differential increases by orders of magnitude when it comes to people lacking some of Blatt's privileges: people who are not white or wealthy or well-educated or heterosexual.

As Blatt's choices emphasize, one's status in a particular market is subject to an important condition. The status market for identity—in which outgroup members have certain advantages—does not occur in a vacuum. Rather, it occurs against the backdrop of a society in which virtually all the important benefits are controlled by the ingroup, ranging from power to money to opportunity. Because outgroup members are often lacking, relative to ingroup members, in these important status indicators, they are more likely to engage in status exchanges related to identity. It's a chance to get ahead.

Endless Black Friends

In the movie *Trainwreck*, Amy Schumer's eponymous character goes to interview a sports doctor, Aaron, played by Bill Hader. In his office, Aaron becomes suspicious of Amy's racial views.

AARON: Do you have a problem with black people?

AMY: No! I love black people. I *prefer* black people.

AARON: Do you have black friends?

AMY: *Endless* black friends.

AARON: Can you show me pictures of your black friends on your phone?

AMY: You want to see pictures on my phone of my black friends?

AARON: Yeah, you must have a lot of them.

AMY [*scrolling and stalling*]: I have so many. I'm just deciding which one, because there's so many.

She then shows him a photo of herself with a white girlfriend. There's a black waiter in the background. Aaron isn't having it. He demands to see another photo. "My phone just died," Amy says.

For ingroup members seeking to improve their status, anxiety is the "why," and—as we now see—identity capitalism is the "how." Like George Constanza, Schumer's character wants to prove her egalitarian beliefs. Within a status market for identity tolerance, members of ingroups want to rise to the top. But it's hard to communicate tolerance directly. This is why we end up with identity capitalism: an opportunity for ingroup members to use proxies to communicate their tolerance. People often use such proxies as a substitute for independent judgments about the relevant characteristics of individuals or institutions. This is true outside the identity context: when a college applicant submits an application, it's far easier to look at their test score and grade point average than to dig into their essays or to interview them. Or when a job applicant submits a resume, it's easier to look at their educational credentials and the status of their references than to observe more complex differences in individual performance.[27]

Proxies require signaling to work. It's not enough to have a nonwhite friend; other people have to *know* you have a nonwhite friend. This is why identity capitalists usually broadcast their affiliations with members of outgroups. We can't probe the inner cognitive processes of a white individual for racist ideation or infiltrate the internal workplace culture of an institution to detect racist norms. So observing a white person's affiliation with a nonwhite individual serves as a proxy for making independent judgments about those factors. The affiliation signals to outsiders that the white person or predominantly white institution is nonracist. If the person or institution was racist, the reasoning goes, they would not seek out an affiliation with a nonwhite person, nor would the nonwhite person agree to affiliate with them.

Signaling about identity is a kind of performance. Racist comments are common in what sociologists Leslie Picca and Joe Feagin call the "backstage"—all-white spaces in which white people feel free to make jokes and comments in areas they would not make in the "frontstage"—a multiracial or multicultural setting.[28] But in the racial "frontstage" white people generally adhere to social norms against overtly racist speech and behavior. A similar phenomenon emerges in relation to sexism. Some men feel free to engage in so-called "locker room talk" in spaces where only men are present; in mixed-gender settings, however, they assume a more respectful tone.

In the age of the Internet, social media provides a prime opportunity for signaling tolerance and affinity for an outgroup. Ingroup individuals pose with members of outgroups—often exaggerating the closeness of their relationship—or ostentatiously opine on social justice issues while doing nothing of substance to advance them.[29] President Donald Trump's twitter feed is a prominent example, featuring a regular stream of photos of the president with Clarence Thomas, Ben Carson, Katrina Pearson, Omarosa, and Diamond and Silk. Michael Cohen, Donald Trump's long-time lawyer turned adversary, tweeted a collage of himself with his supposed black friends to prove that he is not racist (Figure 3.1).[30]

Performative tolerance also arises out of "voluntourism"—the practice of traveling in developing countries while engaging in some nebulous version of "doing good" or "helping the less fortunate." One former volunteer describes, with chagrin, a photo of herself surrounded by black children in a village in Africa:

> Here we have a smiling young white girl with a French braid, medical scrubs, and a well-intentioned smile. This young lady is the center-piece of the photo; she is its protagonist. Her scrubs suggest that she is doing important work among those who are *so* poor, *so* vulnerable, and *so* Other. . . . I'm beaming in the photograph, half towering and half hovering over these children. I do not know their names, they do

not know my name, but I directed a friend to capture this moment with my own camera.[31]

Writer Teju Cole calls this the "White Savior Industrial Complex," observing that too often "Africa serves as a backdrop for white fantasies of conquest and heroism."[32] Pakistani-English columnist Rafia Zakaria explains, "The photo ops, the hugs with the kids and the meals with the natives are part of this package; the helpers can see and touch those they are saving and take evidence of their new nobility home with them. Poverty and its very real indignities give way to a new form of exploitation, those suffering put on stage to provoke a lucky-me gratitude for the voluntourist's ordinary life

FIGURE 3.1. Michael Cohen has no tolerance for racism, and he has a collage to prove it. Source: Twitter, Michael Cohen, August 16, 2017.

back home."[33] As usual, *The Onion* captures both the pervasiveness of the phenomenon and its absurdity: "Local 22-year-old Angela Fisher told reporters Tuesday that her six-day visit to the rural Malawian village of Neno has complete changed her profile picture on Facebook."[34]

Online dating sites provide yet another forum for signaling outgroup affinity. Between 2008 and 2014, users of dating website OK Cupid became significantly less likely to say that they strongly prefer to date someone of their own race. And 84 percent of OK Cupid users say they would not consider dating someone who has vocalized a strong negative bias toward a certain race of people. Yet their actual behavior during the same time period remained the same. For example, all nonblack men rated black women as significantly less attractive and were less likely to start conversations with black women, all women preferred men of their own race, and women were otherwise less likely to start conversations with both Asian and black men.[35] The views that OK Cupid users communicate in their profiles don't reflect their actual behavior when they think no one is looking.

Institutions signal outgroup affinity too. In May 2018, Fox News named Suzanne Scott, formerly president of programming, as its first woman CEO. But Scott's selection did not occur in a vacuum. Rather, it occurred after Roger Ailes stepped down as CEO in 2016 after harassment allegations from several women, including former *Fox & Friends* host Gretchen Carlson, and former star Bill O'Reilly settled the six publicly known sexual harassment lawsuits against him for a total of about $45 million.[36] Lachlan Murdoch—son of media mogul Rupert Murdoch, whose company owned Fox News until 2019—wrote in *Variety* that Scott is "the only woman in our industry running a news division or cable news network. Indeed, her programming changes created the most gender-diverse lineup in all of cable news."[37] Although Scott was also alleged to have aided in retaliating against Carlson for her claims against Ailes, and to have enforced Ailes' "miniskirt policy" for women, Fox News nonetheless lauded her appointment as an achievement for women.

Fox News is not alone. After Travis Kalanick resigned as CEO of Uber in part due to comments about sexual harassment and a raft of studies suggesting racial and gender disparities in the experiences of users, the company replaced him with Iranian-American Dara Khosrowshahi. While Krosrowshahi's reflective and diplomatic style was a contrast to Kalanick's self-described "burn the village" approach, he also brought with him the capital of nonwhite status and an immigrant narrative.

Researchers in organizational behavior have found that corporate boards are more likely to promote women and people of color to top leadership roles when an organization is in crisis[38]—a phenomenon that researchers have termed the "glass cliff."[39] The reasons behind this phenomenon are complex. Some suggest that women and people of color may be more likely to accept a risky appointment because they may view it as their only chance, or that boards may view women as having the positivity and warmth needed to lead in times of crisis. Given the praise that companies generally receive for diversifying, it also seems plausible that such signaling is particularly valuable for struggling companies.

Even beyond times of crisis, research shows that institutions instigate a great deal of signaling. Patrick Shin and Mitu Gulati refer to one signaling practice as "showcasing": institutions gain status by placing women, people of color, and other outgroup members in visible positions. They argue that placing women and minorities in prominent positions in the workplace signals "a certain level of geniality toward members of the showcased individual's group and a certain kind of sensitivity or attitude about diversity in general."[40] This signaling benefits the workplace that engages by communicating that the workplace cares about diversity whether or not it actually does.

Both individuals and institutions engage in signaling. Individuals signal in both public and private life; institutions of all kinds signal, including corporations, colleges and universities, daycare centers, public agencies, movie and film productions, advertisers, and even funeral homes. And signaling can happen anywhere: in a conversation, on social media, on a website, in a board meeting, on a billboard. It sometimes seems that everyone is anxious to tout their tolerance and inclusivity at any opportunity.

The Identity Market

When everyone wants to signal tolerance, one result is a tendency toward identity capitalism—and a related need for people on whom to capitalize. A market for identity is born.

If there is a market for identity, then we can think of identity as a commodity that we all produce. I'm not saying identity *should* be a commodity—just that it's helpful to treat it that way for the present analysis. Identity production is complex and nuanced. Some identity characteristics are visible and mostly immutable—the color of someone's skin, the shape of their eyes, whether they can walk. Other identity characteristics are visible but can be changed—hair style, clothing, mannerisms. Still other identity characteristics are invisible: some are mostly immutable (sexual orientation; ADHD), while other such characteristics can, at least in principle, be changed (religious beliefs).

Collectively, these characteristics determine the value of a particular identity. Individuals are not bystanders when it comes to their own identity. While some characteristics are predetermined, how someone performs identity deeply influences the way that others perceive that identity.[41] Scholars have described three versions of identity performance: passing, covering, and flaunting. "Passing" refers to presenting oneself as an identity that one is not. The practice is historically associated with light-skinned black people who presented themselves as white to better their social and economic opportunities, but today could include, for example, a closeted gay person or a student who does not tell anyone she has dyslexia. "Covering"—a term popularized by legal scholar Kenji Yoshino—refers to presenting oneself in a way that does not deny the existence of a particular identity characteristic, but also intentionally does not make that characteristic noticeable to others.[42] For example, a gay man might be out, but might also refrain from putting a photo of his partner on his desk at work, and might avoid telling his colleagues that he participated in a pride parade. Finally, "flaunting" is the practice of making an aspect of one's identity especially noticeable: soliciting donations from colleagues for a charity benefiting LGBTQ youth, for example, or speaking in an exaggerated accent that connotes a particular race or ethnicity.

Somewhere between covering and flaunting is simply "being"—behaving in the way you would if there were no social pressure in any other direction. Categorizing behavior as one or the other is a difficult task, as one person's flaunting—say, wearing a rainbow pocket square as a signal of gay pride—might be another's way of simply being himself. (For many gay men, acting like Jonathan Van Ness of *Queer Eye* would probably be flaunting, but for Jonathan, one has the impression that he is simply being himself.) But the task at hand is not to distinguish among these various ways of performing identity. Rather, we need to recognize that each decision about performing identity influences the value of that identity as a commodity.

Our leaders do it. President Franklin Roosevelt often met with people while sitting behind the resolute desk in the Oval Office. He was not passing—everyone knew he used a wheelchair—but perhaps he was engaging in an act of covering by declining to make his disability more noticeable than necessary to those around him.

And we regular people also engage in variations of this behavior. A person with a racially identified first name might choose to adopt a nickname—perhaps eschewing "Muhammed" in favor of "Mo"—or a black woman might choose to straighten her hair. Alternatively, Muhammed might choose to go by his given first name, or the same black woman might choose to wear her hair in a style that emphasizes its natural texture. A native speaker of Cantonese might choose to avoid speaking Cantonese to family on the phone in her workplace, or she might emphasize her bilinguality to her employer. In response to inquiries about his weekend, a gay man might choose to tell his colleagues that he participated in a pride parade, or he might just say he hung out with friends. Each decision involves a complex process through which an individual produces the commodity of racial identity. Such decisions might make identity a more valuable commodity in some situations and a less valuable one in others. Put in market terms, identity performance affects the value of identity as a commodity.

Pricing the Priceless

"Money can't buy me love," sang the Beatles. "The best things in life are free," concurred Coco Chanel. And most of us agree with both of them. We tend to place our loftiest ideals beyond the reach of the market.

By contrast, putting a price tag on something places it within the realm of the mundane.[43] Commodifying an item puts it on the same level as everything else you can buy. It may be costly—Chanel went on to observe that "the second best things are very, very expensive"—but it's still for sale.

Commodifying identity—placing a price tag on it—enables exploitation and reinforces inequality. Commodification puts outgroup members in a double bind: perform the identity the way the ingroup prefers or else suffer economic and social consequences. Legal scholars Devon Carbado and Mitu Gulati observe that everybody "works identity" to some degree, but the greatest amount of identity work falls on outsiders to the dominant culture because they are subject to more negative stereotypes that they must work to overcome. Identity work has downsides. It is exhausting and consuming—"the outsider not only has to perform, but she has to perform well."[44] Identity performances can backfire if others view the performance as strategic or calculating.[45]

Performance demands play out in many ways. People of color often talk about code switching—shifting between a performance of race that is palatable to the ingroup and one that is more authentic.[46] As Dave Chappelle says, "Every black American is bilingual. All of us. We speak street vernacular, and we speak job interview."[47] The film *Sorry to Bother You* illustrates Chappelle's observation.[48] The black character Cassius Green gets a new job as a telemarketer but fails to make a single sale until his black coworker Langston suggests, "Use your white voice." Cassius does so, and quickly becomes successful. Examples of code switching drawn from the media make us laugh, but they also describe a significant burden on the outgroup, requiring psychological labor over and above the job description.

To maximize the market value of one's identity, outgroup members must thread the needle: they must be identifiably different to benefit from their outgroup status, yet not so different that they meet with ingroup disapproval. Ann Hopkins was denied partnership at Price Waterhouse two years in a row, even though she was well-qualified on every objective metric and frequently outperformed her male coworkers. Her supervisor told her she needed to "walk more femininely, talk more femininely, dress more femininely, wear make-up, have her hair styled, and wear jewelry."[49] Another partner said in a written evaluation that she needed a "course in charm school." Hopkins eventually brought a sex discrimination lawsuit and won an important case, *Price Waterhouse v. Hopkins*, before the Supreme Court, but her victory was certainly a second best: women want to make partner, not win lawsuits. Her story clearly illustrates the challenges for outgroup members: their identities may be valuable to the firm as a way of signaling diversity, but only to the extent that the identity commodity they produce is congenial to the ingroup.

Beyond the costs to individuals, commodification also harms society as a whole. It replaces productive discourse. Why have a hard conversation about your school's lack of diversity when you can just put up some enticing photos showcasing diversity on the website? Commodifying identity impoverishes our thought and discourse surrounding identity. It infects the way we think about and talk to one another. Commodifying identity causes us to think of it as just another *thing*—like bread, clothing, or furniture—that we can take, use, consume, exploit, enjoy, ignore, disparage, or discard as we wish. This attitude is fundamentally at odds with an attitude of respect for identity, or at the very least an attitude of open conversation about it. The desire for particular identity commodities doesn't reflect worthy feelings about that identity, such as a desire for respect or inclusion. It simply reflects the desire to signal the status and gain the social capital associated with that particular identity commodity.

Commodification of identity also stokes the fires of resentment. Many Asian American women—stereotyped as gentle and submissive—are not only outraged by the abuses of the Trump administration but also particularly angered by his mostly aesthetic effort to diversify his cabinet by appointing Nikki Haley as ambassador to the United Nations and Elaine Chao to Secretary of Transportation. Others are angry at the administration's attempt to use Asian American people as a wedge in affirmative action lawsuits against Harvard and the University of North Carolina. As Yeon Choimorrow, then the interim executive director at the National Asian Pacific American Women's Foundation, said, "We've been called the model minority. We've been pitted against other people of color for the amusement of white people in this country over and over. And I think there is a growing movement in the AAPI community where we are saying that's not who we are. That's not how we want to be identified or associated."[50]

Commodification of identity interferes with progress toward equality between ingroups and outgroups. Legal scholar e. christi cunningham argues that "tokenism leverages undervalued identities," maintaining the racial status quo by parading an exception.[51] By showcasing outgroup employees in prominent positions, employers attempt to get credit for diversity while making minimal substantive changes. Shin and Gulati agree, explaining that showcasing women and minorities for their signaling value treats them as "prized trophies" or "passive emblems." Showcasing subtly reinforces the perception that women and people of color can't succeed in work environments on their own: they're only there because the company needs to look diverse, not because they bring anything of substance. Including outgroup members in this manner reinforces a common and harmful narrative among ingroup members rather than disrupting it. Treating identity as a commodity devalues identity for everyone.

Identity Capitalism: A Summary

Let's review the lessons of social science. Ingroup members experience anxiety about whether they are perceived favorably by and in relation to the outgroup. This status anxiety creates a drive to gain social capital by affiliating with members of outgroups. Such affiliations lead to status leaks: when a high-status person associates with a low-status person, the former cedes some status to the latter. Finally, none of these maneuvers matter without signaling. Signaling is how ingroup members communicate status to the outside world. In a nutshell, this is the how and why of identity capitalism.

This richer theoretical account of identity capitalism also allows a deeper understanding of its harms. What happens when identity becomes a prized way of signaling status? For one thing, identity starts to look more and more like something that can be bought and sold—a commodity. Ironically, treating identity as a market commodity actually cheapens its value.

Status anxiety, social capital, and signaling explain a lot about ingroup motivations for commodifying identity. But what about the outgroup? If ingroup members are avid consumers of outgroup identity, then how does the outgroup respond? We will see next that members of outgroups aren't merely passive targets.

4

IDENTITY ENTREPRENEURS

R EMEMBER SARAH PALIN? Of course you do. The 2008 Republican candidate for vice president was and is a willing and
eager participant in identity capitalism. Palin was neither oblivious
nor passive to the reasons underlying her selection as the nominee for vice
president. She immediately framed presidential candidate John McCain's
selection of her around her gender and presented it as a bold substantive
reform rather than as a purely strategic maneuver. She explained that Mc-
Cain "didn't go with a conventional, safer pick. John believed in change, the
power of independent and committed individuals, the power of women."[1]

Palin frequently took opportunities to make her gender even more salient. In a campaign speech, Palin, flanked by women who supported her,
announced, "Our opponents think they have the women's vote all locked
up, which is a little presumptuous since only our side has a woman on the
ticket. When it came time for choosing a vice president, somehow Obama

couldn't bring himself to choose a woman who got 18 million votes in the primary."[2] She even memorably misquoted Madeleine Albright: "There's a special place in Hell reserved for women who don't support other women."[3]

As Palin shows us, outgroup members are not always passive, unknowing, or reluctant participants in identity capitalism. Sometimes they deliberately use their outgroup identity for personal benefit.[4] They may want a job, a promotion, social status, fame, or simply money. I call these enterprising outgroup members *identity entrepreneurs*—individuals who leverage their outgroup identity to benefit themselves.

Sarah Palin's behavior exposes an important aspect of identity entrepreneurship. For an outgroup member to leverage her identity most profitably, the outgroup identity must be visible to the ingroup, but must also take a form of which the ingroup approves. Palin is a successful identity entrepreneur precisely because her appearance and demeanor are conventionally feminine, because she embraces gender roles such as "mother" and "wife," and because she is unthreatening to ingroup members—here, a wealthy straight white male Republican presidential candidate and others like him. Palin offers her take on gender roles: "Women have a unique perspective. Typically, they are less ambitious for superficial [*sic*] power than men and more focused on providing for the needs of others."[5] While this statement is nominally feminist—it embraces the notion that women should take on leadership roles and wield power—it also unequivocally reinforces stereotypes, evoking an idea of women as selfless caregivers with limited ambition.

By asserting that women are more selfless and less concerned with personal glory than men, Palin comforts men suffering from anxiety that women might prove to be better leaders and replace them altogether. Her version of identity is reassuringly stereotype-affirming to a male-dominated political ingroup. Palin's identity entrepreneurship suggests that to reap the rewards of identity entrepreneurship, it's not enough simply to make one's identity as a woman noticeable: one has to be the *right kind* of woman.[6] As philosopher Kate Manne has argued, men, and sometimes society at large, punish women in various ways for "withholding and failing to give[;] being cold, calculous and heartless; neglecting their natural duty to provide safe haven and nurture"—for failing to act the way women are "supposed" to act.[7]

In this chapter we'll look at identity entrepreneurs from politicians to porn stars, from Shakespeare to *Queer Eye*. Identity entrepreneurs are legion and complicated: it's easy to celebrate the ones we like and condemn the ones we don't. But before imposing judgment, we need to understand better what identity entrepreneurship is, how it works, and the full spectrum of its consequences.

Identity Entrepreneurs: Why, How, and Who?

Identity capitalism creates a market that rewards identity entrepreneurship—the act of leveraging outgroup identity for personal benefit.[8] The word "entrepreneur" is particularly appropriate to describe the outgroup response to identity capitalism because it has neither universally positive nor universally negative implications. Entrepreneurs, particularly small business owners, are respected and even valorized in America. Yet the word "entrepreneurial" is sometimes used in a far less laudatory way to communicate that the person in question is self-promoting, grasping, inauthentic, a climber. The word, like identity entrepreneurship itself, is full of ambiguity.

Sometimes the market that identity capitalists create is obvious. "We need to cast five fabulous gay men for a reality makeover show," a producer might say (and probably did). In such a situation, a gay man who leverages his outgroup identity, making his sexual orientation salient to an ingroup of producers and casting directors, is engaging in identity entrepreneurship. If successful, his behavior may lead to tangible financial benefits in the labor market—more concretely, a role on a television show. At other times the market for identity involves less an explicit quid pro quo and more a promise of future benefits. "We need to add some women who work here to the speaker lineup at the new-employee training because right now all the speakers are men," a human resources professional at a big corporation might say (and undoubtedly has). Here there is also a market, albeit a less tangible one. Women who agree to speak at the training aren't getting paid directly for Speaking While Women, but they may still gain some advantages: the new hires may immediately see them as important people within the corporation, their bosses may hear of and appreciate their contribution to the training, and they may gain the gratitude of the human resources department, all of which might come in handy later on. None of these advantages are economic in the immediate sense, but they might translate to economic benefits in the future, such as a choice assignment or even a promotion. In both these examples, as we learned in the previous chapter, the extent to which outgroup members benefit from identity entrepreneurship depends on the particular way they choose to perform their identity.

Not every outgroup member who is targeted by identity capitalism is an identity entrepreneur. Some subjects of identity capitalism are conscripted without knowledge or consent. George Fitzhugh almost certainly never asked the slaves who he insisted were grateful and happy for their enslavement for permission to share the views he falsely attributed to them. Other subjects of identity capitalism, however, are willing and eager participants. Vocal anti-suffrage women were perfectly willing for men to amplify and rely on their commentary, and they enhanced their social status within certain social circles by doing so. These anti-suffrage women were early identity entrepreneurs: they intentionally made their outgroup identity more noticeable in order to benefit from the ingroup.

We can also approach identity entrepreneurship through the lens of college admissions. Take a college student who is socially identified as Asian—that is, a person on the street would perceive him as Asian—and attends a predominantly white university. If the school photographs the student extensively, features him on its website, and perhaps even photoshops him into a brochure, the student has been recruited—involuntarily, perhaps even unknowingly—into participation in identity capitalism.

Contrast this student's passive involvement with the active behavior of a second student. The second student appears ethnically ambiguous, although his mother is part Chinese, and his surname is not identifiably Asian. Suppose that this person's ethnic background is not particularly important to him. Yet also suppose that he takes affirmative steps to make his Asian identity salient to the predominantly white institutions with which he interacts. For example, he checks only the "Asian" box on his college application, knowing that the schools to which he is applying enroll few Asian students. He writes his personal statement about his Asian heritage. He prominently lists his nominal membership in Asian cultural groups on his resume. He expands further on his Asian identification when he applies for a scholarship designed for underrepresented minorities.

The first student is merely a passive participant in a system of identity capitalism. The second student is an identity entrepreneur. Against a backdrop of identity capitalism in which racial diversity is a commodity valued by institutions, the second student knows that his Asian racial identity is a commodity of value and has chosen to act on that knowledge. By making that identity obvious to admissions and scholarship committees, he reaps tangible benefits in the form of increased chances of admission, more generous financial aid, and perhaps even opportunities for leadership within the school.

I am not judging the choices or behavior of either student. My point is to differentiate between two different forms of involvement in identity capitalism. What distinguishes the two is the deliberate effort of the second student to derive value from his identity by behaving in a way that he would not, but for the incentives and potential advantages created by the ingroup.

Identity entrepreneurship is a common and unsurprising consequence of identity capitalism, but outgroup involvement in identity capitalism is not inherently identity entrepreneurship. And it's important to keep in mind that someone can be both an identity capitalist and an identity entrepreneur.

Outgroup participation in identity capitalism is complicated, contingent, and fraught with ambiguity. Identity capitalism quite often creates a double bind for outgroup members: do they behave in ways that ingroup identity capitalists tend to reward, or do they resist these incentives and suffer the consequences? My goal is not to condemn identity entrepreneurs, but rather to reveal the incentives they are given and the dilemmas they face.

Entrepreneurs Versus Sellouts

Everyone is familiar with the idea of selling out. We all have that friend who refuses to listen to a once-favored indie band whose music supposedly suffered once it got too commercial—that is, once the band "sold out." While we might roll our eyes at our friend, their attitude demonstrates a broader point: the label "sellout" is seldom a compliment.

When it comes to identity, selling out is treacherous. Legal scholar Randall Kennedy defines a "sellout" as "a person who betrays something to which she is said to owe allegiance."[9] He explains that, when used in a racial context, sellout "is a disparaging term that refers to blacks who knowingly or with gross negligence act against the interest of blacks as a whole." He offers examples of those he would categorize as sellouts, including "an African member of a black uplift organization who reveals its secrets to antiblack adversaries out of malevolence or merely for purposes of self-promotion" and "an African American who, believing that a given position is adverse to the interest of blacks, advances that position anyway for patently unjustifiable reasons."[10] For Kennedy, selling out by a black person requires more than simply disagreeing with most other black people and more, even, than doing things that are affirmatively bad for black people in the aggregate.

Selling out is also a familiar concept to other outgroups: when an act by an outgroup member disadvantages the interests of the outgroup as a whole, most outgroup members view selling out as a wrongful act. While outgroup members might disagree about what particular behavior is defined as selling out, once they reach a consensus that selling out has taken place, they have no trouble labeling it as undesirable, perhaps even disgraceful or reprehensible.

In contrast to selling out, identity entrepreneurship as I define it is neither inherently good nor inherently bad. Leveraging one's own identity for personal social or economic gain might be good for a variety of reasons—it might advance a historically disadvantaged outgroup member, redistribute social resources more equitably, or improve society as a whole. But leveraging one's own identity might also have negative consequences—it might advantage an individual at the expense of the group, reinforce harmful ingroup preferences, or create a hierarchy among outgroup members based on their appeal to the ingroup. Identity entrepreneurship can sometimes lead to the same sorts of disadvantages as selling out.

Selling out is a form of identity entrepreneurship, but identity entrepreneurship is not always selling out. Distinguishing between the two requires an examination of the individual actor's motivation and impact. Sellouts intentionally use their identity to gain an advantage for themselves at the expense of other members of their outgroup. Identity entrepreneurs leverage their outgroup identity for any one of a number of motivations and with a wide range of consequences. Selling out is generally a bad thing. Identity entrepreneurship is not always so straightforward.

The distinction between selling out and other forms of identity entrepreneurship is not always obvious. It hinges on the intent of the individual and the consequences of her actions; it must be evaluated on a case-by-case basis. And a participant may not understand that her identity performance benefits the ingroup at the expense of the outgroup. While such false consciousness might affect the way we feel about an outgroup identity entrepreneur—for example, we might feel more sympathy for her, even if we dislike the consequences of her actions—she's still behaving like an identity entrepreneur.[11]

A Sale to Suit Themselves

Before the Civil War, violently subjected to egregious conditions, slaves in America courageously fought to survive from one day to the next. When they learned they would be sold, sometimes their struggle for survival led them to emphasize certain personal characteristics to shape a sale in ways that benefited them. As historian Walter Johnson explains, the slaves "knew what the traders wanted them to say and what the buyers wanted to hear."[12] In a tragic irony, slaves became "the information brokers in the slave market," mediating between traders who wanted them to present themselves in a certain way and buyers who relied on their honesty. Their position of greater knowledge provided an opportunity for slaves to influence their own futures: "[S]laves could create themselves in the slave market, matching their self-representations to their own hoped-for outcomes. Sometimes, at enormous risk, they shaped a sale to suit themselves."[13]

The slave Henry Bibb, after spending months in a slave pen, eventually sought to improve his circumstances by presenting himself to appeal to a prospective buyer who he thought would be relatively humane. He understood that his light skin would cause the buyer to view him as a flight risk, so he truthfully emphasized that he was happily married to a woman who was also for sale, untruthfully claimed that he could not read, and voluntarily disclosed that he had run away once. Pleased by both the content of his answers and his apparent honesty, the master purchased both Bibb and his family.

Henry Bibb teaches us that even slaves, who were literally considered property, could leverage their identities to influence those around them. The people who owned them "were vulnerable to the vagaries of human interaction—deception, manipulation, and misunderstanding." In situations of deplorable unfreedom, under conditions of grievous subordination, outgroup members still found ways to exercise agency to benefit themselves—or, more accurately, to slightly mitigate the unspeakable harms they suffered.[14]

Such self-presentation is a form of identity entrepreneurship, and aptly demonstrates the distinction between identity entrepreneurship and selling out—surely a slave who attempts to shape her own sale is doing the former but not the latter. Like slavery, many of the historical examples of identity capitalism discussed in Chapter 2 reveal a complementary instance of identity entrepreneurship. Within the anti-suffrage movement, for example, some of the most active and ardent opponents of women voting were women themselves. The National Association Opposed to Women's Suffrage (NAOWS) was headed by anti-suffragists Josephine Dodge and Minnie Bronson, and had, at one point, as many as three hundred and fifty thousand members. The NAOWS was influential: examples of anti-suffragist men pointing to the existence of NAOWS are legion.[15]

One might ask why women would oppose their own ability to exercise political power. But an examination of the anti-suffragist movement through the lens of identity entrepreneurship offers a telling answer. Many of the anti-suffragists won praise for their activities from powerful men. Others reaped more concrete rewards. Nearly all were white, middle to upper class, and married to men involved in politics and law. By espousing anti-suffragist views, they maintained both their own social and community status and their husbands' in a politically contentious time.[16] Some even solidified their own social status by leveraging their anti-suffragism to facilitate a "good" marriage. Anti-suffragist Alice Hay Wadsworth built her marriage to the virulently anti-suffragist politician James Wolcott Wadsworth Jr. around their shared views. By lending her identity as a woman to the anti-suffragist movement, she also cemented her status in society and her compatibility with her politician husband.

It would be tempting to consign the anti-suffragists' antics to the dustbin of history. But in recent years women—with varying degrees of seriousness—have also made the argument that women shouldn't be able to vote—nicely supporting the views of various men who would also prefer that women not vote. Conservative pundit Ann Coulter, for example, said in 2007: "If we took away women's right to vote, we'd never have another Democratic president. It's kind of a pipe dream, it's a personal fantasy of mine."[17] Coulter is, of course, an identity entrepreneur. Her status as a woman elevates her within the male-dominated world of conservative punditry, and her willingness as a woman to float even half-jokingly the idea that women shouldn't vote wins her praise and support from a mostly male conservative ingroup that wouldn't much mind if women didn't or couldn't vote.[18] Members of this group buy her books, watch her television appearances, pay her speaking fees, and generally keep her in the public eye.

From slavery to the anti-suffragists, history is replete with examples of identity entrepreneurship. And such entrepreneurship has not diminished in the present day. The increasing complexity and connectedness of our society creates new and tempting opportunities for members of outgroups to leverage identity for personal profit.

An Asian Fantasy

When it comes to sex, people feel entitled to be candid about their identity preferences. If someone said, "I only like to work with men," or "I don't want to be friends with Asians," they would likely face substantial social and perhaps even legal consequences. But it's socially acceptable to say "I only like gay porn" or "I don't like watching porn with black girls"—or at least no more taboo than porn itself. The openness with which people express preferences about the porn they like to watch provides insight into the equally open acts of identity entrepreneurship that adult film stars undertake to advance their careers, both for status and for profit.

Asian and Asian American women are popular commodities in pornography. Scholars attribute this popularity to a confluence of racial and sexual stereotypes. Legal scholar Frank Wu explains one stereotype: "[T]he West knows that Asian women are exotic erotics, alluring coquettes hiding behind their fans. The China Doll or Geisha Girl possesses Oriental sex secrets that make her aggressive in bed, but she is also trained to be obedient around the house."[19] Mainstream media, movies, and television perpetuate this stereotype. While many Asian American women cringe at this characterization, its existence creates an undeniable opportunity within the adult film industry, in which Asian American women are some of the most active identity entrepreneurs.

One early Asian American identity entrepreneur in adult film is Jessica Steinhauser, who literally took the stage name Asia Carrera. Carrera states that she "picked Asia because I'm Asian, and because it's a pretty name."[20] (No one can accuse the porn industry of excessive subtlety.) Many of her films highlight her Asian identity, including *Asian Beauties*, *Asian Persuasion*, *Asian Silk*, and many similarly titled films created over a decade-long career, including a number with all-Asian female casts. Carrera's identity entrepreneurship paid dividends: she's won many awards, including the coveted Adult Video News Female Performer of the Year award in 1995, and even today, decades after she retired from the industry, her net worth is reported at around $1 million.

Following Carrera, the adult film actress Asa Akira further refined the art of identity entrepreneurship. And we know more about Akira's entrepreneurship—or, at least, we know more about how she wants it to be perceived—because of her autobiographical books and her active social media presence. Unsurprisingly, many of the films in which Akira has acted also feature racialized titles. Just a few titles from her extensive filmography are *Asian Anal Assassins*, *Asian Booty* (and, inevitably, *Asian Booty 2*), *Asian Erotic Dreams*, *Asian Fever 37*, and *Asian Girls Are Sexy*. As of 2016, the Internet Adult Film Database reported that Akira had appeared in 451 adult movies, about 50 of which were explicitly racialized by their titles alone. Films that do not have racialized titles might also contain sexualized racialization, as when Akira delivers lines like "fuck my tight little Asian pussy" or explicitly makes her race salient in other ways. Simply by appearing in these films, Akira engages in identity entrepreneurship.

More striking is how much else Akira does to leverage her particular brand of Asian femininity for status and profit. Her website prominently notes that she was born in Tokyo. She often explains in interviews that she is from Brooklyn, but then volunteers that her heritage is Japanese. She has cherry blossoms tattooed on her shoulder—a symbol associated with

Japan. She promotes a fleshlight—a male masturbatory device supposedly molded in the shape of her vagina—which has a "dragon" texture because, she explains, "I'm Asian." Her advertisements and promotional photos often feature Asian decorations (Chinese? Japanese? it doesn't really matter) such as dragons, orchids, incense, geishas, and a font that evokes stereotypical "Asianness," all for the consumption of a presumably heterosexual non-Asian male viewer.

Akira acknowledges her approach in her memoirs *Insatiable* and *Dirty Thirty*, which candidly discuss and blend her on-screen persona with her off-screen life. One passage explains,

> When I first started porn, I resented getting cast as the token Asian. . . . One out of every three shoots was an "Asian" scene. I can't even tell you how many times I've covered my naked body in sushi, or played the role of a mail-order bride. . . . Over time, I've come to embrace it. It's gotten me to where I am today, and it pretty much guarantees me work until the day I quit, since there is always a shortage of Asian girls in the business.[21]

One can hardly imagine a clearer statement of identity entrepreneurship. Akira realized that her identity was a potential source of profit. She then chose to highlight that identity to advance her career.

A Precarious Position

Identity entrepreneurship is perilous in ways that extend far beyond the individual identity entrepreneur. As a condition of their continued success, identity entrepreneurs may find themselves defending behavior and policies that are, they come to believe, indefensible. But what happens when an identity entrepreneur no longer has value to a particular ingroup?

The career of Omarosa Manigault Newman follows this precise trajectory. Omarosa was once a contestant on Donald Trump's reality show *The Apprentice* and, years later, became a member of his campaign and administration. In her memoir, Omarosa reveals that she was perfectly aware that Trump, his campaign, and his administration were identity capitalists. She knew they were using her identity as a black woman to shield the campaign and administration against charges of racism and misogyny. But rather than reject what she calls "Trumpworld," Omarosa chose to leverage her identity both within and beyond, both for personal gain and—if we believe her self-described motives—to advance the interests of the black community.

Omarosa acknowledges that she benefited from Trumpworld's use of her identity from the very beginning. Omarosa says of Trump's days on *The Apprentice*,

> Our relationship was symbiotic; we exploited each other. Trump and NBC used me to promote the show, lobby for an Emmy, and bring in diverse viewers. I used the success of the first season to catapult my Hollywood career on multiple shows, movies, a book deal, and celebrity appearances.[22]

She links Trump's interest in her at least partly to the value she provided to him as a defense against racism, suggesting, "I think it's possible he decided that because he was being called a racist in the press, it behooved him to cultivate a closer relationship with me. It was to his benefit when we created *The Ultimate Merger*, a TV show with a black woman lead and a black cast, which would wind up airing on TV One, a black-owned network."[23] Trump—a member of the ingroup—derived value from Omarosa's outgroup identity. Omarosa—a member of the outgroup—leveraged her identity for personal gain.

When Trump launched his presidential campaign in 2015, part of Omarosa's contribution was her racial and gender identity. She candidly observes that "[t]he campaign must have seen me as a two-pronged solution" because "I was black and a woman." This became even more true after Trump's unexpected presidential victory. Omarosa was proud of the opportunity to be near a president, but also presents herself as serving the black community. She says, "If I didn't go back to DC and be part of Trump's White House, what other black woman in Trump's orbit would? I was the only one in the unique position to keep Trump accountable." Omarosa seems to view her role as one of damage control, crediting herself with partial success at "the struggle [of] keeping Trump from sounding full racist on any given day."[24]

Ultimately, Omarosa left the White House under less than cordial circumstances.[25] But what happens to an identity entrepreneur cast out by the ingroup? Perhaps they try to find another ingroup.

Omarosa's post-Trump book *Unhinged* courted a different ingroup: political liberals who are opposed to the Trump administration and sympathetic to the plight of women, people of color, and other members of outgroups. (We might even characterize the ingroup to which Omarosa now appeals as *white* liberals, given that Omarosa's reputation among black people is highly negative and, in the view of many commentators, unlikely to change.[26]) Omarosa's new attempt to leverage her identity centers around the idea that she came from humble beginnings, shares many experiences with other members of the black community, believes in progressive causes, and entered the Trump administration in good faith with the hope that she could advance the interests of other black people and other women.

Post–White House, Omarosa is still leveraging her identity as a black woman. It's just that the audience is different now, and how she presents her identity has shifted correspondingly. Her circumstances reveal some of the risks of identity entrepreneurship. Her predicament also teaches that identity entrepreneurship is neither inherently good nor inherently bad. Rather, it is nuanced, complicated, and contextual. Let's take a look at some of the benefits of identity entrepreneurship—followed by some of the harms.

A Big Gay Jesus

The stars of *Queer Eye*, better known as the Fab Five, are targets of identity capitalism. They give entertainment and merchandise executives—mostly straight—an opportunity to profit from queer identity. The Fab Five are not passive participants. Rather, each of them is an identity entrepreneur. Simply by identifying as one of the Fab Five, they are leveraging gay identity in a way that the ingroup values. But the Fab Five also do much more than that. By performing an entertaining, camera-friendly version of gay male stylishness, they—individually and collectively—create an opportunity to profit from their own identities.

Good can come of identity entrepreneurship. Affirming the autonomy of outgroup members to leverage their identities—or not—is valuable in itself. A substantial psychological literature has documented the benefits associated with agency and self-determination.[27] That five gay men can become rich and famous (partly) by actively performing gay identity is already a big step in a country where sodomy was illegal in some states until 2003.[28]

Both ingroups and outgroups benefit from recognizing that outgroups are diverse, and identity entrepreneurship can help with this recognition. The Fab Five enrich the popular understanding of what it means to be gay by presenting subtly nuanced versions of gay identity—by helping viewers see gay men as individual human beings. Jonathan Van Ness delights many viewers, but *Queer Eye* wouldn't be so fab if all five stars shared his style, mannerisms, and demeanor.

The Fab Five regularly discuss the heterogeneity of gay identity among themselves on the show. During a scene at the beginning of a show in which they are driving to meet a show participant who lives in the country, they discuss their different reactions to rural Georgia:

JONATHAN: I feel uncomfortable whenever we get too far from a major metropolitan area.

KARAMO: We'll protect you!

ANTONI: I feel safe wherever we go.

[*simultaneously*]

TAN: Because you're white!

JONATHAN: You look straight!

[*laughter*]

KARAMO: Stick with the two brown guys and the gay guy—

JONATHAN: [*gesturing at himself*]—that looks like a big gay Jesus! But the only way I could get you on our level to understand the discomfort would be if I put you in a teeny baby crop top and made you go everywhere.

KARAMO: And then put you in blackface.

ANTONI: I will consider *one* of those things.

EVERYONE: The crop top?

ANTONI: Yeah.

KARAMO: Wouldn't it be horrible if he said the blackface?

[*laughter*][29]

In this forty-five-second conversation, the Fab Five (minus Bobby, who is probably reading CNN on his phone) educates viewers about several ways in which gay men's experiences can differ from one another. Antoni—who is white and can pass as straight—doesn't feel uncomfortable leaving major metropolitan areas. Karamo, who is black, and Tan, who is Pakistani and British, remind Antoni that some of his comfort in areas that are statistically less hospitable to nonwhite people is due to racial privilege. Jonathan then introduces a more complex idea: that the way Antoni chooses to perform his identity—that is, by wearing (trendy) jeans and T-shirts—does not immediately code him as gay to most people with whom he interacts. For someone like Jonathan, who dresses in a more stereotypically flamboyant way, people are more likely to identify him as gay and, in some cases, to treat him less well as a result. Finally, Karamo closes the loop with a gentle reminder of the ugly history of blackface and, with it, a reminder that black people in America have a unique history of oppression, particularly in the South.

These are important lessons for straight viewers. While one might argue that straight people should take responsibility for educating themselves, the reality is that a group of entertaining, charismatic, and likeable gay men can bring home these lessons in ways that many straight people would not receive any other way. Identity entrepreneurship facilitates better ingroup understanding of outgroup realities.

Demanding More

Rap music has long been viewed as the province of young urban black men. Many white people wrongly associate rap with a limited set of themes: lawbreaking, partying, casual sex, and ostentatious wealth. Bill O'Reilly once claimed that "the rap industry . . . glorifies depraved behavior, and that sinks into the minds of some young people"—ironic words, perhaps, from a man whose sexually harassing behavior was too much even for Fox News.[30] Of course, one does not have to know much about rap music to know that it also addresses important political themes, including racism, poverty, police brutality, and the inequities of the criminal justice system.[31] But the small but growing number of rappers who present challenges to the genre also demonstrate the power of identity entrepreneurship to broaden the conversation.

A woman rapping used to be a curiosity.[32] Today Nicki Minaj leverages her identity as a black woman into a commercially successful brand, using the genre to offer broader social commentary through a challenging and controversial lens of femininity and sexuality.[33] She says, "I came into this industry and demanded more. I wanted more for female rappers. I wanted more for black women. I wanted to make more than what men were making. And I did it."[34] She is candid about her identity entrepreneurship and what she did to stand out: "What people don't know is that before I was doing that craziness I was doing me, I was just doing regular sounding rap that anyone could hear and identify with. . . . [T]his is all years of me learning me and my style, and decid[ing] to do something different that would get everyone's attention."[35]

As an identity entrepreneur, Minaj is successful: she has won critical acclaim from predominantly white mainstream media. Jon Caramanica, a white writer for the *New York Times*, has written that Minaj is "a sparkling rapper with a gift for comic accents and unexpected turns of phrase. She's a walking exaggeration, outsize in sound, personality and look. And she's a rapid evolver, discarding old modes as easily as adopting new ones."[36] And she knows her audience: whether one uses sales or awards as a metric, Minaj is the most successful female hip-hop artist in history.

Minaj demonstrates that identity entrepreneurship can challenge dominant conceptions of outgroup identity. As legal scholar Madhavi Sunder has explained, promoting outgroup heterogeneity—what she calls "cultural dissent"—prevents outgroup identity from becoming fixed or monolithic.[37] As a result, identity entrepreneurship enriches the conversation about outgroup identity as a whole.

Other rappers have likewise carved out their own spaces. One such rapper is Leif—pronounced "leaf"—who challenges other preconceptions. The first openly gay rapper to perform on network television, Leif forces ingroup and outgroup members alike to question the heterosexuality and machismo traditionally associated with rap and, by extension, with black masculinity.[38] It's hard to describe what Leif *is*, exactly—it's true that he's a gay black rapper, but beyond that he and his music defy easy classification or description—and this is precisely the point. (Readers who want to get a sense of Leif ought to go watch the video for "Wut" and then come back.

I'll wait.) Certainly Leif is leveraging his outgroup identity for mainstream consumption, but he ultimately transcends identity categories altogether. For many, Leif's defining characteristic isn't his blackness or his gayness— it's his sheer weirdness.

Success Breeds Success

Sometimes identity entrepreneurship yields tangible material benefits to outgroup members. By making money, identity entrepreneurs can give back to their communities. Beyoncé, whose unapologetic performance of black femininity has made her an icon, has donated millions of dollars through her charity BeyGOOD, funding causes that disproportionately affect black people: relief for the Flint water crisis, alleviating homelessness, full-tuition college scholarships.[39] Colin Kaepernick, who leveraged his outgroup identity into a Nike ad campaign, as of 2018 has donated over $1 million to charities that promote social justice work.[40] The singer Rihanna, whom we'll discuss more in Chapter 6, has donated millions to build a cancer research facility in her native Barbados and raised millions for women's education around the world. Her prolific donations have earned her the title of Harvard University's 2017 Humanitarian of the Year.

Identity entrepreneurs can also facilitate broader social progress. Normalizing the presence of rich and powerful outgroup members not only helps the outgroup, it also helps to shape the way the ingroup perceives the outgroup. In the employment context, showcasing outgroup leadership can end up improving the ingroup's opinion of the outgroup.[41] The improved perception of outgroup members can occur regardless of whether the employer is engaging cynically in identity capitalism or whether the employer is sincerely attempting to improve working conditions for outgroup members. Either way, the outgroup member has the opportunity to break down individual ingroup members' conscious or unconscious prejudices.

Likewise, by gaining positions of prominence, outgroup members can provide access and support for other members of the outgroup. In a lengthy essay about people of color in the entertainment industry, comedian Chris Rock describes how Eddie Murphy helped him, and how he, in turn, has tried to help other black aspiring comedians:

I try to help young black guys coming up because . . . people took
chances on me. . . . I'd do the same for a young white guy, but here's
the difference: Someone's going to help the white guy. Multiple people will. The people whom I've tried to help, I'm not sure anybody
was going to help them.[42]

Rock's description of his strategy suggests progress. For the "young black
guys coming up," Rock's presence softens the need for identity entrepreneurship, with the corresponding need to tailor self-presentation to the
preferences of white people. As more nonwhite comedians succeed, aspiring comedians will be more likely to have mentors in the entertainment
industry who identify with their experiences and who are more invested
in helping them get their first break. And by savvy identity entrepreneurship, outgroup members can elevate those who come after them. Minaj,
for example, explains that the same outspokenness that got her fired from
many of her early jobs "made me able to open doors for female rappers, to
get a lot of money, to have a major influence and see that translated into
our bank accounts. I know a lot of girls who are going to reap the benefits
of that 'attitude.'"[43]

For a member of an outgroup, simply seeing people gain power who are
similar to them in socially relevant ways is encouraging. Researchers found
that a substantial performance gap between black and white participants
on a standardized test shrank dramatically during Barack Obama's historic
ascent to the presidency.[44] Participants took a test consisting of twenty
problems drawn from past Graduate Record Exams before the Democratic
National Convention, then again after the convention. At the first testing,
white students outscored black students an average of 12.14 to 8.79. After the
convention, however, black participants who watched the speech did as well
as white students who had watched the speech—12.11 to 10.32, a statistically
insignificant disparity. And black participants who watched the speech did
much better than black students who did not—10.32 to 6.79. Witnessing
success has the potential to breed more success. And outgroup members who
reach positions of power and prominence inspire other members of their
outgroup to do the same, even if the already-successful outgroup members
do not directly mentor those behind them.

A Dude in a Hot Girl's Body

There's a type of woman that seems to appeal to a lot of men. We can glean her traits from any online dating forum. "Independent." "No Drama." "Low Maintenance." "Not Possessive." This ideal feminine creature has a name. In the novel *Gone Girl*, author Gillian Flynn describes the Cool Girl:

> Men always say that as the defining compliment, don't they? She's a cool girl. Being the Cool Girl means I am a hot, brilliant, funny woman who adores football, poker, dirty jokes, and burping, who plays video games, drinks cheap beer, loves threesomes and anal sex, and jams hot dogs and hamburgers into her mouth like she's hosting the world's biggest culinary gang bang while somehow maintaining a size 2, because Cool Girls are above all hot. Hot and understanding. Cool Girls never get angry. . . . [The] Cool Girl is basically the girl who likes every fucking thing [a man] likes and doesn't ever complain. . . . *Go ahead, shit on me, I don't mind. I'm the Cool Girl.*[45]

Cool Girls are identity entrepreneurs. And from workplaces to schools, classrooms to gyms—anywhere men are the ingroup—Cool Girls are rewarded. Women who fit in with the guys—as one commentator puts it, the Cool Girl is essentially "a dude in a hot girl's body"—win attention, admiration, respect, and social status. Those who protest male behavior or, more generally, seek gender equality, are labeled "difficult," "high maintenance," or—worst of all—feminists. Cool Girls win male approval and the benefits associated with it: social status, professional success, economic security.

The Cool Girl is not a new invention. She has existed in literature as long as literature has existed. Think of Penelope, patiently weaving by day and unweaving by night, for *twenty years*, while Odysseus enjoys a seemingly endless series of exotic adventures. And then she welcomes him back with hardly a word of remonstrance. Shakespeare's *The Taming of the Shrew* offers an ode to the Cool Girl, delivered by reformed shrew Kate: "I am ashamed that women are so simple / To offer war where they should kneel for peace / Or seek for rule, supremacy, and sway, / When they are bound to serve, love, and obey." And Ernest Hemingway is a notable creator of Cool Girls.

Brett, the heroine of his acclaimed novel *The Sun Also Rises*, loves drinking and sex, refuses to take emotional relationships seriously, and earns the desperate loyalty of men wherever she goes. These literary models impart ideals—and ideas—to members of social outgroups.

Cool Girls are women who can take a joke, women who (figuratively, or maybe even literally) don't mind a friendly pat on the butt. Why can't all women be as understanding as the Cool Girl? We would all get along so much better if women could just be more reasonable. In the meantime, though, Cool Girls get rewarded for being so cool.

The Cool Girl's behavior often caters to heterosexual male sexual preferences. Writer Leah Fessler recalls of her college sexual experiences, "On weekends I'd text him around 10pm, usually somewhat drunk. We'd meet at one of our dorm rooms, debate philosophy and Fleet Foxes lyrics, talk about our families and aspirations, and then have sex until he came. . . . I cycled through this routine with at least five guys by senior year."[46] Yet these experiences were not carefree for Fessler. "After I began having sex with these guys, the power balance always tipped. A few hookups in, I'd begin to obsess, primarily about the *ambiguity* of it all. My friends and I would analyze incessantly: Does he like me?" She writes, "I wished that I could be like the guys, who seemed not to care at all." In other words, she wished she was a Cool Girl.

Heterosexual hookup culture presents many women with a dilemma. Researchers generally agree that, while both men and women participate in hookup culture, women are more likely to want a hookup to turn into a traditional relationship, while men are more likely to resist such arrangements.[47] Against this backdrop, a woman's willingness to hook up wins attention from men, and being a Cool Girl about it—not getting emotionally attached, not demanding a relationship, not demanding anything really—wins male approval and social standing. As sociologist Lisa Wade explains, "Hookups are decidedly not about finding any sort of romantic connection. . . . They're often not so much about pleasure in particular for women. They're very much about status."[48]

Within hookup culture, identity entrepreneurial women reinforce the male ingroup's preference for the Cool Girl by conforming to them. Watch porn? Oh, yes, I'd love to. Text racy photos? I love sending nudes, it's a huge turn-on for me! Mind if I stop by drunk at 1 AM? Come on over, I'm just sitting around in lingerie and full makeup. Cause drama? I wouldn't dream of it, I'm not one of *those* girls. Yet by entertaining these male preferences, identity entrepreneurial women reinforce them. They emphasize that men are reasonable to *expect* these things of women—indeed, to feel *entitled* to them. By conforming to male ingroup preferences, identity entrepreneurs legitimate and perpetuate what men want. "If I don't do it, some other girl will," one woman said sadly, explaining why she often gave in to her hookup partner's sexual demands.

No doubt some women genuinely find casual hookups fun, fulfilling, and liberating.[49] But for women who defer to male preferences for social reward rather than genuine desire, hooking up can lead to unappealing options for women. Embracing hookup culture too enthusiastically can lead to women being labeled "sluts" or "easy" by men and other women alike.[50] For other women, attempting to adopt a Cool Girl attitude comes with a cost: sublimating their own physical and emotional needs to those of a man who is accustomed to women who do so. As one woman explained, "I think girls know when they're being used. And I think it feels bad to be used. But I think the alternative is that nobody wants to use you. And that means that you're not hooking up with anybody. And I think that's worse."[51]

Yet opting out of hookup culture is also fraught. Women who decide to stop hooking up are often giving up physical intimacy and the status that comes with male companionship. One woman commented in *Vanity Fair* that criticizing hookup culture feels like admitting a personal shortcoming: "[I]t's like you're weak, you're not independent, you somehow missed the whole memo about third-wave feminism."[52] Similarly, women who refuse to participate in hookup culture are sometimes called "prudes" or "virgin-shamed." An anonymous Reddit post laments, "I've had friends look at me like an alien from another planet because I've never had a one-night stand."[53] Other women who are tired of hookup culture and want a relationship are pejoratively described as needy, clingy, or desperate. "Clingy. It just feels like a dirty word, doesn't it?" *Glamour* magazine asks us, rhetorically. But never fear: the media are here to help women control their unfortunate emotional tendencies. *Glamour* instructs: "[W]e can try to keep our behavior in check for all the right reasons and avoid the clingy label as best we can."[54]

Women often encounter the dilemmas of hookup culture on college campuses, where the ability to appeal to men often provides access to status and shapes the entire college experience. Sociologists Elizabeth Armstrong and Laura Hamilton document the way in which "fraternity parties place men in more powerful positions over women."[55] To be included in the parties that formed the backbone of the university's social scene, "women needed to be alluring, friendly, and flirtatious," while "[w]hen women failed to appeal to men's sexual interests, they reported feeling scorned." This power dynamic extends to male control of the hookup power dynamic: one college woman in an ongoing hookup situation explained that she didn't want to bring up to her partner the question of whether they were in a relationship "because I know guys don't like that question."[56] Sociologist Kathleen Bogle likewise observed that college women frequently did not bring up the status of their relationship with a hookup partner "in anticipation of a negative reaction."[57]

The ingroup is not oblivious to the double standard around hooking up, nor to the power dynamic it creates. One man observed, "The double standard is real. If I'm a guy and I'm going out and fucking a different girl every night, my friends are gonna give me high fives and we're gonna crack a beer and talk about it. Girls do the same, but they get judged. I don't want it to be like that, but sometimes the world is the way it is and I can't change it, so I just embrace it."[58] Identity entrepreneurship by women reinforces the current distribution of sexual power.

Black CNN?

Identity entrepreneurship can also divide outgroups. Rap and hip-hop music offer a microcosm of such division. Despite the best efforts of Leif and Nicki Minaj, rap and hip-hop remain a source of strong disagreement among black people. Sociologist Michael Eric Dyson observes that hip-hop "has been a source of controversy since the beats got too big and the voices too loud for the block parties that spawned them."[59] Some embrace the genre and find it lucrative and empowering, emphasizing the benefits of material success and fame, the ability to give back to the outgroup, and power of the genre to articulate black experiences. Rapper Chuck D, of Public Enemy, once called hip-hop "black CNN."

Many prominent black scholars and commentators concur with this view. Tricia Rose, a professor of African Studies, argues that hip-hop "is a cultural form that attempts to negotiate the experiences of marginalization, brutally truncated opportunity, and oppression" within African American identity.[60] For Rose, rap music "brings together a tangle of some of the most complex social, cultural, and political issues in contemporary American society." Legal scholar Paul Butler agrees, emphasizing that hip-hop is both a social and a political movement with particular implications for the criminal justice system. He writes that not only does hip-hop culture "point . . . out the incoherence of the law's construct of crime," but it also "describes, with eloquence, the problems with the current regimes, and articulates, with passion, a better way."[61] In the view of both Butler and Rose, hip-hop has the power to radically transform society for the better.

Others argue that the genre perpetuates stereotypes of black culture as violent, promotes misogyny and homophobia, and offers yet another opportunity for white people to profit from black creativity.[62] Riché Richardson, a scholar of Africana studies, finds much to celebrate in rap music, yet resists the genre's emphasis on "black-on-black crime," which she argues undermines the "subversive potential" of rap music, and further describes herself as "troubled" by the "hegemony of hip-hop as a paradigm in contemporary African American music [and] culture" due to its violence, misogyny, and materialism.[63] Acclaimed jazz musician Wynton Marsalis, long critical of rap music, goes a step further. Marsalis recently said of rap, "I don't think we should have music talking about niggers and bitches and ho's. . . . To me that's more damaging than a statue of Robert E. Lee."[64]

In an impressive entrepreneurial maneuver, Trump campaign spokesperson Katrina Pierson, who is black, leveraged her identity both as a black person and as a woman to defend Donald Trump shortly after the *Access Hollywood* tape in which he claimed to "grab [women] by the pussy." She argued, "I find it quite rich that we have Democrats and the left talking about rape culture when . . . this rape culture is purported [*sic*] by none other than the entertainment industry, none other than hip-hop music, which you can hear on local radio."[65] "This is insane," responded April Rye, the other guest on the show, also a black woman. The host eventually cut away, saying, "That conversation was going nowhere."[66]

Identity entrepreneurship can make it harder for outgroup members to talk to one another because some of them are heavily invested in serving ingroup interests. While dissent can be healthy, it can also reduce outgroups to internal fighting that helps no one. Identity entrepreneurship fractures communities already vulnerable to seeds of discontent sown by calculating members of ingroups.

Linked Fate

Identity entrepreneurship takes up space. Versions of identity that please the ingroup crowd out other portrayals that are more fragile because they are not buttressed by stereotypes or rewarded by the ingroup. Ingroup-pleasing versions of identity risk freezing stereotypes in a way that perpetuates ingroup power. For the identity entrepreneur, the disempowerment results because his reward is contingent on continuing to please the ingroup. In order to keep making money, the Fab Five have to keep dressing and behaving in a way that pleases the predominantly straight people who constitute their fan base, as well as the mostly straight executives and advertisers who have a stake in their show's success. If Jonathan Van Ness suddenly opted to wear ratty gym shorts and stained T-shirts, he—and *Queer Eye*—would lose some of their allure. The Fab Five's continued popularity depends on their continued performance of gay identities that their straight fans and financial backers approve.

We shouldn't spend too much time crying for the Fab Five, who by all appearances are comfortable with themselves and making plenty of money doing something they enjoy. But we can still question the effect of their identity performances on other gay men. What about the gay man who wants to play football? What about the gay man who wants to run for president? What about the gay man who just wants to sit around in his boxers while he drinks Natty Light and plays *Assassin's Creed* in the basement of a frat house? Social acceptance of these other gay men may be more difficult because of the stereotypes that the Fab Five have reinforced.

Individual instances of identity entrepreneurship don't occur in a vacuum. No matter how much an identity entrepreneur might claim that she is just doing her own thing, any one person's decision to leverage identity affects other members of their identity group. Sarah Palin's performance of gender identity affects the way that people, particularly men, view women politicians. Asa Akira's performance of Asian female identity affects the way that people, particularly white people and non-Asian men, think about Asian women's sexuality. Perhaps Palin and Akira's performances work well for them, but they may work much less well for other members of their identity groups. Researchers have examined a phenomenon that some call "linked fate"—the idea that the behavior of some outgroup members inevitably affects other outgroup members, and that the fate of the group of a whole affects the fates of individual outgroup members. Linked fate means that when Asa Akira presents an image of Asian female submissiveness and hypersexuality, consumers of her films—particularly those who have minimal firsthand contact with Asian women—may accept as true the image she projects. Although Akira's portrayal of her identity may ring true to her, others may interpret it as not only true for Akira, but true for Asian women in general. Akira may believe that she is only playing for herself, but her participation can't fail to affect the others in the game.

Identity entrepreneurship sometimes limits both identity entrepreneurs and outgroup members who don't choose to become identity entrepreneurs. Identity entrepreneurship limits opportunities for human development. As Mari Matsuda has written, "[N]o person is free until the last and the least of us is free."[67] While identity entrepreneurs might prefer to focus only on themselves, the reality is that identity entrepreneurship has consequences for other members of their outgroup too. As we'll see in the next chapter, this linkage is vividly apparent when an outgroup member tries to vindicate her rights through antidiscrimination law.

5

UNEQUAL PROTECTION

TERESA SOTO WORKED on the "kill floor" at a meat-packing plant in Iowa. Sometimes she worked "scissors position": as pig carcasses came down a conveyor belt, her job was to slice the torso from the neck through the legs. Other times she worked "stick hole": she would cut a hole in the neck of each pig carcass, slice the mouth open, and remove any ear tags. Still other times she worked "kidneys": she stood on an elevated platform as pig carcasses approached and removed the pig's internal organs with knives. All of Teresa's assignments on the kill floor required her to use knives, hooks, scissors, or a combination of the three. The work was difficult, stomach-turning, and dangerous, but Teresa needed a job.[1]

Unfortunately, not all the pigs on the kill floor were dead. Teresa's supervisor, Leonard Tanner, frequently stared at her, blew her kisses, offered her his phone number, came up behind her and untied her apron, and made comments such as "muy bueno panoche"—slang for "really good pussy." On one memorable occasion, Leonard held up a pig's penis and told Teresa that it was for her. Another time, he saw a mark on the back of her neck and yelled across the floor to other male workers that Teresa had a hickey; he then asked her how she got a hickey on the back of her neck and asked if she "did it doggie style." Similar comments continued for the next several weeks. Leonard made a habit of discussing how he liked "eating pussy all night long" in front of Teresa and other coworkers.

Other men got in on the fun. A different supervisor once grabbed a female employee by the hips, laid her on a table, and simulated sexual intercourse while other employees on the kill floor laughed and encouraged him. A USDA inspector had a habit of approaching female employees and yelling things like "all night long" or "you like to get eaten out." The same inspector also liked to look at female workers while sticking out his tongue and wiggling it around.

Teresa responded to Leonard's behavior and the behavior of others in her workplace by trying to ignore it. But Leonard didn't like being ignored. He became angry when Teresa needed to miss work because her high blood pressure and asthma were aggravated by the strenuous conditions on the kill floor. Sometimes he would give Teresa more difficult and dangerous assignments when she returned after an absence. Eventually, after Teresa needed to leave work for a family emergency, Leonard told Teresa's boyfriend that she was fired and needn't come back.

Teresa noticed that not all the women at work took her approach of ignoring Leonard's behavior. "I saw that all the women that went along with what was going on got favored and got easier jobs and all the other ones had to do the harder work," she said. Teresa pointed out a woman named Sida. Sida wore sexy clothes to work and played along with Leonard's games. One day Teresa was upset because she had to leave work early for her high blood pressure and Leonard was angry with her. Teresa told Sida what happened. Sida said, "Oh honey, all you got to do is give Leonard a hug and a kiss and he will never tell you nothing. That's what I do and he'll just melt." According to Teresa, Sida could miss any day or go home early without any negative consequences from Leonard. But Teresa never considered taking Sida's advice. "Hell no," was Teresa's response to Sida's suggestion that she give Leonard a hug and a kiss. "I am not gonna kiss no one to make him happy. That's sexual harassment."

In the #MeToo era, it's tempting to sympathize with Teresa and to look at Sida as complicit in the sexualization of the workplace and indifferent to her female coworkers. Yet Sida is also worthy of sympathy. Like Teresa, Sida needed a job. Like Teresa, she was tasked with hard and dangerous work. And like Teresa, Sida was just trying to survive in her workplace. Teresa and Sida chose to deal with their circumstances very differently, but they shared the same dilemma.

In a now familiar pattern, Leonard was an identity capitalist: a male ingroup member who benefited from the women in his workplace. Most obviously, he enjoyed having women around as a target for crude jokes and sexualized power plays. Moreover, Leonard seemed to enjoy having a particular *kind* of women around—women who dressed in a way he liked; women who played along with his jokes. Leonard preferred this kind of woman because she tolerated his behavior and because he could point to her as evidence that he did not have a problem with women. "I get along great with most of the women here," an identity capitalist such as Leonard might explain, "so clearly I don't have a problem with *women*. It's just this one *particular* woman who is difficult."

This kind of identity capitalism leaves both Teresa and Sida with an unpalatable choice. Resist sexually harassing behavior in the workplace and suffer the consequences? Or become the "right" kind of woman and play along? Sida became the right kind of woman—an identity entrepreneur who leveraged her femininity to get along with Leonard and gain benefits in the workplace, like easier assignments and permission to leave early. Teresa instead responded by resisting Leonard and, eventually, filing a lawsuit. These contrasting choices were different battles against the same enemy.

No Winning

Antidiscrimination law is a collection of constitutional provisions, statutes, and cases ostensibly meant to create and maintain equality among people. In principle, antidiscrimination law prohibits treating people differently and worse because of characteristics such as race, sex, gender, or sexual orientation. Antidiscrimination law includes such landmark provisions as the

Equal Protection Clause of the Fourteenth Amendment to the Constitution, which was ratified to address ongoing unequal treatment of black Americans after the Civil War and which has subsequently been interpreted to limit governmental discrimination on the basis of other identity categories.

Antidiscrimination law also includes federal statutory provisions such as Title II of the Civil Rights Act of 1964, which prohibits discrimination in public accommodations (places such as hotels, restaurants, movie theaters, and sports arenas), and Title VII of the same Act, which prohibits discrimination in the workplace. And antidiscrimination law includes a host of state and municipal laws that also prohibit discrimination, with a great deal of variation among states. Twenty-eight states, for example, have no state law prohibiting employers from discriminating against LGBTQ employees.[2] Meanwhile, the city of San Francisco has a municipal statute prohibiting discrimination on the basis of age, AIDS/HIV status, ancestry, color, creed, disability, domestic partner status, gender identity, height, marital status, national origin, race, religion, sex/gender, sexual orientation, and weight.[3]

We are much better off with antidiscrimination law than without it. The patchwork of statutes I have described, and the cases they have prompted, protect many people from worse treatment on the basis of who they are. Without antidiscrimination law, nothing would prevent a big company from declining to hire an Asian American person, or a woman, simply because the CEO doesn't like having them around.

Yet antidiscrimination law is a poor bulwark against the harms of identity capitalism. Ironically, it often provides incentives for identity capitalist behavior. Another problem is that it fails to protect *both* the Teresas *and* the Sidas of the world. Whether an outgroup member becomes an identity entrepreneur or whether she rejects identity entrepreneurship, she is often out of luck when conditions become intolerable and she wishes to sue. When the law doesn't restrain identity capitalism—or when the law actually creates incentives for identity capitalism—there's often no winning for the outgroup.

Some of the most bitter antidiscrimination disputes arise in the workplace, and that's where this chapter will focus, although antidiscrimination disputes also arise in contexts from criminal law to intellectual property law to the First Amendment. Workplaces often throw together people of radically different backgrounds who wouldn't encounter one another in any other setting. This integration can be wonderful, or, if poorly managed, it can result in immense tension. Workplace tensions sometimes flare into litigation, and—as we'll see—litigation sometimes results in the dyad of identity capitalism and identity entrepreneurship.

Identity as Legality

In November 1976, the Navy Ship Engineering Center issued an announcement for a management position.[4] Seven people applied for the position, including Margaret Young, a black woman, and Christopher Iekel, a white man. In accordance with Navy procedures, ranking officers convened a selection panel of three men. After the panel turned in its recommendations, a supervisor noticed that one of the panelists had written "my guess she's black" on a ranking form. The supervisor was concerned that this racial notation was "improper." An Equal Employment Opportunity officer went further, concluding that the panel's process was tainted. Eventually, the ranking officers decided to throw out the first panel's work and convene a new selection panel.

The new panel was diverse in both race and gender, including a black woman, a white man, and an Asian American man. The panel selected Christopher Iekel, the white man, for the position. Margaret Young filed a lawsuit, arguing that she was better qualified and had in fact been ranked first by the previous panel. The Fourth Circuit panel that heard the case said the following about the composition of the second panel: "[T]here is no evidence of improper racial motivation in forming the second panel. Panel member Monk is black, Stoutmeyer is white, and DaRosa is Asian. . . . It is clear that the second panel was correctly selected."

With those words, the Fourth Circuit created a considerable incentive for identity capitalism. The mere presence of racial diversity on the second panel could not only rebut accusations that the second panel was improperly formed, but also remove whatever taint of discrimination may have lingered from the improper notation on the first panel's work product. The Navy may or may not have formed the second panel with an eye toward the optics of a diverse panel, but the Fourth Circuit provided a road map for the Navy—or anyone else—to engage in identity capitalism in order to insulate personnel decisions from legal challenges down the road.

Companies swiftly turned to identity capitalism, with satisfying results. Including an outgroup member in an employment decision often helped persuade courts that no discrimination had taken place. Following are a few examples:

- Walmart won a race discrimination claim brought by a black woman; the court emphasized that "an assistant store manager [who was] a black female" testified that the standard procedure had been followed.[5]
- Walmart won another race discrimination claim brought by a black man; the court said, "The promotion decision was primarily made by a black assistant manager . . . which while not dispositive, indicates an absence of discrimination.[6]
- The Alabama Department of Public Safety won a race discrimination claim brought by a black police officer who was transferred to a less desirable assignment; the court noted that the captain who reassigned him was a black man and stated, without evidence, that "when a minority manager is involved . . . the likelihood of intentional discrimination is substantially less."[7]
- The Department of Veterans Affairs won a race discrimination claim brought by a Hispanic man who did not receive a promotion for which he claimed he was well-qualified; the court noted that "the promotional decision was made by a Hispanic," which "indicates an absence of discrimination."[8]

Even when courts do not explicitly say that the race of a supervisor helps to prove that there was no discrimination, they often gratuitously call attention to the identity characteristics of a supervisor to imply that there was no discrimination. "Plaintiff, a black male, was terminated by his black male supervisor after Plaintiff received three consecutive negative evaluations," one court said pointedly.[9] Similarly, in holding against a lesbian who was discharged from a Bumble & Bumble hair salon, another court observed that the supervisor who discharged her was a "pre-surgery male-to-female transsexual"; that other individuals she accused of discriminating against her included a gay man and a bisexual woman; and that a number of other

LGBTQ people also worked at the salon.[10] It is implausible, the court suggested, "that in this milieu of nonconformists she was a victim of sexual discrimination because she does not conform to gender norms."

The identity capitalism in these cases relies on a crude assumption: if a black person is involved in firing a black person, or a woman involved in firing a woman, or a nonstraight person involved in firing a nonstraight person, then the decision could not have been motivated by discrimination. Yet research shows that the assumption is wrong. Women, for example, are sometimes harder on other women than they are on men. Several large studies have found that women report more incivility from other women in the workplace than from men, while men report less incivility overall and a roughly similar amount of incivility from women and from other men.[11] Similarly, members of a particular racial outgroup sometimes disparage a member of the group who fails to conform to outgroup norms.[12] The notion that a member of a particular outgroup is more likely to favor other members of her outgroup relies on wrongheaded assumptions that all members of outgroups are the same. This does not comport with reality: within racial outgroups, for example, there is substantial intraracial diversity. A microcosm of intraracial tensions emerged in the fallout from the Los Angeles riots of 1992. As the *Los Angeles Times* explained,

> Many Chinese-, Japanese-, and Vietnamese-Americans say their shops were damaged because rioters thought they were Korean. And some have accused Korean immigrants of making trouble for all Asian Americans by treating blacks badly. What is more, Chinese-Americans complained that Koreans turned them away from a Koreatown relief center, and Chinese-American groups boycotted a dinner with President Bush because he visited Koreatown but not Chinatown after the unrest. Some Koreans felt deserted by other Asian-Americans, while others had not even thought to expect their help. Rumors swirled during the riots that buttons were being printed that said: "I'm Not Korean." On the Saturday after the riots, when Korean-American groups held a massive peace rally, organized Asian-American groups were notably absent. As usual, Filipinos, the second-largest

Asian-American group in Los Angeles, who lost a number of stores in or near Koreatown, felt invisible and ignored.[13]

Looking at outgroups also does not account for the important effects of intersectionality—the idea that someone might be uniquely affected by the combination of two or more identity categories.[14] A heterosexual Asian American man from a privileged background may have a workplace experience very different from that of a bisexual Asian American woman with a working-class background, even though they are both Asian American. And these differences may breed animus within a particular group, often of a kind that is invisible to the ingroup.[15]

Yet many courts accept as meaningful the idea that an outgroup member is less likely to discriminate against a member of their own group. And this means that employers have a strong incentive to keep doing it. An employer that is content to have a management cohort composed of entirely white men might be well-served to promote a token or two simply to provide cover when it comes time to fire someone.

Personal Best

For twenty years, Darlene Jespersen worked as a bartender in the sports bar at Harrah's Casino. Jespersen was excellent at her job. Both supervisors and coworkers praised her performance. Customers even wrote that Jespersen influenced their decision to return to Harrah's and spend money at the casino.

From the time Jespersen was hired in 1979, Harrah's encouraged but did not require female beverage servers to wear makeup. Jespersen found that wearing makeup made her feel so uncomfortable that it interfered with her work as a bartender—she said that it made her feel "ill," "degraded," and "violated"— and she opted not to do so. For twenty years, her employer never complained.

This changed in February 2000, when Harrah's implemented a "Beverage Department Image Transformation" regimen, which it dubbed the "Personal Best" program. All bartenders had to wear a uniform of black pants, white shirts, a bow tie, and comfortable black shoes. But the program also required female beverage servers to wear their hair "teased, curled, or styled"; to wear makeup, including foundation, blush, mascara, and lipstick; and to wear colored nail polish and stockings, presumably under a skirt rather than the pants required of men. Male beverage servers were required to wear their hair short and wear no makeup or nail polish.

Jespersen refused to follow the policy. In July 2000, she was terminated from the bartending job she had held successfully for twenty years. Soon after she filed suit in federal court.

Eventually her case ended up before the Ninth Circuit. The court recognized that Jespersen's record as an employee was "exemplary," but ultimately held that Jespersen could not prevail on her claim of sex discrimination. The court rejected two possible theories of discrimination. First, the court held that the grooming policy did not place an unequal burden on women, emphasizing that employers can maintain different grooming standards for men and women and refusing to acknowledge that Harrah's particular grooming policy created a greater burden for women. Second, the court held that the Harrah's policy was not impermissible sex stereotyping because both men and women had to adhere to the policy and the policy was not particularly sexualized.

Several judges dissented, arguing both that the grooming policy placed an unequal burden on women and that the makeup requirement constituted sex stereotyping. One dissenting judge observed, "[I]s there any doubt that putting on makeup costs money and takes time? Harrah's policy requires women to apply face powder, blush, mascara and lipstick. You don't need an expert witness to figure out that such items don't grow on trees."

By ruling against Darlene Jespersen, the Ninth Circuit put a judicial stamp of approval on a particularly insidious form of identity capitalism: the power of the ingroup to dictate how the outgroup behaves. The decision allows Harrah's to leverage the female identity of its employees by requiring them to dress in stereotypically feminine and sexualized ways. This permission came at the expense of individual employees' autonomy. The irony of Harrah's naming its program "Personal Best" is that the program was neither personal to Jespersen, nor did it bring out her best.

Antidiscrimination law often fails to intervene in identity capitalism. When, for example, an identity capitalist employer is attempting to extract additional value from outgroup members by requiring them to behave in particular ways—styling their hair, wearing makeup—the law implicitly gives permission not only for the employer to take advantage of having women working for them but also for the employer to require those women to act in the ways that maximize its profits.

By refusing to invalidate grooming policies using antidiscrimination law, courts go even further. They allow identity capitalists to create incentives for the way they would like to see particular outgroup identities performed. These structures benefit identity entrepreneurs—for example, those who are happy to wear makeup—and harm those like Darlene Jespersen whose aversion to wearing makeup is so intense that they would rather quit a job they performed well for two decades than put on the makeup. The stakes of this denial have tangible workplace consequences, disadvantaging those who refuse to play the identity entrepreneurial game.

The Fifth Black Woman

Legal scholars Devon Carbado and Mitu Gulati pose the following scenario.[16] In a single year, a law firm promotes four black women to the partnership. The promotion of four black women makes quite a splash: previously the firm only had two black partners, both men, and the firm touts this year as "the year of the black woman." Probably it announces the year of the black woman on its website and in its promotional materials, complete with glossy photographs. By now, we can all recognize the law firm as an identity capitalist.

In the same year, the firm denies a fifth black woman—a lawyer named Mary—promotion to the partnership. The problem, Carbado and Gulati explain, is that while identity capitalism may be working well for the law firm and for the first four black women, it is not working so well for Mary. In their hypothetical, the other four black women differ from Mary in important ways (see Table 5.1).

Suppose that Mary believes she was the victim of race and gender discrimination. Over the years there have been a number of comments insinuating stereotypes about black women, incidents in which she was given unfavorable assignments, and recurring social slights. Yet the presence of the four black women who did make partner will make Mary's lawsuit, should she choose to file one, a very difficult one to win.

As legal scholar Kimberlé Crenshaw has observed, antidiscrimination law does not acknowledge intersectionality—that is, Mary can sue for discrimination because she is black *or* because she is a woman, but not because she is, specifically, a *black woman*.[17] Black women are the victims of expectations and stereotypes that affect neither nonblack women nor black men. And often black women suffer animosity that would be directed at neither a woman nor a black man.

TABLE 5.1. A comparison of the five black women from Carbado and Gulati's scenario.

	THE FIRST FOUR BLACK WOMEN	MARY
Hair	Relaxed	Dreadlocks
Casual Friday Attire	Blue jeans or khakis	West African–influenced attire
Institutional Identity	No comment on racial or gender demographics of firm	Driving force between committee for recruitment and retention of women and minorities
Social Identity	Typically attend law firm happy hour	Never attends law firm happy hour
Sports	Tennis; golf; country club membership	No memberships
Education	Harvard, Yale, or Stanford law graduate	Large local state law school graduate
Family	Married	Single mother
Residence	Live in predominantly white neighborhoods	Lives in the inner city, which is predominantly black
Religion	Various Christian denominations	Nation of Islam

Source: Nancy Leong.

Yet even if a court did acknowledge black womanhood as a distinct target for discrimination, Mary would still be unlikely to win her lawsuit because the law currently ignores variations in identity performance. Because the firm promoted four other black women, the court will likely draw a strong inference that Mary did not suffer discrimination on account of being black, a woman, or a black woman. Mary and the other women are not necessarily in the same position simply because they are all black women. Rather, the law firm may prefer the first four black women to Mary because they perform their identities as black women differently. Many people feel one way about a married black woman who plays tennis at the country club and goes to an Episcopalian church on Sunday and a different way about a black single mom who lives in the inner city and belongs to the Nation of Islam. If Mary is treated worse than the other black women, her poor treatment may still be *because of* her race and gender. But the reason for Mary's poor treatment is more nuanced. She is treated poorly because she is the *wrong kind* of black woman—the kind the ingroup disfavors.

As the tale of the fifth black woman teaches, the law's failure to acknowledge identity performance fosters identity capitalism. Promoting four black women is valuable to the law firm because the firm reaps all the benefits of signaling diversity and trumpeting its excellent record on diversity. Antidiscrimination law also enables the firm to engage in whatever it sees as the most profitable form of identity capitalism. Nothing in the law prevents a law firm from punishing an outgroup member who doesn't perform her identity the way the institution would prefer. If Mary's law firm likes the way the first four black women perform their identity and dislikes the way Mary performs her identity, no significant obstacle prevents the firm from distinguishing among them. The law ignores that an employer can like some black women while still disliking a black *woman*, and moreover can do so precisely *because* she is a black woman who does not conform to their preferences.

This tale of the fifth black woman reveals another way that the law encourages identity capitalism. The first four black women are valuable to an identity capitalist firm because promoting four black women it likes provides cover to deny promotion to a fifth black woman it dislikes. A court will see the promotion of four black woman as strong evidence that the fifth black woman was denied promotion for reasons other than her race and gender. The result is a particularly ugly form of identity capitalism: using favored members of an outgroup to mask discrimination against a disfavored member.

Against the backdrop of unchecked identity capitalism, black women are often forced to choose how to react. The law privileges outgroup members who act like identity entrepreneurs over those who resist ingroup pressure. Carbado and Gulati's description also suggests that the four black women who made partner may be identity entrepreneurs. Given that black women often face discrimination in the workplace, they may have deliberately chosen to leverage outgroup identity, but to do so in a way that comforted rather than threatened those in power. Mary, by contrast, is not an identity entrepreneur. Her identity as a black woman undoubtedly attracts attention, but she does nothing to conform to ingroup preferences—indeed, she actively disregards them.

In contrasting the first four black women with Mary, Carbado and Gulati consider the way the women choose to style their hair. Black women's hair is the subject of intense debate, providing a microcosm of the identity performance dilemma faced by the first four black women and by Mary.[18] Many black women attest to the cultural and emotional significance of the decision whether to wear a relaxed, braided, or natural hairstyle. "The decision to stop relaxing your hair is overwhelming," says hairstylist Edris Nichols, "but going natural can be like coming out—a positive and life-changing affirmation."[19]

But the way the world reacts to black women's hair—no matter how it is styled—is often infected by identity capitalism. Ingroup members often have strong reactions to black women's hair. Halle Berry, the first black woman to win an Academy Award, recalls her manager's reaction to cutting off her long hair: "You're never going to work. You're no longer commercial."[20]

These norms extend beyond Hollywood. Correctly or incorrectly, people tend to see a black woman who relaxes her hair as more assimilated to dominant cultural norms, while one who wears her hair in an Afro may be stereotyped as angry, militant, or radical. In many contexts, the former version of identity is worth more to an identity capitalist. A large law firm, for example, may want to showcase black women on its website, but not just *any* black women—it wants to showcase black women who communicate a message of both diversity and assimilation to their prospective clients. A black woman who relaxes her hair, then, is more valuable to an identity capitalist than one who does not. And some employers actively police the hair of the black women who work for them. American Airlines went to court in order to uphold a policy banning all-braided hairstyles among female employees—a policy that clearly had a disproportionate impact on black women.[21] There are signs of hope: several states have proposed legislation to explicitly ban race-based hair discrimination, and California and New York have signed such legislation into law.[22] A black woman's seemingly personal decision about how to style her hair can be an act of identity entrepreneurship or an explicit rejection of identity entrepreneurship.

Outgroup members are often punished for failing to behave as their supervisors and coworkers think that outgroup members should. Here the law allows and even encourages identity capitalism. As a result, even when two workers are the same race, gender, sexual orientation, or combination of identity categories, their decisions regarding identity performance—and, more specifically, identity entrepreneurship—may lead to more favorable treatment of one worker over another.

He Thought She Wanted It

Donnie Mangrum was a single mom. She worked as a used car salesperson at Chuck Clancy Ford for fourteen years. Within the department, swearing, sexual innuendo, and dirty jokes were common. Words like "ass" and "prick" and "fuck" were so common that no one even noticed them. When she was at work, Donnie played along. She swore and talked trash just like one of the guys. Sometimes she sat on coworkers' laps. Other times she gave them massages or scratched their backs. She sometimes asked for massages in return. It was all part of fitting in.[23]

But then in September 1998, Scott Wilson became Donnie's supervisor. Scott made Donnie increasingly uncomfortable. He hugged her and patted her butt. Sometimes he said things to her such as, "I know what you need" or "I'd like to give you a good fucking." Two different times, Wilson came into her office and told her to "lay back on the desk, we'll knock out a little piece right quick." One time he sexually propositioned Donnie's nineteen-year-old daughter in front of her.

Scott's conduct started to affect Donnie's job performance. Once he asked her for a blow job while she was trying to close a deal with a customer, and when she refused, he immediately increased the price of the vehicle so that she lost the deal. Another time he asked Donnie to set him up with a woman who was buying a car, and when she refused, he would only approve unfavorable terms for the sale, which then fell through. Several times, when Donnie came to him to get the terms of a sale approved, Scott said that he would only approve the sale if Donnie would perform sexual favors. Often, when Donnie sought approval for a sale, he would ask her, "What's in it for me?" On one occasion, customers overheard him and Donnie's sale again fell through.

Throughout all of this, Donnie tried to take Scott's comments and actions "with a grain of salt." Normally she would just "laugh it off and went on with it, just let it go." Occasionally she would say something like "pervert, why don't you leave me alone?" But sometimes she hugged him and gave him back rubs and massages, and scratched his back, just like she did for other employees. Donnie later explained, "It was a game. You went along with it. You did the best that you could. That's what I had to do in order to keep my job."

On November 8, 1998, a rainy Saturday afternoon, Donnie sat in a van in the used car parking lot. She waited for customers and watched a football game to pass the time. Late in the afternoon, Scott got into the van, pulled down the blinds, and asked Donnie for sex. When she refused, he unzipped his pants and exposed himself. Donnie felt trapped. She was afraid to move. She was afraid that he would be "right on top of her" if she tried to open the door or get out of the van. When he finally left, Donnie got her purse, left the dealership where she had worked for fourteen years, and never came back.

Donnie Mangrum tried to be a Cool Girl. She played along in order to fit in with a highly sexualized workplace culture. For quite a while it worked. She loved her job and was successful at it. She got used to the joking. She was a successful identity entrepreneur. But Scott Wilson came along, and when he did, Donnie didn't know what to do.

Eventually what she did do was find a lawyer and file a lawsuit. Here, though, Donnie Mangrum ran into trouble, like many women in similar situations. Decades ago, the Supreme Court explained in *Meritor v. Vinson* that any plaintiff bringing a sexual harassment claim must show that the alleged sexual advances were "unwelcome." It held that a complainant's "sexually provocative speech or dress" is "obviously relevant" in determining whether a particular instance of sexual conduct in the workplace is welcome, and therefore not sexual harassment.[24]

Legal scholars and advocates have denounced the welcomeness standard. Susan Estrich compares the welcomeness standard to rape laws that ask whether a woman expressed her nonconsent or resisted sexual behavior powerfully enough.[25] She says, "Unwelcomeness has emerged as the doctrinal stepchild of the rape standards of consent and resistance, and shares virtually all of their problems." In sexual harassment cases, the welcomeness standard shifts attention from the behavior of the supervisor—usually a man—to the behavior of the plaintiff—usually a woman. Estrich writes, "She, rather than he, goes on trial" and her behavior—ranging from lifestyle to attire—becomes part of the inquiry.

Plaintiffs in such cases bear the burden of disproving welcomeness. The implication is that women in the workplace are sexually available unless they prove they are not.[26] This inference is particularly problematic because welcomeness can be read into all sorts of behavior, much of which is socially conditioned or simply unavoidable. For example, women are relentlessly conditioned to smile (by the man taking their photo for the second-grade yearbook; by the man yelling at them on the sidewalk outside their college dorm). Indeed, within the workplace, women are often penalized for being unfriendly or insufficiently nice.[27] Yet smiling or laughing politely at jokes in the workplace also comes with a price. Even this small act of identity entrepreneurship—attempting to be more pleasant, in ways rewarded by the ingroup—may make it more difficult to disprove welcomeness if a male harasser purports to interpret these gestures as flirting and claims that a woman encouraged his advances.

Beyond polite smiling and laughing, the *Meritor* court's emphasis on "sexually provocative speech or dress" creates a further dilemma. Estrich asks, "Does the Court mean that women who wear short skirts intend to invite sexual advances? That tight sweaters may justly be pled as provoca-tion for otherwise offensive conduct? That men are legally entitled to treat women whose clothes fit snugly with less respect than women whose clothes fit loosely?"[28] What about women who have gained weight lately, who have recently been pregnant, who cannot afford new clothes, or who simply like a more tailored fit in their clothes?

The notion of provocative speech or conduct raises another host of prob-lems. All sorts of behavior might qualify. Complimenting a man might sig-nify welcomeness. Having dinner alone with the boss on a business trip might signify welcomeness. Swearing in the workplace might signify welcomeness. Eating with the men in the breakroom might signify welcomeness. Laughing at dirty jokes (however uncomfortably) might signify welcomeness. Con-tinuing to wear your only suit after the boss compliments it might signify welcomeness. Smiling awkwardly in response to sexualized comments, or simply remaining silent, might signify welcomeness. Yet the welcomeness requirement persists and continues to preclude recovery for plaintiffs in many sexual harassment lawsuits. And the welcomeness requirement presents a particular challenge for lawsuits in a world where the structures of identity capitalism encourage women to become identity entrepreneurs.

Donnie Mangrum, unfortunately, learned this through experience. The court held Donnie's identity entrepreneurship against her. "Because Plaintiff participated in and, in some instances, initiated inappropriate language and activity, she cannot show that Wilson's actions, other than his alleged exposing himself to her, were unwelcome," the judge wrote. "[T]here is no evidence that Plaintiff, at any time, let Wilson know that his sexual banter was unwelcome." Donnie argued that she *had* tried to tell Wilson "no," but the court didn't buy it: "[H]er own evidence shows that when she did tell him 'no,' she also said such things as 'I'm busy,' or 'not now,' comments which tend to negate the effect of the initial 'no,' making her intentions less than clear." Because Don-nie played along to fit in with her workplace culture, the law ultimately failed her. "[E]ven after telling Wilson 'no,'" the court admonished, "she continued to participate in the sexual banter common in the workplace."

Donnie's dilemma is the same one faced by women and other outgroup members in workplaces everywhere. Like Donnie, some women become Cool Girls, and sexual joking and occasional horseplay are par for the course.

A Cool Girl just laughs off that kind of thing. Maybe she doesn't even mind so much, or at least tells herself that she doesn't. But if more serious sexual harassment starts, the Cool Girl is in trouble: laughing off a crude joke is a lot easier than laughing off a demand for oral sex that comes attached to a performance review. And if the harassment becomes so serious that the Cool Girl files a lawsuit, her initial amused, tolerant approach to a sexualized work environment becomes a liability. Like Donnie Mangrum, many Cool Girl plaintiffs lose because a court finds that they "welcomed" sexually harassing behavior by participating in a sexualized workplace culture. As Donnie learned the hard way, courts do not look kindly on such behavior. The list of Cool Girls turned Title VII losers is a long one, and Donnie Mangrum's name is now on the list. (If Sida, who recommended giving the boss a hug and a kiss in the narrative at the beginning of the chapter, ever brought suit, she would likely encounter obstacles similar to Donnie's.)

It's easy to say that Cool Girls deserved what was coming to them. "Why did she play along with it if she didn't like it?" some might ask. "She contributed to this environment and now she wants to complain about it?" But we have to consider the alternatives. What if Donnie had lectured her coworkers about their coarse language, sexual banter, and massage exchanges on the second day of the job? The friendly relationship she developed with many of them during her fourteen years at the dealership would likely never have materialized. Her colleagues might have labeled her a prude, a scold, or—worst of all—a *feminazi*. Had she developed this reputation, her work environment would have become tense. Her colleagues and supervisors might have turned on her with sarcastic comments and insults. They might have retaliated against her by boxing her out of sales opportunities. Donnie's fourteen enjoyable years at the dealership would never have materialized. In many instances Cool Girl behavior is the best choice among bad alternatives.

Covering Their Tracks

Shenavia Moulds, a black woman, worked at Walmart as a receiving department clerk. After she'd been there for about a year and a half, a manager position came open. Moulds thought she was perfect for the job: she knew the receiving department well, and she already had experience substituting for the previous manager. Yet the managers ultimately promoted

Bill Humenansky, a white man. He had only worked at Walmart for nine months, some of that time as a janitor.

After she was denied promotion, Moulds filed suit. Humenansky, in her view, was vastly underqualified. He was not even familiar with all of the receiving manager's duties. In fact, *she* had to train *him* after his promotion. The decision to promote Humenansky could only have been the result of racial bias, she argued.

The court wasn't interested. While noting that "subjective evaluations involving white supervisors provide a ready mechanism for racial discrimination," the court emphasized, with evident relief, that in this particular case another black woman in the department had testified that the department followed standard practice in this instance. The court further noted that six out of fourteen black people were promoted to the department manager position that the plaintiff wanted, and that out of four customer service managers, at all times at least two had been black.[29]

Courts often ignore potentially relevant differences among members of the same identity group—whether black women or some other identity category. In a case against a nursing facility, for instance, the court found that a black employee who had been terminated could not win on a claim of race discrimination. While the court based its decision partly on the employee's performance, it also gave weight to evidence that her supervisor "hired several other black employees including one to replace a white employee, attended a black employee's graduation, and received positive reviews from other black employees."[30] This simplistic analysis verges on a black best friend defense.

The message from the court is clear: if an employer treated a few people of a particular identity group reasonably well, it will be difficult for a member of that identity group to win a discrimination lawsuit against that employer.[31] The strategy for identity capitalist employers is obvious. They should find a few members of outgroups—women, racial minorities—on whom to bestow promotions and favorable treatment. In many instances that will insulate the employer from complaints by members of those identity groups down the road, even if there are material differences between outgroup members, as with the fifth black woman and, perhaps, with Shenavia Moulds.

Sometimes identity capitalist employers also escape liability by retroactively treating an outgroup employee well. After an Alabama state trooper filed a complaint with the EEOC claiming that higher-ranking officers discriminated against him by assigning him to work in Birmingham rather than Montgomery, he was promoted to sergeant over eleven white men who also applied for the position. The court took this as evidence that the commander and others on the police force did not discriminate against the trooper. Yet by giving credence to things that happen *after* the beginning of legal proceedings, including administrative proceedings such as EEOC complaints, courts again provide a road map for identity capitalists to cover their tracks. In a particularly ironic instance of identity capitalism, Alabama's state police force benefited from the identity of a black man to defeat that very black man's own discrimination lawsuit.

One might argue that it's actually good for employers to have this incentive. If they make efforts to show that they don't actually harbor animus toward an outgroup employee in order to benefit themselves in litigation, then in the process those efforts will also undo discrimination toward the employee and others like her. The incentive might even cause employers to overcorrect by behaving solicitously to a litigious employee simply to avoid the cost of litigation. But this argument overlooks that the cost of discrimination is never *just* the burdensome job assignment or lost promotion. Discrimination is also a harm to dignity, a cause of immense stress, a burden on other aspects of an employee's life. If litigation ensues, the financial and emotional costs are profound.

The incentive to change course and treat an employee well as a defense encourages employers to engage in identity capitalism after the fact and in the face of litigation. It does nothing to reduce the likelihood of discrimination before it happens. It also creates incentives for employers to make such litigation more difficult in the first place—by implementing mandatory arbitration agreements, which have proliferated in workplaces despite legal challenges, with one study finding that the use of such agreements increased from 16.1 percent of employment contracts in 2012 to 42.7 percent of contracts in 2014.[32] Litigation ensues, large companies have more resources to devote to the dispute, and can often drag out litigation with time-consuming motions and discovery requests until an exhausted plaintiff is forced to settle just to cover her lawyer fees—and this is true even when a number of plaintiffs file suit together as a class action. As for that rare litigious employee who receives a windfall: while a few such individuals may exist, the financial and emotional cost of litigation is so great that they will remain few and far between. At a talk I attended last year, an experienced attorney who had spent a career representing plaintiffs in employment discrimination lawsuits was asked whether her clients were happy they had sued. "Never," she said. "Not a single one. Not even the ones who won. They all regretted it in the end."

Every so often, the use of identity capitalism as a litigation defense is so obvious that even a court cries foul. Joy Owens worked as a teacher in Alabama's Jackson County School District beginning in 1988.[33] From May 2010 through May 2012, she unsuccessfully applied for sixteen different administrative positions in her school district: seven as a school principal, six as an assistant principal, and three in supervisory roles at the central office. According to Owens, her supervisor, Superintendent Kenneth Harding, said that "he did not want females in administration positions," that "females do not make good administrators because they are too emotional and hardnosed," that "females don't have the personality and fortitude to be principals," and that he "had a lot less problems out of the male principals."

The sixteen positions for which Owens applied unsuccessfully were eventually filled by fourteen men and two women. While Harding tried to point to his hiring of two women as evidence that he had not discriminated against Owens, the court was having none of it. It wrote:

> As for the two women who were hired Owens' brief points to evidence in the record suggesting that in both instances unusual circumstances overbore Harding's discriminatory attitude. According to an affidavit from a teacher familiar with the hiring of the first woman, Harding was going to hire a man, but a state senator personally lobbied Haring [sic] and persuaded him to hire the woman. The record indicates that the other woman was hired after Owens filed an EEOC charge. Owens argues in her brief that, based on the timing, it can be inferred

that the woman was hired to minimize the appearance of discrimination if Owens filed a lawsuit.

As noted, some identity capitalism is so painfully obvious that it will not pass judicial scrutiny. But the threshold at which a court will refuse to play along with identity capitalism appears to be the point at which it won't even pass the laugh test.

Weak Victories

Teresa Soto, the woman whose story began this chapter, fared far better than most Title VII plaintiffs. She was fortunate in several ways. She had a lawyer: many Title VII plaintiffs are pro se, meaning that they represent themselves. She also had a *good* lawyer: Teresa was represented by counsel from Munger, Renschmidt & Denne, an experienced employment litigation firm that has a strong track record of obtaining large verdicts in sexual harassment cases.[34] Teresa was also fortunate in the judge she randomly drew for her case: Judge Mark W. Bennett was a liberal judge with a deep understanding of the way law and society can leave outgroups vulnerable. Appointed by Bill Clinton, he is perhaps best known for his refusal to apply the 100:1 powder/crack sentencing disparity. After retiring from the bench, he took a full-time position at Drake Law School, where he trained judges and lawyers about implicit bias to improve understanding within the criminal justice system.

Teresa was also fortunate that Leonard Tanner was not a better advocate for himself and that the company did not really try to stand behind him. A few months after she filed a charge with the Iowa Civil Rights Commission, the company interviewed Leonard. He changed his story from a previous interview, in which he'd denied everything, and admitted some of the conduct. After interviewing several of Leonard's coworkers on the kill floor, the company terminated his employment.

And Teresa was also relatively fortunate in the case's outcome. Judge Bennett denied the defendants' motion for summary judgment on her sexual harassment claim, meaning that the case could proceed to trial. Only 6 percent of cases filed in federal court actually go to trial, and the judge believed her lawsuit was sufficiently plausible to be one of them.[35]

Simply because Soto fared better in the legal system than almost everyone else did not mean that her situation was desirable. She suffered six months of sexual harassment. She went through the struggle of finding a lawyer and the stress of litigation. When women go to work, they don't dream of one day winning a sexual harassment lawsuit. They just want to do their jobs and be treated with respect. No doubt dismembering pig carcasses on the kill floor was brutal and dangerous, but Teresa was there to work—not to be treated like a piece of meat herself.

Identity capitalism undergirded Soto's poor treatment, as with many other workplace outsiders. And most such outsiders are not able to recover anything for the economic losses, lack of respect, and other harms they suffer. Courts, unfortunately, make the situation worse. They create incentives for identity capitalism and fail to provide remedies for its harms.

A More Equal Protection

Antidiscrimination law is rife with identity capitalism. But all hope is not lost. Workplace antidiscrimination law also offers opportunities for reforms to discourage identity capitalism, remove incentives for identity capitalism, and mitigate the harms of identity capitalism.

Outgroup Decisionmakers

When considering a claim of workplace discrimination, courts should not take into account whether the decisionmaker was a member of the same outgroup. Providing special deference to outgroup decisionmakers encourages employers to tokenize outgroup members. Even a relatively high-ranking outgroup member may not feel that they can protest an employer conscripting them to lend legitimacy to an adverse employment decision. And if a particular incident leads to litigation, the employer may wish to showcase the outgroup decisionmaker for its own benefit, creating an even greater dilemma for the outgroup decisionmaker.

Social science evidence indicates that shared outgroup membership does not necessarily mean that an outgroup member will receive equal treatment. The implication that it does reinforces unsupported views about outgroup heterogeneity and solidarity that continue to result in limiting stereotypes about outgroup members in the working world and beyond. The law is both a substantive and a communicative tool: better laws implement a more just society, and they also communicate ideas about identity that make society more just beyond the courthouse doors.

Identity Performance

To discourage identity capitalism, courts should incorporate identity performance into their analysis of discrimination. Such performance might include identity-correlated behavior that has a particular social significance: hairstyle, fashion, makeup, accent, vocal inflection, mannerisms, disclosure of personal details, and many other aspects of personhood that affect how a particular person is perceived. Courts should be open to the possibility that just because an employer rewards a black woman who straightens her hair, shops at Ann Taylor, and plays tennis for fun, that does not insulate the employer from charges of discrimination against a black woman who wears her hair in cornrows, wears jewelry she purchased in Senegal, and is open about her attendance at Black Lives Matter rallies. If an employer only rewards the "right kind" of black women, the employer is still discriminating on the basis of race and gender.

Identity is more complex than courts currently presume, and the result is identity capitalism—invoking positive treatment of one black woman to obscure poor treatment of another. The solution is to engage in a deeper analysis of whether two people who belong to the same identity categories are actually similar. Such an analysis will inherently be nuanced and fact-bound. But this is what judging *is*: judges undertake complex inquiries regularly. Encouraging parties to introduce evidence about identity beyond crude race and gender categories will enrich courts' consideration of identity performance and ultimately create incentives for more nuanced thinking about identity.

Welcomeness

Courts should revise both the burden and scope of the welcomeness defense. Currently the burden lies with the plaintiff to demonstrate that they communicated to the alleged harasser that the behavior in question was unwelcome—and as discussed earlier, that can be quite difficult to do when courts are willing to look at clothing, smiles, and laughter (however uncomfortable) as evidence of welcomeness.

Instead, the defendant company should be required to show that allegedly sexually or racially harassing behavior was welcomed, and that the plaintiff consented to it verbally, unambiguously, and without coercion. The inquiry is analogous to the affirmative consent inquiry that some campuses have adopted, like the University of California. While some people have argued that affirmative consent is going to Ruin Good Sex Forever, I know of literally no evidence that Good Sex has been Ruined on college campuses, let alone Forever. And even if the affirmative consent requirement were to chill some sexual behavior on college campuses (horrors!), that does not mean that we should dismiss a workplace analog. We do and should expect more formality in a workplace than in a college dorm, and more stringent rules are appropriate. If someone wants to tell dirty jokes or give massages at work, it should fall on them to make sure the person on the receiving end of their behavior is a willing participant.

The standard I am proposing would also rely on clear verbal consent—not inferences from behavior, dress, and body language. If someone wants to make racially or sexually provocative comments at work—and if they choose to do so without getting clear verbal consent—then they are choosing to take on the risk that their colleague may not welcome their comments and behavior. A shifting of burdens in the workplace is long overdue.

Track Records

Courts should stop taking into account employers' track records in assessing whether an employer engaged in discrimination. Whether an employer has treated other outgroup members well is generally irrelevant to whether a particular outgroup member was the target of discrimination. As the discussion of comparators reveals, there might be something about a particular outgroup member that an employer dislikes. Alternatively, different personnel within an employment setting may have quite different reactions to various categories of outgroup members.

The exception to the otherwise blanket prohibition I have proposed is when a plaintiff (or group of plaintiffs) relies on statistics or other track records to show that an employer engaged in discrimination. For example, if a plaintiff argues that a large company promoted a disproportionately low number of women to its upper management, the company might respond with statistics indicating that women are more likely to leave the company before reaching the point in their career trajectories when they would typically be eligible for promotion to upper management. We might ask *why* women are more likely to leave the company at that point, but then we are no longer making inferences from track records—we are talking about something of substance. This shift will both allow better legal decisions and avoid reinforcing the idea that a good track record is a defense against a specific instance of discrimination.

Removing track records from the legal conversation will increase attention to the situation of the actual plaintiff, not the usually irrelevant facts surrounding it. Ultimately, this will remove a powerful incentive for identity capitalism and replace it with an incentive for companies to engage substantively with the way it treats outgroup members within its walls.

These four reforms certainly will not cure everything that ails antidiscrimination law. However, they demonstrate how antidiscrimination law can mitigate the harms of identity capitalism and treat identity entrepreneurs with sensitivity. These reforms would lay the foundation for developing principles to mitigate identity capitalism beyond antidiscrimination law. As we're about to see, identity capitalism is not limited to antidiscrimination context, and many other areas of law likewise cry out for reform.

6

THE LAW OF
IDENTITY CAPITALISM

I N 2018, organizers of a Trump rally in Tennessee played Rihanna's
huge hit "Don't Stop the Music." It's not hard to see why. "Don't Stop
the Music" sounds young and cool. Many would say that it sounds
black. For Trump's aging white supporters, the song might evoke the feeling
that they are part of something happening, something fashionable, perhaps
a multiracial club scene very unlike the rally—a place they'd never go but
wouldn't mind bragging that they'd been.

Rihanna wasn't happy. After she learned that "Don't Stop the Music"
played at the rally, she tweeted, "Not for much longer . . . me nor my people would [n]ever be at or around one of those tragic rallies, so thanks for
the heads up!"

Rihanna has vocally opposed Donald Trump and his policies. She participated in the Women's March in New York City in 2017. After Trump
signed an executive order banning immigration from seven majority-Muslim

countries, she described him as an "immoral pig" and tweeted, "Disgusted! The news is devastating! American is being ruined right before our eyes!" She supports policy views that Trump and his supporters largely reject. She appeared in a video protesting police brutality called "23 Ways You Could Be Killed If You Are Black in America." She vocally expressed disagreement with Indiana's Religious Freedom Restoration Act, which has been criticized for allowing religiously motivated discrimination against LGBTQ people. She declined an invitation to headline the 2019 Superbowl halftime show to support Colin Kaepernick and protest the NFL's controversial anthem policy.

Rihanna is unapologetically political—President Obama called her "a powerful force in the fight to give people dignity"—and unapologetically black. On Instagram she posted a meme with the words "I'm Black Every Month," with the caption "black history month or naw." (It was clear that Rihanna went with "naw.") She is alert to race discrimination in her industry: "'You know, when I started to experience the difference—or even have my race be highlighted—it was mostly when I would do business deals. . . . And, you know, that never ends, by the way. It's still a thing.'"[1] Shorter version: "[E]veryone's cool with a young black woman singing, dancing, partying, looking hot, but that when it comes time . . . to broker a deal, she is suddenly made aware of her blackness."[2]

As an artist, Rihanna invests great effort in her music, her image, and her entire persona. And her work has paid off: she has sold millions of records; she has won nine Grammy Awards; she is the most-streamed female artist of all time on Spotify and Apple Music. Her elaborate music videos made her the first woman to pass two billion views on the music video website VEVO. She is a fashion icon: one critic observed that "Rihanna's wardrobe is the most talked-about, influential and dissected in pop"; whatever she wears "is immediately reproduced on the high street, because it sells."[3] She has launched a highly successful makeup line and four perfumes. Rihanna is always working. In a *New York Times* profile, interviewer Miranda July reveals, "Almost every night, when you're asleep, Rihanna is in the studio. She was headed there after our meeting and [her assistant] said she'd be there until morning." And even these remarkable accomplishments aren't enough. Rihanna said, "I used to feel unsafe right in the moment of an accomplishment—I felt the ground fall from under my feet because this could be the end. And even now, while everyone is celebrating, I'm on to the next thing. I don't want to be lost in this big cushion of success."[4]

Rihanna's life's work is the product of Rihanna. From a purely pragmatic perspective, she would suffer a serious injury if people believed that she endorsed Donald Trump or his political cronies. Her audience is young and multiracial—a demographic with whom Trump polls particularly poorly.[5] If her fans believed she was a Trump supporter, some might find her views distasteful and stop buying her music. If she lost her fans she might lose endorsement deals, public speaking opportunities, leverage to pursue various humanitarian projects, and other career benefits. Rihanna carefully cultivates her sound, appearance, and public persona. If her song is played in a context that radically contravenes her image, her image suffers.

Losing fans and profits is already a harm, but Rihanna's opposition to Donald Trump suggests that having the song played at his rallies could be an injury to her *self*. As a black woman, perhaps Rihanna doesn't want her work used at the rallies. For centuries, unconsenting black women's bodies were used as entertainment for white people. Rihanna may find the use particularly problematic for that reason. Even if no one would mistake playing the song as support, perhaps she just doesn't want to be associated with Donald Trump in any way.

Yet Rihanna likely has no legal recourse for these injuries to her brand and her person. As long as a political campaign obtains a so-called "blanket license" from the performing rights organization of which the copyright holders of the musical work are members, the license allows the campaign to play any song in the performing rights organization's repertoire. If "Don't Stop the Music" were used in a campaign advertisement, then Rihanna might have a claim. But American copyright law, which protects only economic interests rather than other, more personal, interests, fails to recognize the injury caused by the misuse of Rihanna's music.

Lawyers and legal scholars don't necessarily think of copyright law as related to identity and discrimination, although some scholars have rightly pointed out that copyright law has disparate effects on different identity groups.[6] Yet copyright law frequently enables identity capitalism by allowing ingroup members to use outgroup members as they please. As a result, outgroup members' identities are not entirely their own. Rihanna describes the experience of being used within and beyond the music industry. "In the beginning . . . I didn't feel like an artist, I felt like a tool. I just felt, hey, here I am, this money-making vehicle for this big record label [and] I'm not even having fun, because I'm not able to be who I am."[7]

In the previous chapter, we saw how identity capitalism infects antidiscrimination law. Now, we're about to see that antidiscrimination law was just the tip of the iceberg. The influence of identity capitalism throughout our laws and our legal system is breathtaking. I won't attempt a comprehensive survey, but I've selected some examples that will give a sense of the magnitude of the problem. Think of it as a curated exhibit of identity capitalism in the law.

Identity capitalism affects legal doctrine from copyright law to constitutional law to criminal law. Identity capitalism affects the way cases are adjudicated from beginning to end, from litigation strategy to the writing of decisions. Identity capitalism infects the legal system writ large—both the law and the mechanisms for implementing it. It starts at the very beginning, with strategic selection of plaintiffs to bring particular claims.

I Needed Asian Plaintiffs

Edward Blum is on a crusade to reshape laws relating to race. The *New York Times* described Blum, who is not lawyer, as "a one-man legal factory with a growing record of finding plaintiffs who match his causes, winning big victories and trying above all to erase racial preferences from American life."[8] Blum was involved in litigation that struck down a major portion of the Voting Rights Act of 1965—a law that subjected certain states and counties to federal scrutiny when they modified voting procedures. The law was intended to prevent states from implementing procedures that disproportionately burdened racial minorities. Blum's victory likely played a part in oversight—or lack thereof—affecting key races throughout the south in the 2018 midterm elections.

Blum has also turned his attention to affirmative action. He backed an unsuccessful lawsuit brought by Abigail Fisher, a white student who was denied admission to the University of Texas. At the time the University of Texas admitted every student who finished in the top 10 percent of their high school class and used a holistic review, including consideration of race, to fill the remaining slots. Fisher, who failed to finish in the top 10 percent of her class and received a score of 1180 out of 1600 on the SAT, almost certainly would not have gained admission even if race were not a factor in the admissions process.

Perhaps realizing that an unexceptional white student was not a particularly appealing plaintiff, Blum turned to a different strategy. As he put it, "I needed plaintiffs; I needed Asian plaintiffs . . . so I started" the Project on Fair Representation, which included a network of websites to recruit plaintiffs for litigation that prominently feature photos of Asian American students (Figure 6.1). Blum treated Asian American people like items on his shopping list: he needed them so he went out and got them.

In service of such litigation, he also founded Students for Fair Admissions, which originally had a board of directors comprising only three members: Blum, Fisher, and Fisher's father, none of whom is Asian American. While the organization now claims to have over twenty thousand members,[9] it appears to be funded almost entirely through Blum's efforts, and as this book goes to press its website does not list any information about the number of members who are either students or Asian American, let alone both.

Students for Fair Admissions subsequently brought lawsuits against Harvard and the University of North Carolina, in both instances alleging that the schools "intentionally discriminate against Asian-American applicants."[10] While neither case has yet reached a final disposition, the origin and evolution of the litigation strongly suggest that, at least from Blum's perspective, this lawsuit is not really about Asian Americans. What Blum and his allies actually care about is dismantling affirmative action programs. Nothing in Blum's career trajectory suggests that he cares about Asian American well-being. He has not, for instance, advocated for employment protections, fair housing, immigration, or a host of other issues that affect Asian Americans. And his vigorous advocacy against the Voting Rights Act—which protects the rights of minority voters, including Asian Americans—indicates that he does not care about Asian American political power.

Rather, Blum is an identity capitalist. When it comes to affirmative action, Asian Americans are valuable to him because they provide an optical improvement. Rather than arguing that affirmative action programs are unfair to white people—which looks rather like white people complaining

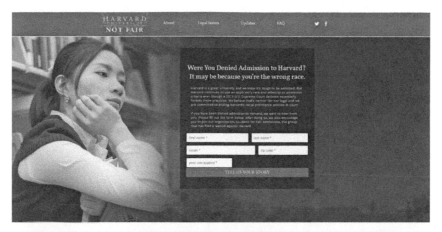

FIGURE 6.1. Screenshots from the Harvard Not Fair website. Source: Nancy Leong.

that groups they have systemically disadvantaged for decades or centuries might now have that disadvantage taken into account—Blum would rather assume the mantle of a crusader for racial justice. The narrative is now that Blum is advocating on behalf of hardworking Asian Americans who suffered discrimination at the hands of elite universities.

Beyond the courts, Blum's identity capitalist plaintiff selection has public relations benefits. He partially neutralizes one group who might otherwise be opposed to his efforts: Asian Americans themselves. Particularly for recent Asian American immigrants who are not informed about the long history of race discrimination in America and the resulting reasons for affirmative action, Blum may look like an ally in putting a stop to discrimination.

More importantly, though, introducing Asian American plaintiffs provides white opponents of affirmative action with a rhetorical tool. "Affirmative action is so unfair to the Asians," they can say, without actually caring about Asian Americans in literally any other setting. Identity capitalism in plaintiff selection allows white opponents of affirmative action to reframe their opposition as a racial justice issue. They no longer have to come out and say that they don't like affirmative action because it threatens the racial status quo—specifically, a status quo that privileges white people. Here, identity capitalism is a way of obscuring true motives and obstructing honest conversations about race.

Identity capitalism both advances the interests of white affirmative action opponents and usurps the actual preferences of Asian Americans. A majority of Asian Americans support affirmative action. In 2016, Karthick Ramakrishnan and Janelle Wong led research that asked Asian American registered voters: "In general, do you think affirmative action programs designed to increase the number of black and minority students on college campuses are a good thing or a bad thing?"[11] Fifty-three percent supported such programs; 33 percent were opposed. There is a sharp divide in opinion between Chinese Americans and everyone else. While Chinese American support for affirmative action declined from 78 percent in 2012 to 41 percent in 2016, support remained constant between 70 percent and 73 percent for every other subgroup. Even under the most generous reading of the data, Blum and his collaborators are advancing the preferences of only a third of Asian Americans. That one-third is not a representative cross-section of Asian Americans (as they imply by describing plaintiffs as "Asian American") but rather a subset that is disproportionately Chinese American and socioeconomically advantaged. This tactic erases other Asian subgroups: Japanese, Filipino, Vietnamese, Thai, Burmese, Korean, Indian, Cambodian, Laotian, and so on. These groups are overwhelmingly supportive of affirmative action, a fact you would never know from SFFA's lawsuit or the surrounding publicity. As I wrote in 2016, "[I]t is unclear to me why people who are not Asian Americans should get to decide whether Asian Americans are injured."[12]

Blum's fervor to free Asian Americans from affirmative action is particularly dissonant with his relative indifference to legacy admissions. Research has found that legacies account for a great deal of racial inequality within society. As former Princeton admissions officer T. H. Rawls wrote: "There is . . . one deliberate and robust admission policy used at many colleges that in effect constitutes white affirmative action: That is the preference given in admissions decisions to children of alumni of the college."[13] Rawls explained that the legacy pool is overwhelmingly white, and estimated that 5 to 10 percent of admitted students were legacies who would not otherwise have been admitted.[14] Some opponents of affirmative action do express opposition to legacy preferences as well. But they aren't spending millions of dollars to oppose it in court. Actions speak louder than words, and here affirmative action opponents' phony solicitude for Asian Americans speaks loudly indeed.

While any plaintiff is entitled to file a lawsuit, courts should not draw a more favorable inference simply because the plaintiff is not white. Legal journalists should also strive for transparency. They should not imply that a case is more likely to further racial justice simply because the plaintiff is not white. Affirmative action is not only a legal battle—it's a public relations battle. Coverage of the lawsuits by Students for Fair Admissions should include the organization's history and strategy so that the public can make up their own minds about what is actually fair.

Handy Race-Neutral Explanations

In the entire history of America, Curtis Flowers is the only man in America to stand trial six times for the same crime. Accused of murdering four employees of a furniture store in Mississippi in 1996, Flowers was found guilty in his first three trials, but in each one the conviction was overturned on appeal. The fourth and fifth trials resulted in hung juries sharply divided along racial lines. The sixth and most recent trial—which took place in 2010—resulted in a conviction in just half an hour.[15] Flowers challenged his 2010 conviction, and the Supreme Court agreed to hear his case. But his claim—that the jury that convicted him was selected in a racially biased manner—was an uphill battle to win. In 2019, the Supreme Court finally held that the prosecutor, who is white, unconstitutionally kept black people off the jury.[16] But the Supreme Court's decision does not mean the ordeal is over for Flowers. As this book was being written, he was released from prison on bail after twenty-three years, six trials, and four death sentences, and prosecutor Doug Evans recused himself from future proceedings. But the state of Mississippi is still deciding whether it wants to try Flowers a *seventh* time.

During a trial, each side can eliminate a certain number of jurors using what are called peremptory strikes. A peremptory strike allows the party to eliminate a juror for any reason—except, as the Supreme Court held in *Batson v. Kentucky*, their race.[17] (A later case held that jurors also could not be struck because of their gender.) The Supreme Court's holding places the emphasis squarely on prosecutor's intent: What was the prosecutor thinking when she struck a particular juror? Did she strike the person because of their race? Or did she have literally any other reason? If the latter, the court will hold that the peremptory strike was not unconstitutional.

The effect on the ground is that jurors have been removed for their race for as long as there have been juries, and this has continued long after *Batson*. The problem is particularly acute—and particularly high stakes—in criminal cases, in which people of color are stereotyped as more sympathetic to defendants and consequently removed by the prosecution. According to a recent report, one county in Alabama struck 80 percent of African Americans qualified for jury service in death penalty cases, and in one county in Louisiana, 80 percent of all criminal cases have been tried before all-white juries.[18] Mississippi—the site of Curtis Flowers' trials—is no exception. The Mississippi Supreme Court concluded in 2007 that "racially motivated jury selection is still prevalent twenty years after *Batson* was handed down."[19]

But the Supreme Court has been extremely lenient in determining what counts as a reason other than race. One judge, vexed by "the charade that has become the *Batson* process," speculated ironically that new prosecutors are given a manual titled "Handy Race-Neutral Explanations" or "20 Time-Tested Race-Neutral Explanations." According to the judge, the manual would include reasons prosecutors have actually offered for strikes: a prospective juror is too old or too young, is divorced, has "long, unkempt hair," is a freelance writer, holds certain religious views, is a social worker, is a renter, lacks family contact, attempted to make eye contact with defendant, "liv[es] in an area consisting predominantly of apartment complexes," is single, is over-educated, lacks maturity, displays improper demeanor, is unemployed, wore improper attire, lives alone, misspelled their place of employment, lives with a girlfriend, has an unemployed spouse, has a spouse employed as school teacher, is employed part-time as a barber, is friends with a city council member, failed to remove a hat, lacks community ties, has children in the same "age bracket" as a defendant, has a deceased father, and has an aunt receiving psychiatric care.[20] The judge's sardonic comments highlight a serious problem: race-neutral reasons are abundant and hard to disprove. Commentator Gilad Edelman observes, "The most remarkable thing about *Batson*, it turns out, is how easy it has been to ignore."[21]

Courts often examine not only the prosecution's stated reason for a strike but also the surrounding context—which creates a powerful incentive for identity capitalism. Many courts have held that the defendant cannot show race discrimination if the prosecutor only strikes one or two people of a particular race. As one commentator observed, "This ruling in effect allows the prosecutor one or two 'free shots' to discriminate on the basis of race."[22] If a prosecutor seats one or more people of a particular race on the jury, courts take that to mean that other jurors were not excluded due to their membership in the same racial group. One court rejected a defendant's claim of race discrimination because "the prosecutor could have, but did not, strike all of the black members of the jury pool."[23] Another agreed: "The fact that the government accepted a jury which included two blacks, when it could have used its remaining peremptory challenges to strike these potential jurors, shows that the government did not attempt to exclude all blacks, or as many blacks as it could, from the jury."[24] If a prosecutor wants to eliminate some prospective jurors of a particular race and get away with it, the safest way to do so is to include one or two more "palatable" members of that race on the jury.[25]

Prosecutors explicitly acknowledge the incentives that the law of jury selection creates for identity capitalism. Ronald Sievert prosecuted four cases that resulted in the jury imposing the death penalty in Texas. Sievert first preemptively defends prosecutors from allegations of race discrimination, explaining that race "was not discussed and I never saw the slightest hint that it was even subconsciously considered."[26] (The conclusion that *subconscious* racism did not happen because no one saw the slightest hint of it is dubious at best, but one better addressed by a different book.) Sievert then goes on to say, "I must admit that after a time many of us started to go out of our way to look for blacks to put on the jury. We might have an honest fear that a particular minority juror might not be fair but we now resolved that conflict in favor of achieving highly integrated juries."[27]

Identity capitalism in jury selection raises the same concern as does much identity capitalism elsewhere: it is fundamentally dishonest. "It just makes such a farce of the system," prominent defense attorney Stephen Bright says of *Batson*. "Nobody—the judge, the prosecutor, the defense lawyers—nobody thinks the reasons are really the reasons they strike the people. They strike the people because of their race. I mean, we all know that. And then you try to come up with a good reason for doing it and see if you can get away with it."[28]

If courts want to make sure the jury selection process is actually fair, the solution is simple. They should look at whether the resulting jury provides a roughly representative cross-section of the relevant community with respect to race, gender, age, and other factors. Looking at the resulting jury—rather than at a sham selection process tainted with identity capitalism—is the way to ensure that people are not unfairly excluded on account of their identity.

Slanted Trademark Law

Native American activists first asked the Washington Redskins to change the team name in 1972, and first filed suit in court to ask the United States government to withdraw the team's trademark registration in 1992.[29] The activists claim that "Redskins" is a racial slur; that the name is offensive and disparages a group that has already suffered atrocities at the hands of white immigrants; that it makes Native Americans into mascots rather than full human beings; and that it allows a non-Native person to profit from Native American identity.

When the first group of plaintiffs lost for reasons unrelated to the merits of the case, a second group—led by a woman named Amanda Blackhorse—subsequently brought suit. Blackhorse and her co-plaintiffs relied on a provision of federal trademark law stating that trademarks cannot be registered if they "[c]onsist of or comprise immoral, deceptive, or scandalous matter" or "disparage or falsely suggest a connection with persons, living or dead, institutions, beliefs, or national symbols, or bring them into contempt, or disrepute."[30] Under these provisions, she argued, the government should deny trademark protection to the Washington Redskins.

Blackhorse won. The U.S. Patent and Trademark Office canceled the team's trademark registration, agreeing that their name and symbols are disparaging to Native Americans.[31] As legal scholars were quick to note, this did not mean that the Washington Redskins had to change their name. They can continue to use "Redskins" as the name of the team, sell "Redskins" branded merchandise, and refer to "Redskins" in advertising. Rather, it simply meant that they could not claim the protection of trademark law. This makes it more difficult for the Redskins to protect their brand or prevent other people from creating "Redskins" merchandise. As legal scholars Robert Tsai and Christine Haight Farley explain, "[T]he cancellation of the trademark's registration doesn't actually inhibit anybody's ability to utter a single word."[32] Rather, denying trademark registration "simply denies the federal government's support for disparaging trademarks." So while the Redskins team "can choose to define itself by reference to a racial epithet," Blackhorse and other leaders in the Native American community believed that the victory served an important signaling function, validating the idea that disadvantaged groups (or, for that matter, anyone else) should not be used as mascots.

Yet the victory was short-lived. An artist named Simon Tam—the lead singer of the band The Slants—brought suit over the Patent and Trademark Office's decision to deny a trademark to his band on the same grounds: that the name of the band was an offensive racial epithet for Asian people and thus disparaging. In *Matal v. Tam*, the U.S. Supreme Court unanimously ruled the disparaging-trademarks provision was unconstitutional on the ground that it violated the First Amendment's guarantee of free speech.[33]

The result was a win for Tam, the Slants, and the Redskins. In the future, the government will not be able to deny a trademark because a name is disparaging. This opens the door to the registration of all kinds of racist, sexist, homophobic, and otherwise offensive language. In the month after the Supreme Court decision, people filed trademark applications for "gutter sluts," "chink," and, in at least five instances, "nigga."[34] There may be other reasons that a trademark application would not be granted—for example, if the term is already in common usage—but that it is disparaging is no longer one of them.

The troubling consequence of the decision is that outgroup members who are identity entrepreneurs receive greater protection than those who are not. Tam is an identity entrepreneur: he offers a version of outgroup identity that appeals to the ingroup. Tam's version suggests that racial slurs aren't problematic as long as a few members of the outgroup like to use them. Without question, reclaiming a racial slur can be powerful. But what is good for identity entrepreneurs is not always good for the outgroup as a whole. A privileged and relatively prominent musician might benefit from trademarking a racial slur. But an Asian kid bullied by racists now has more difficulty trying to explain that the name hurled at him is deeply problematic. "There's even a band that won a lawsuit because they wanted to be called 'The Slants,'" the bullies can now point out if they get in trouble for name-calling, and they'd be correct.

The other problem with invalidating the "disparagement" clause is that, by arguably helping one identity entrepreneurial outgroup member, it harms many others. The holding of *Matal v. Tam* applies regardless of whether the person using the term is doing so in a way that is harmful or helpful to the outgroup. One can make a case that reclaiming "The Slants" is helpful to some Asian American people. It's very difficult to argue that the same is true of "The Redskins."

Identity capitalists like *Matal v. Tam* because it gives them cover for seeking legal protection for offensive speech without seeming racist. In an interesting coincidence, attorney Lisa Blatt (remember her? Brett Kavanaugh's feminist female friend?) represented the Washington Redskins. She commented that the lower courts' conclusion "is not a cultural referendum," suggesting that an appellate court would have overruled the lower court decision. Blatt also referred to polls supposedly showing that an "overwhelming majority" of Native Americans do not find the team's name offensive.

Blatt was probably referring to polls like the one conducted in 2016 by the *Washington Post* that found that nine out of ten Native Americans do not find the name offensive.[35] But the methodology of most polls has drawn intense criticism from Native Americans: 56 percent of respondents were not members of any tribe or could not name what tribe their ancestors claimed, more than half of respondents were over the age of fifty, only 12 percent of those polled were from the Mountain West, where eighteen out of twenty of the most heavily populated Native American reservation communities are, and 36 percent of respondents were from the South, where only 13 percent of the total estimated Native American population lives.[36] Other Native Americans object to the use of polls in itself: Louis Gray, an Osage Indian, says, "Why would you take a poll to see if something is racially offensive? You wouldn't do that with any other race."[37] Blatt is engaged in identity capitalism: she found a poll of nominal outgroup members that agreed with her and leveraged the identities of those polled to support her position, rather than actually engaging with the serious critics of her substantive position.

The real issue with the polls, though, is that even if they had accurately captured public opinion, they fail to take account of the more serious harms of the Redskins name, as well as other sports team names invoking Native Americans that are not in themselves racial slurs, such as "Braves," "Chiefs," and "Indians." Research has shown that American Indian students are negatively affected by mascot representations of American Indians.[38] One study found that American Indian students attending a high school on a reservation had positive associations with Chief Wahoo—a cartoon caricature representing the Cleveland Indians Major League baseball team—and Pocahontas, yet they suffered decreased self-esteem and feelings of community worth when shown their images.[39] Another study found that American Indian college students shown images of Chief Wahoo or Chief Illiniwek (at the time, still the mascot of the University of Illinois) and then asked to think about what they would be like in a year were less likely to think of themselves in terms of achievement, such as "find a job," or "get good grades." The authors suggest that American Indian mascots negatively affect American Indian students' well-being "because, in the contexts in which they appear, there are relatively few alternative characterizations of American Indians."[40]

In *Matal v. Tam*, trademark law incorporated the structures of identity capitalism. The decision privileged identity entrepreneurs above those who don't seek the approval of the ingroup and removed a tool for disadvantaged groups seeking the dignity of legal recognition. The argument by Tam—and the Redskins—that the *government* has to recognize subordinating speech by bestowing a trademark trivializes the harm that such speech causes. The way to get identity capitalism out of trademark law is simple: *Matal v. Tam* should be overruled.

For Her Own Good

Some of the most overt identity capitalism in the law involves reproductive rights. Members of the Supreme Court who have little regard for women in most other areas suddenly become very concerned about the welfare of women who seek access to abortion. Such concern is woven into the foundational decisions upholding a woman's right to choose. In *Casey v. Planned Parenthood*, the Court stated that "the State has legitimate interests from the outset of pregnancy in protecting the health of the woman."[41] The Supreme Court—which at the time included only one woman—relied on women's own welfare as a reason to regulate abortion.

In the years since *Casey*, antiabortion judges, legislators, and other opponents have used women to bolster their argument for restricting reproductive rights. They have used this strategy even though a majority of women believe abortion should be legal: in a 2018 Pew poll, 60 percent of women say that abortion should be legal in all or most cases, while 36 percent say it should be illegal in all or most cases.[42]

Undoubtedly some women vehemently oppose abortion. But opponents of abortion—especially men—often choose to showcase the views of women who oppose abortion and to ignore or disparage the views of women who support access to abortion. This blatant identity capitalism should prompt a feeling of déjà vu. Similar to the historical debate over women's suffrage that we saw in Chapter 2, men are relying on the views of a minority of women in order to buttress their own arguments.

In 2008, the Supreme Court decided *Carhart v. Gonzales*, which upheld the constitutionality of the Partial-Birth Abortion Ban Act—legislation prohibiting a particular late-term abortion procedure. In a 5-4 decision, the Court reasoned that women should be prohibited from certain procedures on the ground that to allow women to seek such procedures would be bad for women themselves. Writing for the majority, Justice Kennedy explained,

> Whether to have an abortion requires a difficult and painful moral decision. While we find no reliable data to measure the phenomenon, it seems unexceptionable to conclude some women come to regret their choice to abort the infant life they once created and sustained. Severe depression and loss of esteem can follow.[43]

The Court, without "reliable data," still held that whether women can obtain certain abortion procedures should be limited because women themselves may regret it. The Court went on,

> The State has an interest in ensuring so grave a choice is well informed. It is self-evident that a mother who comes to regret her choice to abort must struggle with grief more anguished and sorrow more profound when she learns, only after the event, what she once did not know: that she allowed a doctor to pierce the skull and vacuum the fast-developing brain of her unborn child, a child assuming the human form.[44]

The decision included a paean to the type of women the court favors: Good Mothers, not women who get abortions. "Respect for human life finds an ultimate expression in the bond of love the mother has for her child. The Act recognizes this reality as well."[45]

Justice Kennedy's conclusions did not come out of thin air. Rather, he and the other five justices in the all-male majority gave space to the views of Sandra Cano—the plaintiff in *Doe v. Bolton*, a case heard simultaneously with *Roe v. Wade*—and 180 other "post-abortive" women.[46] That brief argued that "the health exception in fact creates serious adverse consequences to women's health." It also presented an affidavit from the 180 women, which describes their experiences post-abortion, often involving guilt, shame, substance abuse, abusive relationships, depression, anxiety, and a range of other mental health issues.

The Court's leveraging of outgroup identity—here, the identity of women—to support its decision follows a now-familiar model. I do not discount the trauma and real pain the women amici express, and Sandra Cano's account describes inexcusable conduct by her attorney—conduct for which an attorney should probably be disbarred, if true. Yet the Court, and Justice Kennedy, gives disproportionate credence to the views of a small minority of women as a way of bolstering its opinion. Available evidence suggests that the views of the women in the brief—again, I do not question their authenticity—do not represent the experiences of most women in relation to abortion. For example, a 2015 peer-reviewed survey of 667 women found that 95 percent did not regret the decision three years after the fact.[47] Many other studies have reached similar conclusions.[48] Yet rather than turning to research representing the experience of many women, much of which was also called to the Court's attention by amici,[49] Justice Kennedy's opinion instead highlights the experiences of the few women who regret abortion because these women support the Court's result. This tactic allows the Court to reframe its opinion: it's no longer an opinion about five men on the Supreme Court restricting women's choices; now it's an opinion that reflects what *women* want.

The Court's identity capitalist opinion in *Carhart* has metastasized. Several other courts have now given doctrinal weight to Justice Kennedy's self-described data-free commentary about women's regret. In a case called *Texas Medical Providers v. Lakey*, the Fifth Circuit relied on regret. The challenged Texas law required doctors to display a sonogram and make audible the heartbeat of the fetus, to explain the procedure to the woman, and imposed a twenty-four-hour waiting period.[50] In upholding the law, the court articulated a four factor test, of which one factor was premised on ensuring that a woman seeking an abortion didn't regret it later: "[T]he state furthers the legitimate purpose of reducing the risk that a woman may elect an abortion, only to discover later, with devastating psychological consequences, that her decision was not fully informed." *Lakey* demonstrates how the Supreme Court's data-free musing that did not directly affect the result can be translated by lower courts into a more concrete and more consequential part of the test. More broadly, the progression from *Carhart* to *Lakey* shows how identity capitalist comments can start out as rhetoric and quickly become part of the doctrine itself.[51]

The Court's identity capitalist methodology has spread to state legislatures and courts. Opponents of abortion argue that it's "better for women" to mandate a whole host of procedures that are really designed to deter abortions: ultrasounds, fetal heartbeat laws, waiting periods, provision of state-mandated information designed to deter women from having abortions, requiring that doctors have admitting privileges. The supposed focus on what is good for women also extends beyond courts. Louisiana—which has very restrictive abortion laws—provides information on a Department of Health page called "Women's Right to Know," which includes a long list of risks associated with abortion.[52] The page then lists the potential complications associated with pregnancy. It begins, "Although every pregnancy has some risk of problems, continuing a pregnancy and delivering a baby is usually a safe, healthy process." The website provides no similar statement at the beginning of the list of abortion-related health issues, although the risks associated with pregnancy are much greater than those associated with abortion. The implication is that abortion is bad for women's health, even though available evidence shows otherwise. As Amanda Marcotte summarizes, "[T]he main strategy for scraping away at women's rights was to claim that it was being done for women's own good."[53]

The doctrinal problem associated with the abortion cases is one of proportionality. If judges are going to reason from the feelings and values of some women, judges should acknowledge the views of all women, including those who strongly support reproductive rights. They should even consider those who regret *having* children—a minority group, but certainly not a nonexistent one. Cherry picking the views of women who agree with the position the court adopts—and then predicating part of the reasoning of a decision on them—should not form the basis for an opinion about reproductive choice.

Beyond abortion doctrine, judges themselves are also targets of identity capitalism. Many opponents of abortion wanted Trump to appoint Amy Coney Barrett, an accomplished former Notre Dame professor later appointed by Trump as a federal judge on the Seventh Circuit, to fill the seat vacated by Anthony Kennedy on the Supreme Court. Commentator Ramesh Ponnuru wrote, "The main reason I favor Barrett, though, is the obvious one: she's a woman . . . it cannot be good for conservatism that all three women now on the court are liberals. If *Roe v. Wade* is overturned—as I certainly hope it will be, as it is an unjust decision with no plausible basis in the Constitution—it would be better if it were not done only by male justices, with every female justice in dissent."[54] Ponnuru's claim is not a logical, legal, or even moral one. It's a claim about optics. Similarly, commentator Liz Mair observes, "Let's say the Supreme Court overturns Roe 5-4. The five justices in the majority will all be conservative men, and two of them will be accused sex harassers, while all the women justices will be stacked on the minority, pro-*Roe* side." She concludes, "Trump, and Senate Republicans, should have learned the biggest, easiest lesson from #MeToo: When in doubt, just pick the woman."[55] Identity capitalism does not only infuse the doctrine of abortion. It also influences who gets to make that doctrine.

Speaking Truth from Power

AutoAdmit is an online message board that purports to be about law school. In reality most of the posts have next to nothing to do with law school. One commentator observed that there are hundreds of threads with despicable racist, homophobic, misogynist, and otherwise bigoted slurs in the titles.[56] The board is also very interested in Jewish people, whom posters frequently describe using vile anti-Semitic language.

In 2009, AutoAdmit posters became obsessed with two Yale Law students: Brittan Heller and Heide Iravani. Anonymous commenters, using pseudonyms such as "Patrick Bateman," "playboytroll," "Remember when I said I would kill you last? I lied" and "HitlerHitlerHitler," wrote countless sexualized and false posts about the two women.

The site's first thread about Heller was titled "Stupid Bitch to Attend Yale Law." Subsequent posts were replete with sexualized comments about Heller, many of them violent. They included comments such as "i'll force myself on her, most definitely," "I think I will sodomize her. Repeatedly," and "just don't FUCK her, she has herpes." A poster lied that Heller had bribed her way into Yale Law School and had a secret affair with the dean of admissions. Another said that "[c]learly she deserves to be raped so that her little fantasy world can be shattered by real life." Another said, "I would like to hate-fuck Brittan Heller but since people say she has herpes that might be a bad idea." When Heller contacted the moderators of the site and asked for the content to be removed, they repeatedly refused.

The site's first thread about Iravani was titled "Rate this HUGE breasted cheerful big tit girl from YLS." Posters linked to photos of Iravani on another social networking site. As with Heller, posters frequently posted about having sex with Iravani. For instance, "I'm trying to decided if Id rather do her doggystyle or cowgirl. Cowgirl, the funbags would be in my face. Doogystyle, they'd swing furiously as I pounded her from behind." Another poster in the same thread encouraged the previous poster: "cowgirl but honestly if you had a shot with her do it both ways." Posters also claimed that Iravani has gonorrhea, is addicted to heroin, and had given Yale Law School's dean oral sex in exchange for a passing grade. "Heide Iravani deserves to be raped," stated one. On a thread titled "Heide Iravani, YLS 1L, you're a fucking cunt," one poster said, "I'm doing cartwheels knowing this stupid Jew bitch is getting her self esteem raped." Posters started false rumors that she had died or committed suicide. When Iravani contacted the moderators of the site and asked them to remove the posts, not only was her request refused, but also she was told that future requests would be posted to the site.

Heller and Iravani sued, claiming copyright infringement, appropriation of their names and likenesses, disclosure of private facts, false light invasion of privacy, and intentional and negligent infliction of emotional distress. The case settled, so we do not know whether they would have won any or all of the claims. But the AutoAdmit complaint highlights an important distinction. Heller and Iravani likely could have proceeded on some of their claims. But they had little legal recourse otherwise because the problem with the speech was the speech itself, and the Supreme Court has held that the First Amendment of the United States Constitution protects speech that is "merely" hateful and misogynistic. Again and again, the Supreme Court has struck down statutes that attempt to regulate expressions of identity-motivated hatred. In *Virginia v. Black*, for example, the Court struck down a Virginia statute prohibiting people from burning a cross with intent to intimidate.[57]

The Court's reasoning in these cases expresses a set of common assumptions about free speech. Free speech absolutists typically argue that freedom of expression is the most fundamental right protected under the Constitution; the correct response to harmful speech is more speech; and there is no principled basis for distinguishing "good" from "bad" ideas, therefore the government cannot regulate any speech at all.[58] The result is tolerance of racism, misogyny, homophobia, and other bigotry in the name of free speech. "More speech" is held up as a panacea.

While a thorough review of free speech doctrine and commentary over the past decades could fill many books longer than this one, what is clear is the identity capitalism that animates it. Justice Scalia wrote in *R.A.V. v. St. Paul* that "it is the responsibility, even the obligation, of diverse communities to confront such notions in whatever form they appear," yet "that confrontation cannot consist of selective limitations upon speech."[59] In other words, disempowered and stigmatized minorities have to solve their own problems; the government isn't going to help level the playing field.

Many commentators across the political spectrum sign onto the disingenuous view that the "more speech" view is really for the good of women, people of color, LGBTQ people, and other historically and currently disempowered groups. Jay Stanley, senior policy analyst at the ACLU, argues, "If we don't stand up for racist speech when it is censored, it is the weak, the powerless, minorities, and those who seek change who will be hurt most in the end."[60] John Samples, of the Cato Institute, agrees: "We must resist solutions that embrace censorship, as hate speech laws fall hardest on those they aim to protect."[61] Even Barack Obama has said, "The strongest weapon against hateful speech is not repression; it is more speech—the voices of tolerance that rally against bigotry."[62]

What this position ignores is that the ability not only to speak but also to make oneself heard is not distributed equally in American society. Perhaps everyone has the same First Amendment rights, but not everyone has the same ability to use them. Hate speech silences the voices of the disempowered—people of color, women, LGBTQ people, and other marginalized groups. It's true that anyone can make a Twitter account, but if a woman of color's tweet produces ten times as much harassment, she's not as free to speak. As legal scholar Mari Matsuda has written, the tolerance of toxic expression "is not borne by the community at large. It is a psychic tax imposed on those least able to pay."[63]

Certainly there are powerful examples of effective counterspeech by oppressed groups. But we can also see that these measures are not always effective and they are not always "for the good" of the individual group member. When Heller and Iravani spoke out against the harassment against them, they suffered for it.[64] The harassment on the AutoAdmit board got worse. Various law professors criticized them. Free speech absolutists—ironically, the very people who think Heller and Iravani's best remedy is to speak out in the marketplace of ideas—chastised them for doing so. Anthony Ciolli, one of the people in charge of the AutoAdmit message board (his exact role is disputed, but evidence shows that he had some authority over the operation of the board) countersued Heller, Iravani, their lawyers, and a number of other parties who had supported them. Jarret Cohen, another site administrator, said that posters should not have to use their names because "People would not have as much fun, frankly, if they had to worry about employers pulling up information on them"—a consequence that Heller and Iravani actually experienced. Whatever the value of free speech, its principles here did nothing for the women whose voices it supposedly protects.

First Amendment doctrine is the product of centuries; it can't be revised in a few sentences. But a good first step would be to get the identity capitalism out of it. Let's drop the pretext that the First Amendment is an unqualified good for underrepresented minorities. Let's drop the pretext that hateful speech is the price we pay for free speech when the "we" paying the price is often the disempowered groups victimized by hate speech, and the people benefiting from free speech often pay little or no price at all. If free speech doctrine is to protect hate speech, then courts and commentators should engage in a more honest reckoning with the costs of so-called free speech.

Judges as Identity Capitalists

Judges are fond of quoting Martin Luther King Jr. They are particularly fond of doing so while reaching a decision that tends to disadvantage black people. In *Christian v. United States*, a case in which two white Army officers challenged an affirmative action policy that they claimed unfairly advantaged people of color, Judge Loren Smith began: "This case, and the constitutional claim raised in this case, is not about race."[65] Then the judge quoted extensively from King's famous "Letter from a Birmingham Jail":

> An unjust law is a human law that is not rooted in eternal law and natural law. Any law that uplifts the human personality is just. Any law that degrades human personality is unjust. All segregation statutes are unjust because segregation distorts the soul and damages the personality. It gives the segregator a false sense of superiority and the segregated a false sense of inferiority . . . and ends up relegating persons to the status of things.

Smith went on to strike down the Army policy that supposedly disadvantaged the white plaintiffs—as though there was no possible way of distinguishing the segregationist laws against which King protested and a modern affirmative action policy designed to help undo centuries of racial subordination. Smith wrote, "Dr. King himself repeatedly observed that the moral cause of racial justice cannot be fought by immoral means, and that freedoms of whites and blacks are 'inextricably bound' to one another." Reading the decision, Jeremiah Goulka describes his reaction: "This guy has got to be a Republican." Goulka was right.[66]

King made an appearance in *Vera v. Richards*, in which Judge Edith Jones, writing for a panel of three Republican appointees, struck down a Texas redistricting law that created three minority-majority congressional districts. In reaching that result, Jones quoted King, stating that the Voting Rights Act of 1965 "marked the full maturity in American political life of . . . the Rev. Martin Luther King's hope that his children would be judged by the content of their character, not the color of their skin."[67] Jones wasn't done with King yet. "Racial gerrymandering is unconstitutional, but it is also morally wrong, inconsistent with our founding tradition and Martin Luther King's vision," she wrote. "The color of a person's skin or his or her ethnic identity is the least meaningful way in which to understand that person." Jones' opinion went on to hold that the districts in question were racially gerrymandered so badly that they bore "the odious imprint of racial apartheid."[68]

For Judges Smith, Jones, and many of their colleagues on the bench, citing King is a way of claiming racialized moral legitimacy. It uses a black man's words to reach a result of which that same black man almost certainly would not have approved.

King is a particularly obvious example of the broader truth that judges are identity capitalists too. Legal scholar Justin Driver has uncovered substantial variation in the circumstances when courts do and don't choose to explicitly identify the race of people discussed in their opinion. In *Ricci v. DeStefano*, for example, the Supreme Court held that the New Haven fire department's decision to ignore standardized test results that disparately affected racial minorities violated Title VII. Justice Kennedy's majority opinion discussed the testimony of three experts on standardized testing, yet only identified the race of one of the three—the one whose testimony best supported the majority's result—by stating that he "is black." This pointed identification is particularly striking because one of the other experts was *also* black, and yet the majority did not identify her by race. As Driver observes, "This identification is striking because, in a decision that cautions against the dangers of racially disparate treatment, it treats [the experts] disparately by race."[69] It hardly surprising that the law is threaded through with identity capitalism when judges themselves are some of the most notorious identity capitalists.

Most judges' thinking is relatively impoverished when it comes to identity. To return to the Brett Kavanaugh Supreme Court confirmation hearing, Kavanaugh appears to believe that hiring a lot of women law clerks insulates him from charges that his record on abortion restricts women's rights, or that a long list of women who like him insulates him from the charge that he sexually assaulted a few women. The identity capitalist logic is almost painfully shallow: the fact that a judge helps women in one way—perhaps strategically—does not mean that he cannot restrict women's rights in another way. A lot of women liking him does not mean that he could not have abused others while drunk. Kavanaugh's identity capitalist performance is a lot of sound and fury signifying next to nothing.

Unsurprisingly, judges' reductive thinking finds its way into judicial opinions. Kavanaugh has publicly signaled his racial virtue by calling attention to a concurrence he wrote stating that even a single instance of the n-word could create a hostile environment. But getting people to avoid the n-word is the easy part. The hard part is changing the culture in which anyone would want to say the n-word in the first place. To this end, most judges are behind the times when it comes to thinking about substantive equality rather than the aesthetic equality that characterizes identity capitalism. And it shows in their opinions.

Identity Capitalism Is the Law
Identity capitalism permeates both the substantive law—the statutes, regulations, and doctrines that govern us—and the legal process itself—the way the law is invoked, enforced, applied, and modified. But with identity capitalism rooted so deeply in law and legal process, the law itself is also a powerful tool for addressing identity capitalism.

A comprehensive plan for reforming the law to subvert identity capitalism is beyond the scope of this book, or, indeed, a set of encyclopedias. But the next chapter begins the effort. Read on to learn about four principles—honesty, apology, education, and authenticity—that can improve both the law itself and society beyond the law.

7

BOYCOTT

THE LAW is both a powerful tool and a limited one. We can't discontinue identity capitalism without eliminating it from the legal system. But we also can't discontinue identity capitalism using the legal system alone—at least not in our complicated democracy, which I'm going to assume we want to keep. Beyond compelling or encouraging people to discontinue identity capitalism using the law, what else can we do to disentangle identity capitalism from our social fabric?

The four principles for reforming the law that I previewed at the end of the last chapter—honesty, apology, education, and authenticity—provide guidance for reforming society beyond the law. While these principles are not an exhaustive list, they provide a foundation for replacing superficial identity capitalism with deeper, more substantive progress toward equality.

Honesty

Devin Friedman titled his ad "Looking for an African American Friend" and posted it in the "Activities" section of Craigslist.[1] According to Friedman, the ad was literally true. He wanted a black friend. The thirty-six-year-old *GQ* writer confessed, "I had a cocktail party the other night. A natural moment to look around at the demographics of your life. And I thought: Jesus Christ, there are a lot of white people in this room." What follows is a humorous—or, depending on your perspective, "humorous"—chronicle of his attempts to make black friends. (Spoiler: he succeeds, assuming that making one black friend fits your definition of success.)

Friedman's quest is easy to dismiss as crude identity capitalism, particularly given that chronicling one's life for the entertainment of *GQ* readers is a self-interested act. The simplest explanation is that Friedman wanted a black friend because he felt bad that all his friends were white and he also wanted to write an article about his journey.

Yet the episode also bears closer inspection. It's not bad to want a life enriched by a racially diverse circle of real friends. America is plagued by a lack of cross-racial understanding. One reason is the lack of interaction, let alone friendship, between people of different races. Research reveals that 75 percent of white people have zero nonwhite presence in their social networks.[2] (Perhaps this is why nonwhite people are in demand at weddings.) Chris Rock's joke has an uncomfortable truth wrapped up in it: "All my black friends have a bunch of white friends. And all my white friends have *one* black friend."[3]

But the real problem with Friedman's approach isn't that he wanted to make a black friend. It's that he failed to confront honestly the underlying reasons that his social circle only included white friends—and then do something about those reasons. Friedman could, for example, start volunteering for a political cause or charity—one that he agrees with, of course—that tends to attract racially diverse support. He could start going to more diverse bars and clubs and make an effort to meet people there. He could choose to live in a racially integrated neighborhood. (He lives in New York City, after all.) He could choose to work out at a racially diverse gym. He could take a class at a racially diverse community college.

Instead, Friedman tried to take a shortcut. He thought the solution to not having any black friends was to make a black friend. Then he went the Craigslist route, targeting the symptom of the problem with surgical precision, without ever examining the root causes of the disease.

Given the long history of racial segregation and discrimination in America, the lack of interracial friendship is—to some degree—understandable. But addressing social segregation requires honesty about the underlying reasons it lingers. Residential segregation is partly to blame, and white people are much to blame for residential segregation. For years racially restrictive covenants intentionally prevented nonwhite people from living in some neighborhoods. "White flight" took place because white parents were unwilling to have their children attend integrated schools; for example, Kevin Kruse has painstakingly documented white flight to the suburbs of Atlanta.[4] Even today, research shows that white people prefer to live in all-white neighborhoods, while black people prefer racially mixed neighborhoods.[5] Moving to a racially diverse neighborhood, as a white person, with goals including but not limited to making friends of other races, is a more authentic way to build friendships with people of other races. As Willie Jennings, a professor at Yale Divinity School, has written, those committed to a racially just society must "transgress the boundaries of real estate, by buying where we should not and living where we must not, by living together where we supposedly cannot, and being identified with those whom we should not."[6]

As many parents have advocated, a related way for white people to meet and make friends with nonwhite people is to leave their kids in public school and get involved with the school. Public schools are generally more diverse than private schools. Indeed, many are majority minority. Today's reasons for moving to neighborhoods with "good" schools are not overtly racist. Nor are the reasons for pulling kids out of public schools and putting them in private schools. But they still reflect a lack of honest self-examination about why some schools are good and others less so. To some degree this is a collective action problem: nobody wants to be the one parent who doesn't pull their child into private school. But much of it reflects some parents' inflated sense that their children are simultaneously very special and very sensitive—so much so that a lack of sufficiently advanced classes and a "rough" environment will cause harms that outweigh the advantages of a racially diverse learning environment and a racially integrated group of friends. As parents of children enrolled in public school have argued, others ought to consider the ethics of giving their children advantages simply because they can when other people—no less worthy—can't afford those advantages. Allison Benedikt writes, "Whatever you think your children need—deserve—from their school experience, assume that the parents at the nearby public housing complex want the same."[7]

At the end of the day, perhaps interracial friendship is overrated. Damon Young, a black writer and editor, observes, "[I]nterracial friendship is great if it happens organically, but racial empathy and kindness are more important. And racial empathy and kindness can (and should) exist without friendship."[8] While friendship is a site of identity capitalism, we could partially address identity capitalism in that arena simply by adopting the view that racial empathy is more important than how many photos of black people our Instagram pages include.

Beyond social interaction, imagine the effect that complete honesty could have for a business—say, the website of a technology company. To implement my brief suggestion from Chapter 1, imagine that such a company spoke honestly about diversity. Rather than broadcasting empty words about their commitment to diversity and showcasing unknowing and unconsenting employees, imagine a company that said the following about gender diversity:

Historically, we haven't been a very diverse company. We've been particularly weak in this area, even within an industry that's not very diverse. We know this, and we know we need to do better. We're proud of the fact that in the past five years we've increased the number of women at our company by 30 percent, but we won't be satisfied until our workforce is half women. Moreover, we know it's important to have women in leadership roles, not just as employees. Right now our leadership is only 12 percent women, but we have created a pipeline program to mentor women for leadership roles. We've also initiated a number of programs that will address some of the structural issues that have traditionally held women back: for example, our company now offers twenty weeks of paid parental leave for everyone—men and women alike—which we hope will make it easier for all of our employees to balance parenthood and a fulfilling career. Finally, we've implemented programs to broadening the pool of people who are interested in working for our company down the road. For example, we've partnered with four local colleges to develop summer internship programs specially designed to attract women and other gender-diverse students who might not otherwise consider working in a tech company.

The level of honesty in this statement is almost unimaginable in today's climate. But what if it weren't? It's entirely consistent for a company to acknowledge its shortcomings while communicating a commitment to do better. Women have read enough boilerplate diversity statements to be grateful for one that is both honest and communicates concrete, substantive commitments to improve. It wouldn't hurt to find out how people would respond to one like this.

Apology

In 2017, H&M launched an ad campaign showing a young black boy in a sweatshirt that read, "Coolest Monkey in the Jungle." Backlash was swift and intense, condemning the ad for its insensitivity to the long and disparaging association between black people and non-human primates.

The outrage was appropriate. Racists have long compared black people to monkeys as a way of communicating their inferiority.[9] Research reveals that today white people associate black people and monkeys, even white people born after the Jim Crow era.[10] Writer Bee Quammie wrote, "From grotesque depictions of Black people as apes, to bananas being thrown at everyone from Black athletes to Black government officials . . . monkeys have been utilized by racists around the world to dehumanize Black people for generations."[11]

The ugly comparison persists today. President Barack Obama and First Lady Michelle Obama were frequently likened to monkeys and apes by various commentators, often with little consequence for the perpetrators. Pamela Ramsey Taylor, a government employee in Clay County, West Virginia, wrote on Facebook, "It will be so refreshing to have a classy, beautiful, dignified First Lady back in the White House. I'm tired of seeing a [*sic*] Ape in heels." Taylor was suspended for the post but was back at her job six weeks later.[12] Scholars emphasize that such comparisons are more than symbolic. Race scholars Gregory Parks and Danielle Heard have argued that Obama's unprecedented death threats result in part from dehumanizing language and imagery that portray him as a gorilla or a chimpanzee.[13]

H&M's initial apology foundered. "This image has now been removed from all H&M channels and we apologize to anyone this may have offended," H&M said. This did little to reassure anyone. But a second apology, a few days later, went much better. On its website, H&M wrote:

H&M is committed to playing its part in addressing society's issues and problems, whether it's diversity, working conditions or environmental protection—and many others. Our standards are high and we feel that we have made real progress over the years in playing our part in promoting diversity and inclusion. But we clearly haven't come far enough.

We agree with all the criticism that this has generated—we have got this wrong and we agree that, even if unintentional, passive or casual racism needs to be eradicated wherever it exists. We appreciate the support of those who have seen that our product and promotion were not intended to cause offence but, as a global brand, we have a responsibility to be aware of and attuned to all racial and cultural sensitivities—and we have not lived up to this responsibility this time.

This incident is accidental in nature, but this doesn't mean we don't take it extremely seriously or understand the upset and discomfort it has caused.

We have taken down the image and we have removed the garment in question from sale. It will be recycled. We will now be doing everything we possibly can to prevent this from happening again in future.

Racism and bias in any shape or form, conscious or unconscious, deliberate or accidental, are simply unacceptable and need to be eradicated from society. In this instance we have not been sensitive enough to this agenda.

Please accept our humble apologies.[14]

The apology did not satisfy everyone, but it won praise from many. As journalist Leah Fessler put it, the second apology "models the most essential element of an apology: taking full responsibility for your actions, and not attempting to justify the ways in which your wrongs may have been right."[15]

Apologies are powerful. They shape reactions and move emotions. The medical profession has long faced a conundrum involving apology: after a medical mistake, doctors are often afraid to apologize because they are worried about getting sued, but sometimes people only sue because they are angry that they never even got an apology. States that passed so-called "I'm sorry" laws saw the rate of settlement prior to litigation increase 20 percent, and average settlements decreased by about $20,000 for moderate injuries and by $50,000 for major injuries.

Legal scholar Eric Yamamoto studies what he calls "race apologies"— apologies for incidents involving racial bigotry, discrimination, or more serious historical wrongs. In 1997 Yamamoto catalogued seventy-six instances of American and international apologies for issues relating to race, a list that, in the subsequent twenty years has grown exponentially.[16] Some apologies are governmental, such as the United States' apology to and reparations for Japanese Americans wrongfully interned during World War II and Congress' apology to Native Hawaiians for the illegal overthrow of the sovereign Hawaiian nation. Others come from religious institutions such as the Catholic, Southern Baptist, and Mormon churches for various acts and policies of racial discrimination. Still others come from entertainers such as Ice Cube, for the lyrics of his song "Black Korea," which referred to Asian people as "Oriental one penny countin' motherfuckers," or *Duck Dynasty* star Phil Roberts for his comments that, prior to the civil rights era, black people "were godly, they were happy, no one was singing the blues." Some apologies come from regular people whose actions—particularly in the age of Internet virality—attract attention.[17]

Apologies sometimes involve identity capitalism. In 1995, Michael Jackson drew criticism for the anti-Semitic lyrics of his song "They Don't Care About Us." As originally released, the song included the lyrics: "Jew me, sue me, everybody do me / Kick me, kike me, don't you black or white me." Jackson defended himself, saying, "I'm not anti-Semitic because I'm not a racist person." In a now-familiar litany, he explained, "My accountants and lawyers are Jewish. My three best friends are Jewish. . . . I was raised in a Jewish community." Jackson also announced that he would re-record the song to omit the offending lyric, and a sticker explaining his lack of racist intent was added to copies of the album already in warehouses.[18]

But when it comes to apologies, identity capitalism is counterproductive. Researchers suggest that to be effective, an apology must be costly to the apologizer in some way.[19] It might compensate the wronged party. It might diminish the status of the apologizer—for example, saying something like "It was really ignorant of me not to realize that this was offensive" risks harming the apologizer's reputation. Or it might express a commitment to do better in the future. The apologizer has to have skin in the game for the apology to advance the ball. Research also indicates that the structure of the apology is important: the most effective apologies are victim-centered, rather than offender-centered. They also involve what sociologists Karen Cerulo and Janet Ruane call "mortification," meaning that the person apologizing must "unequivocally admit shame and guilt and explicitly ask the public for forgiveness."[20]

The apology by the United States for the internment of people of Japanese ancestry during World War II contains many of the elements of an effective apology. The apology was public: it took the form of legislation signed by President Ronald Reagan. The apology was costly to the United States in more ways than one: It provided for $20,000 compensation to each of more than a hundred thousand people of Japanese descent who were incarcerated in internment camps, and it acknowledged wrongdoing. The legislation describes internment as "a grave injustice" that was "motivated by racial prejudice, wartime hysteria, and a failure of political leadership." And the apology was expressly victim-centered, with its purpose "to acknowledge the fundamental injustice of the relocation and internment of citizens and permanent resident aliens of Japanese ancestry during World War II" and to "make restitution to those individuals of Japanese ancestry who were interned."[21]

By contrast, the United States government has never offered a unified apology for slavery. Both the House of Representatives and the Senate have separately passed resolutions apologizing for slavery, but the two were never reconciled, never resulted in a law of any kind, explicitly excluded the consideration of financial reparations, and as a result were dismissed by many people as purely symbolic.[22] Indeed, the Senate resolution included a disclaimer: "Nothing in this resolution (A) authorizes or supports any claim against the United States; or (B) serves as a settlement of any claim against the United States." Sometimes the law stands in the way of social progress, and here the legalese conveys that the Senate is trying to get credit for an apology while thoroughly covering itself from a legal perspective—by any measure, a feeble effort. After this uninspiring apology, the rampant identity capitalism we currently see from our government officials, from the president on down, is—if anything—more offensive. Real apology acknowledges the complexity of racial relations and offers a first step in solving them. Identity capitalism avoids racial problems by implying they have been fully resolved or never existed in the first place.

Apologies by governments and institutions provide a powerful opportunity to move beyond identity capitalism. So do apologies by individuals. Kari Wagner-Peck blogs about her son, Thorin, who has Down Syndrome.[23] One day she wrote an open letter to Chuck Klosterman, then the writer of the *New York Times Magazine*'s "Ethicist" column, pointing out instances in which he had used the words "retard," "retarded," or even "fucking retard." "Today people with cognitive disabilities and their allies are asking members of society to refrain from using the word retarded," Wagner-Peck wrote. "Is it ethnical to contribute to the denigration of the vulnerable?"[24]

Klosterman could have gotten defensive, claimed his tone was facetious, and apologized "if anyone was offended." As a means of "proving" his claims, he could have engaged in identity capitalism and referred to his friends or relatives with disabilities. He did none of these things. Instead, he wrote this email to Wagner-Peck:

Dear Ms. Wagner-Peck:

I have spent the last two days trying to figure out a way to properly address the issue you have raised on your web site. I've slowly concluded the best way is to just be as straightforward as possible: I was wrong. You are right.

I should not have used "retard" pejoratively. It was immature, hurtful, and thoughtless. I have no justification for my actions. I realize the books that contain those sentiments were published over 10 years ago, but that is no excuse; I was an adult when I wrote them and I knew what I was doing. I feel terrible about this and deeply embarrassed. I take full responsibility for my actions and understand why this matters so much to you. I'm truly sorry.

Feel free to re-post this message on your web site. I deserve the criticism I am receiving, and I want other people to know that I realize I was wrong. I would also like to donate $25,000 to whatever charity you feel is most critical in improving the lives of people with cognitive disabilities—[redacted] or any other organization you recommend. I have done something bad, so help me do something good.

Again, I apologize—and not just to you and your son, but to anyone else who was hurt by this.

—Chuck Klosterman[25]

Klosterman's apology includes several of the elements identified earlier. It offers a form of compensation (the donation); a status consequence, alternatively described as mortification (Klosterman's repeated statements that he was wrong and deserves criticism); and a commitment to do better in the future. Moreover, he expresses real empathy for Wagner-Peck and her son. This is particularly important because what is often lacking in identity-related apologies is the sense that the person apologizing genuinely understands the conditions of an identity group to which they don't belong.

Apologies are delicate things. If overused or poorly done, they can backfire or be worse than nothing.[26] But done properly, they are a vast improvement over the identity capitalism defense that too many people currently use rather than an apology.

Education

Many years ago, I was in some airport restroom during a flight delay, exhausted, disheveled, and ready to get on the final leg of my flight home. I wanted nothing more than to mind my own business as I washed my hands at the sink.

Next to me a white woman was pulling her white daughter's hair into a ponytail. The girl, maybe seven years old, exclaimed as her mom pulled up the sides of her hair, stretching the skin of her face, "I look like a Chinese person!"

The mom instantly hushed her daughter. "Shhhhhh, don't say that here!" she exclaimed. I glanced up and met her eyes in the mirror. She was looking at me anxiously. Had the sort-of-Chinese-looking lady heard? Her daughter was also looking at me, not anxiously, but curiously.

We were the only three people in the restroom. It was deadly quiet as I finished washing my hands and went over to the dryer. I dried my hands. Then I said to the woman, "I hope you teach your daughter not to be racist." Her face was mortified.

The little girl's comment didn't make me angry. Children inevitably notice physical differences among people and sometimes comment on them, and sometimes they do so in ways that are unintentionally embarrassing to their parents. But her mother's response was a different story. What she communicated to the little girl was that the problem wasn't her comment per se. The problem was that she'd made the comment *here*, in front of a (partially) Chinese American person. I realize now that my response did not make any of that clear: it certainly made the woman feel bad and it probably confused her daughter. With another fifteen years of life and immersion in identity scholarship, I hope that today I would respond differently and more productively.

Members of dominant groups should take responsibility for educating their children and the less-informed members of their own identity group. Parents are generally in the best position to educate their children, and the sad truth is that it's often easier for white people to educate other white people about racial issues, for men to educate other men about gender discrimination, for straight people to educate other straight people about issues of sexual orientation, and so on. Formal institutions of education can help as well. Drawing a distinction between explicit bias—or blatant prejudice—and implicit bias—prejudice that operates at a subconscious level—will help people understand why identity capitalism is such a troubling tactic. While educating people about identity is difficult, at a minimum, educational institutions can ensure that their students have access to accurate information.

Beyond individuals and formal institutions of education, we as a society also should think seriously about when we need retribution and when we need education. Sometimes retribution is the right course of action. Some people deserve punishment. Take Harvey Weinstein or Bill Cosby: their wrongs are so grievous and so numerous that rehabilitation is not an appropriate part of the conversation—not now, and probably not ever.

But for others, the circumstances may be quite different. Often, the way we respond to difficult social moments is an important moment for collective learning. In a pre-Halloween episode of her show on NBC, television personality Megyn Kelly said she was "a little fired up today." She proceeded to make ignorant comments about blackface that offended many of her viewers. "But what is racist?" Kelly asked rhetorically. "Because you do get in trouble if you are a white person who puts on blackface for Halloween, or a black person who puts on whiteface for Halloween. Back when I was a kid that was OK, as long as you were dressing up as, like, a character." Her all-white group of guests seemed surprised. "It sounds pretty racist to me," said Jacob Soboroff. "I think there are limits to how far you want to go if you are making people feel bad," Jenna Hager Bush agreed. None of them, however, unpacked the particular problems with blackface.[27]

Kelly was instantly castigated online and chastised by other employees of her own television network. On *NBC Nightly News* with Lester Holt, Al Roker said that, while Kelly had apologized to her coworkers at NBC, "she owes a bigger apology to folks of color across the country." Craig Melvin agreed, calling her comments "stupid" and "indefensible."[28]

Blackface has a long and racist history, partly as a result of its use in minstrel shows. Frederick Douglass once said that blackface was perpetrated by "the filthy scum of white society, who have stolen from us a complexion denied to them by nature, in which to make money, and pander to the corrupt taste of their fellow white citizens."[29] Indeed, the term "Jim Crow"—used to refer to the era of legal racial segregation—literally came from an 1832 blackface minstrel production.[30]

Experts agree that blackface is rooted in racism. "Blackface was a deliberate attempt to represent Black people as bizarre and deviant, while appropriating their cultural forms for profit and to get a laugh," explains Philip S. S. Howard, a scholar of race and education. "Minstrel performers would . . . use ungainly movement, exaggerated accents, malapropisms and garish attire to further ridicule Black people."[31] In light of this history, casually wearing blackface on Halloween trivializes an era of considerable suffering and inequality for black people. David J. Leonard explains that there is no such thing as an innocent use of blackface: "Blackface is never a neutral form of entertainment, but an incredibly loaded site for the production of damaging stereotypes . . . the same stereotypes that undergird individual and state violence, American racism, and a century's worth of injustice."[32]

Critics censured Kelly for failing to learn in her forty-seven years that blackface is unacceptable for Halloween costumes. Yet polling suggests that many Americans share her views: in 2015, one poll found that 47 percent of Americans believe that blackface is "acceptable" in a Halloween costume, including 52 percent of white people and 27 percent of black people; 33 percent of white people and 55 percent of black people think that blackface is unacceptable.[33] In other words, a majority of white people, more than a quarter of black people, and a substantial minority of Americans overall think blackface at Halloween is acceptable.

The frequency with which blackface incidents occur also indicates that many people share Kelly's confusion. Many people have worn blackface and faced public backlash. In 1993, actor Ted Danson wore blackface and repeatedly said the n-word during the opening monologue at a roast for his romantic partner, Whoopi Goldberg. Although the event was not recorded, reception was reportedly icy and Danson at one point said, "Whoopi dared me to do this."[34] Mel Kuhn, the mayor of Arkansas City, Kansas, wore blackface and drag for a costume competition sponsored by a charitable fundraiser in order to portray a character he dubbed "Smellishis Poon."[35] Actor Julianne Hough donned blackface as part of a Halloween costume portraying the character Crazy Eyes from the TV show *Orange Is the New*

Black.[36] University of Oregon law professor Nancy Shurtz—who had been honored with the school's Martin Luther King Jr. Award—wore blackface as part of a costume portraying Damon Tweedy, a black doctor who was the subject of *Black Man in a White Coat: A Doctor's Reflections on Race and Medicine* at a Halloween party for faculty and students at her house in 2016. Shurtz said that her costume was intended to educate her students and that she had never heard of blackface.[37] Megan Luloff, a first-grade teacher in Iowa, wore blackface at a Halloween party in 2018, reportedly to portray a character from *Napoleon Dynamite*.[38] In a trend dubbed "blackfishing," some white Instagram influencers have posed in makeup, hairstyles, and fashion that suggests they are black or biracial, drawing criticism for attempting to appropriate black cool to gain a following.[39] One Internet commenter put it this way: "People like the look and swagger of blackness but not when it comes from actual black people."[40]

The list of blackface wearers—many recent—is long and getting longer, and we could argue that Kelly should have been on notice from following the news that blackface is problematic.[41] We could also argue that Megyn Kelly should be better informed than most Americans, and that even if she'd somehow missed the many instances of blackface in the news, her significant platform carries with it significant responsibility to educate herself proactively. Still, while we should condemn Kelly's ignorance, she is hardly the only one in need of an education. Even if she *should* have been better informed, she wasn't. The question is what we should do about it.

In some ways, how we respond to a racial screw-up says as much about us as it does about the person who screwed up. It's easy to say that Megyn Kelly should have taken the time to educate herself about blackface before talking about it on national television. I think she should have too. But the problem with simply condemning her and firing her is that many people won't learn anything from the event. Indeed, such a response even potentially casts Kelly as a victim without doing anything to combat racial ignorance. In one poll, 45 percent of Americans—probably including many who do not, themselves, understand what is wrong with blackface in a Halloween costume—thought that NBC canceling Kelly's program "would be too harsh of a consequence for her comments"; far fewer, 26 percent, said that canceling "would be the appropriate consequence for her comments."[42]

Kelly apologized, first to her colleagues at NBC and then on her show the next day. As apologies go, it wasn't bad: she accepted responsibility, didn't make excuses, and indicated that she had been and would be listening. She then hosted a segment on her show in which two black commentators— Jonathan Martin and Amy Holmes—explained why blackface is offensive. Martin described blackface as a "caricature" of black people and black culture and described it as a "constant assault—this degradation and this demeaning of how we look and how we act." Holmes pointedly suggested that talking about racial issues required information and sensitivity—two tactics that Kelly didn't display in the original show. "We I think are in total denial about how deeply embedded this is in the DNA of American and how it impacts so many things that are done in this country," Martin said, and the mostly white audience listened. This was an opportunity to educate the half of Americans who don't understand what is wrong with blackface, and as conversations about race go, it wasn't bad. It could have been the beginning of a productive dialogue about race. It could have reached the suburban white women who tend to like Kelly and her show—many of whom are among the 75 percent of Americans who have no nonwhite friends. As Martin noted, many Americans live in "silos," and it's rare when we voluntarily say, "I need to learn more about you." The show might have been a good starting place for a project of racial education.

Yet instead that show was Kelly's last at NBC. The network decided to negotiate her departure, perhaps in part because, even before the blackface incident, her show was reportedly faltering and she didn't get along with some of her colleagues at NBC. This reaction cut short conversation about the substance of Kelly's comments and her reaction to their fallout. It missed an opportunity for education. NBC prioritized not taking heat for Kelly's remarks over the possible benefits of keeping her on. Indeed, the company ended up paying Kelly the entire value of her $69 million three-year contract—even though she was only on air at NBC for seventeen months—meaning that they paid tens of millions of dollars simply to take her off the air rather than to educate her audience.

In addition to teaching valuable lessons about the history of blackface and why many people view it as problematic, a more educative response to Kelly would have cut the legs out from under identity capitalism. Here,

NBC effectively used Kelly's firing as an opportunity for identity capitalism: it disassociated itself from a white woman who had made racially offensive statements and showcased black commentators who explained, in sound-bite form, why Kelly was wrong. But none of this required NBC to back the challenging long-term project of educating people about blackface and race more generally. Nor did the network confront its other racially questionable actions in the past, such as its cancellation of Melissa Harris-Perry's popular show, or its decision to replace Al Roker and Tamron Hall with Kelly in the first place.[43] Firing Kelly was a way for NBC to signal that it was on the racially correct side while doing very little in the way of substance to support racial progress.

To be clear, I am not necessarily arguing that Kelly should have been retained. Rather, I think that NBC should have responded to the event with a great deal more thoughtfulness. Ultimately, rather than directly replacing Kelly with someone more racially informed, NBC simply shuffled its existing personnel, and—months later—added to Kelly's former time slot both Dylan Dreyer—a white meteorologist—and Sheinelle Jones—a black woman whose assignments have been mostly on the lighter side, ranging from meeting her doppelganger to learning how to drive a stick shift on air. One might argue that Kelly's departure opened an opportunity for Jones to increase the representation of people of color on television, a worthy goal. But one wonders whether a more important goal might have been achieved by adding Jones, retaining Kelly in some capacity, and deliberately involving both—together and separately—in more content featuring complex issues relating to identity. Committing to such a project of education would represent a turn away from identity capitalism and a turn toward substance.

Authenticity

In the weeks after the 2018 midterm election, commentators pointed out a striking contrast between the two parties' newly elected members of Congress. Of the one hundred new senators and representatives, sixty-four were Democrats and thirty-six were Republicans. The incoming class of Republicans included thirty-four men and two women (5.6 percent women), while the Democratic class included twenty-six men and thirty-eight women

(59.4 percent women). The Republican class included only one person of color, while the Democratic class included twenty-two (Figure 7.1).

The 2018 midterms included a number of other firsts for the Democrats. Ilhan Omar and Rashida Tlaib are the first Muslim women elected to national office. Tlaib is also the first Palestinian American. Ayanna Pressley is the first black woman from Massachusetts elected to national office. Sharice Davids is a Native American lesbian from Kansas. (Let that sink in.) All three newly elected Democratic senators were women, bringing the total of Democratic women senators to seventeen, or 36.2 percent of the caucus. (Only seven Republican senators are women, or 13.2 percent of the caucus.) Jared Polis of Colorado became the first gay man elected governor. Kyrsten Sinema of Arizona became the first bisexual woman elected to the Senate—and, along the way, the first woman senator from Arizona. Voters elected thirty-six new LGBTQ state legislators—all Democrats—in twenty-six states.[44] The tally included three transgender women: Gerri Cannon and Lisa Bunker in New Hampshire, and Brianna Titone in Colorado. Although Stacy Abrams fell short of her effort in Georgia to become the first black woman governor, her campaign came close enough to raise the specter of a recount and exposed egregious abuses in the state electoral system.[45]

The 2018 midterm results underscore an ongoing trend. The overall number of Republican women in Congress dropped to twenty-one. Remarkably, of the forty-two women of color serving as voting members of Congress, none is a Republican.[46] All ten LGBTQ members of Congress are Democrats.

The demographic differences between Republican and Democratic elected officials explain why Republicans are more likely to practice identity capitalism than Democrats: they are a mostly homogeneous group, and they prefer not to acknowledge that fact or its implications. If someone wanted to take a photo of a group of Democrats that included women and people of color, they could just point the camera in the direction of the caucus. To do the same with Republicans would require significant staging.

The lack of authentic diversity among Republicans results in contorted attempts to manage the party's image while conducting legislative business. After Christine Blasey Ford accused Brett Kavanaugh of sexually assaulting her, the Senate Judiciary committee held additional hearings about the

FIGURE 7.1. A photo of a flier that circulated on Capitol Hill shortly after the 2018 mid-term election depicts some of the freshman members of Congress, revealing a stark contrast between the Republican and Democratic representatives-elect. Source: Melina Mara.

accusations. But the Republicans worried that they had a problem: there were no Republican women on the judiciary committee. Indeed, there had *never* been a Republican woman on the judiciary committee.[47] The Republicans worried about the optics of ten white men and Ted Cruz questioning an alleged survivor of sexual assault.

Led by Senate Majority Leader Mitch McConnell and Senate Judiciary Committee chair Chuck Grassley, the Republicans' solution was to hire Rachel Mitchell—a prosecutor from Arizona—to question Ford. "We have hired a female assistant to go on staff and to ask these questions in a respectful and professional way," McConnell said. This was textbook identity capitalism, with mixed results. Because the committee rules dictate that the senators ask questions alternating by party and in order of seniority, the result was an odd proceeding in which Mitchell alternated questioning time in five-minute increments with the Democratic senators on the committee. The pageant grew even stranger when Kavanaugh's turn for questioning came. After some of Mitchell's questions appeared harsher to him than anticipated, Republicans suddenly decided not to cede their time to her, essentially sidelining the woman they had brought in to improve the optics of the situation.

The reason that the Democrats did not feel the need to engage in identity capitalism is that their membership on the judiciary committee was authentically diverse. Of the ten Democrats on the judiciary committee, four were women—including ranking member Dianne Feinstein—and three were people of color. A political party doesn't need to bring in a woman as a ringer when several women already have seats at the table.

Perhaps some will criticize me for singling out Republicans as identity capitalists throughout this book. It's certainly true that I've spent more time talking about Republicans, though I've hardly done so exclusively. And the photos in Figure 7.1 tell a powerful story—one indicating that my examination of Republicans is appropriate. Republican political leaders are mostly white and mostly male, and their identity capitalism is often an attempt at disguising this. Democrats engage in identity capitalism too, but Republicans have more need to do so. The lack of diversity within the Republican Party is a symptom of the problem, not the problem itself. The real problem is the policies and values that the Republican Party has—at least during the last several decades—come to represent.

If every American institution were authentically diverse, people would have no motivation for identity capitalism. One way to avoid identity capitalism is to avoid the conditions that create its perceived necessity. We see this play out in the Republican Party. Republican policies tend to disproportionately disadvantage groups that are already disadvantaged. Republicans in several states enacted restrictive voting laws that made it more difficult for nonwhite people to vote. Republicans opposed the Affordable Care Act, which would have improved health care for women and people of color. Republicans oppose LGBTQ rights. A Republican-controlled Senate confirmed Republican Supreme Court justices who decimated the Voting Rights Act. Many people believe that the Republican appointees in the majority on the Supreme Court will soon roll back protections for reproductive rights.

In recent years, more Republicans have expressed openly misogynist and white supremacist views. Steve King, a representative from Iowa, displayed a Confederate battle flag on his desk for many years. He endorsed for mayor of Toronto a woman who claims Canada is undergoing a white genocide. He retweeted a self-described neo-Nazi. While in Europe, King met with members of a far-right Austrian political party founded by a former Nazi officer and told the party's affiliated publication that "we can't restore our civilization with somebody else's babies." On a podcast popular with white nationalists, he referred to the Congressional Black Caucus as a "grievance committee."

King has company. Cindy Hyde-Smith, senator from Mississippi, posed wearing a Confederate hat and a rifle at the Jefferson Davis homestead in Biloxi: "Mississippi history at its best," she said on Facebook. While campaigning for reelection in 2018, she announced that she would be in the "front row" of a "public hanging" if a supporter asked her—never mind Mississippi's history of lynching—and said that she wouldn't mind if some other college students didn't vote—the context of the statements suggesting that she meant students at nearby historically black colleges.[48] Representative Matt Gaetz invited a Holocaust denier to the State of the Union Address who was banned from Twitter after issuing an apparent threat against a black civil rights activist; the same person later attended a Gaetz fundraiser. Senator Charles Grassley and Representatives Kevin McCarthy and Louie Gohmert have spread conspiracy theories about Jewish billionaire George Soros. Even after nine accusations of sexual misconduct, including from women who alleged that he sexually assaulted them when they were just fourteen and sixteen, Roy Moore still very nearly won a special election in Alabama. And the fish rots from the head: Donald Trump described as "very fine people" neo-Nazis in Charlottesville; he mocked a reporter with a disability; he spread racist birther conspiracies about Barack Obama; of women, he announced that "you can grab them by the pussy"; and twenty-three women have accused him of sexual assault.[49]

Republicans who don't engage in appalling behavior themselves still tolerate their colleagues rather than calling for their censure or even making efforts to distance themselves. In a different era, Republicans denounced David Duke in his campaign for governor of Louisiana and publicly pledged to vote against him. The Republican Party of the twenty-first century seems unable to take these simple steps—even when it comes to accused child molesters and avowed white supremacists.

Republican leaders have bemoaned the difficulty in recruiting women and nonwhite people to the Republican Party. Mitch McConnell described the lack of Republican women in the Senate as "a great frustration," and added that he is hoping to persuade more Republican women to join the committee but hasn't had much success in the past because "they just haven't been interested."[50] Other leaders echoed his sentiments.[51]

I am only a law professor, not a savvy political strategist, and so this is just a guess on my part, but perhaps if Republicans didn't tolerate and enable racists and misogynists, their party would become more diverse organically. If their platform didn't demean racial minorities, women, and other disadvantaged groups, they wouldn't need identity capitalism to thinly cloak the way their party treats outgroups. They wouldn't have to bring in a hired gun to question an alleged survivor of sexual assault before the judiciary committee. They wouldn't have to create ads proclaiming that "Republicans Are Black." They wouldn't have to bring up the increasingly noticed Frederick Douglass, who was a Republican literally more than a hundred years ago.

Authentic diversity and substantive attention to the interests of out-groups makes identity capitalism obsolete. Although Diamond and Silk would be out of a job, I suspect that the Republican Party would be better off if its members recognized the importance of a diverse range of life experiences and perspectives. Again, it's just a guess.

Closer to Home

It's relatively easy to talk about strategies for combating identity capitalism—honesty, apology, education, and authenticity—when they relate to other people. But what about when the issue is distinctly more personal? To answer the question, let's bring identity capitalism closer to home. We're going to talk about identity capitalism as it relates to me and to you.

Conclusion

WE, IDENTITY CAPITALISTS

"Privilege is not in and of itself bad; what
matters is what we do with privilege."
—*bell hooks*

A FEW YEARS AGO I was in St. Louis for work. I called an Uber to go meet a friend for dinner. It was after dark and I didn't know St. Louis at all. If you've ever taken Uber, you know the Uber app tells you the make, model, and license plate of the car that's coming to pick you up so that you can make sure you're in the right car.

That night, when the car arrived, it was the right make and model, but the license plate on the car didn't match the app. I pointed this out to the driver, who had an explanation that I didn't understand—something about how the temporary plate signified a disability and Uber hadn't changed the information in the app. I felt nervous about it. Finally I said, "I'm sorry, I don't feel like I can get in the car because the plates don't match."

Something changed in the driver's face. "It's not the plates. You don't want to get in the car because I'm black. You're racist. You're racist!" The driver was shouting. A group of people passing on the sidewalk looked over curiously.

What I felt in that moment was pure outrage. How could this person call *me* a racist? "I'm *not* a racist. I literally write about race discrimination for a living," I wanted to say. "I wrote a fifty-page article called 'Race Discrimination in the Platform Economy' because I want businesses like Uber to treat their black employees *like you* better. I don't care that you're black. I ride with black drivers all the time! I'm not getting in the car because your fucking plates don't match."

I didn't say any of that. I am grateful today for the impulse (a rare one) that caused me to bite my tongue. I stepped back on the sidewalk and held up my hands in a way that meant "we're done." The driver yelled "Racist!" at me one more time and drove away.

I felt awful. Physically sick to my stomach. Because I'd been yelled at, because I'd been called a racist, and, just as painfully, because I was worried that I *had* acted like a racist. Immediately I went on the mental defensive. I told myself that I would be crazy to get in a car with the wrong license plate. I was allowed to be cautious. I told myself that a lot of people—although *definitely* not me—were racist, that probably this driver got treated badly all the time. That was why the driver reacted so strongly and negatively. I knew about this experience because I studied race, not to mention that I was a woman of color myself. I gave myself points for my commendable empathy.

At dinner, I told my friend what happened. She commiserated. It was good I hadn't gotten in a car with a stranger with the wrong license plate in a strange city in the dark. It didn't matter that the driver was black. This wasn't about race, or for that matter about disability. It was about safety.

Would I have gotten in the car if the driver had been white? I don't know. I want to say no: that the issue was just the plates. But we never really know for sure what we're going to do until we're in a situation. I *do* know that, as I type these words, I feel anxious about making sure you understand my dilemma. I'm worried you'll think I'm racist.

While I still don't know whether I should have gotten in the car, I do know that my reflexive mental response to the driver's accusation of racism was wrong, and that my impulse to justify myself in these pages is counterproductive. My research and writing about race discrimination, my work that takes me to conferences that are naturally diverse, my wonderful friends of all races—none of these things means that I don't do and say and think racist things. I try not to, but, like everyone else, I am the product of a racist society. Social science documents how, from the first hour of our first day, American society teaches us to think, say, and even do racist things. Researching race discrimination for years doesn't insulate me from the charge of acting in racist ways. It certainly doesn't save me from thinking racist thoughts.

That night in St. Louis, though, I felt differently. I felt compelled to invoke my life's work and the racial identities of the people I hope to elevate. I felt an impulse to invoke my racially diverse colleagues and friends. I felt attacked and I wanted to defend myself. For a few hours that night—and even now, today—I felt a powerful urge to be an identity capitalist.

Identity Capitalism and Me

Nobody gets a free pass to ignore identity capitalism, let alone to actively encourage it. Not me, and not you. But I try—imperfectly—to live out in my own life the four concepts for replacing identity capitalism with racial reform that I described in the previous chapter.

Some interactions, like my troubled interaction with the Uber driver, are unsalvageable. We lack time. We intersect with one another only briefly. It's easier to simply disengage. Sometimes, due to the constraints on our behavior imposed by mechanisms such as rideshare apps, we have no option but to disengage. And the thoughts and urges I—or anyone—might have during those interactions are reflexes. I don't mean to excuse the way that I—or anyone—might behave in one-off interactions. But at the end of the day often the best we can do with our reactions is contain them—to prevent thoughts from becoming words or actions. That interaction with the Uber driver was bad. It would have been much worse if I started yelling about my black friends.

But there are other, better, opportunities for preventing identity capitalism, if we're willing to be uncomfortable and to do difficult things because they're right.

Not that long ago I was in a meeting with some other professors and administrators at the law school where I teach. One topic on the agenda was the perennial difficulty of dividing first-year students into sections. At most law schools, students' first-year sections take all their classes together. The people in your first-year section profoundly affect your first-year experience.

For reasons relating to history, geography, cost of tuition, limits on our ability to offer financial aid, and many other factors, my school has long been predominantly white. I don't like this—indeed, no one who teaches here likes this—but change is a slow process and as an individual I have minimal influence.

I have slightly more influence over how we as an institution deal with our overwhelming whiteness. The demographic situation is frankly alienating for most of our nonwhite students. It is severely exacerbated by our practice of—as far as I have observed—dispersing nonwhite students as evenly as possible among first-year assigned sections. The result is that the few students of color are spread thin and often feel isolated. I recently taught a first-year class of thirty-five people, of which only three were people of color. Over the years, many students of color have expressed their frustrations to me, explaining that they weren't going to talk in classes about race discrimination because when they did, they were viewed as spokespersons for their race as motivated purely by self-interest.

At the meeting, according to my notes, white administrators defended the practice of spreading our students of color evenly throughout the sections. One claimed that the whole reason we even bothered to admit a racially diverse student body was so that *all* the students would benefit from a racially diverse class, and concentrating the nonwhite students in a few sections would deprive the *white* students in the other sections of that benefit. In other words, we *had* to spread the students of color around, because otherwise how would the *white* students benefit from their presence? (That particular administrator's tone suggested to me a skepticism of this benefit—another topic, perhaps, for another book.)

I suspect that this particular white administrator was also concerned about how concentrating students of color in some sections would *look* to the white students in the other sections. If we concentrated the students of color in a few sections so they would feel less isolated, then some other sections would have no students of color at all. And having no people of color in the room might make the white people feel uncomfortable, a lot like my friend at her wedding.

In addition to focusing on the white people at the expense of the people of color, this administrator was advocating an approach that flies in the face of a wealth of sociological research.[1] Those who research diversity have found that a critical mass of students of color in a classroom is necessary for those present to avoid feeling like tokens. The precise threshold for critical mass might vary from one situation to the next, but surely it would consist of more than three out of thirty-five, or 8.5 percent. In my career, I have taught classes of a hundred students of whom only one was black; I wondered how frequently the white administrator had been the only white student in a room of a hundred. (My best estimate was "never.") In short, the administrator's comments were incredibly misinformed. What the administrator was advocating was unreflective identity capitalism, and the victims would be our perennially isolated students of color.

I spoke up. In a room full of white people, I knew this would probably be an exercise in futility. But I still tried my best to steer the ship away from what I saw as a bad situation for our students of color by applying the four principles I discussed in Chapter 7: honesty, apology, education, and authenticity.

I tried to be honest. "The approach of dispersing the students of color privileges white students' interests over their classmates of color," I said bluntly. I tried to educate by explaining the concept of critical mass and how it harmed our students of color when we fell short of meeting it. I advocated authenticity by arguing that we should own up to our shortcomings when it came to diversity: if we didn't have a critical mass of people of color at our school, then we shouldn't lay the burden on our students of color to offer the impression that we do for the benefit of our white students. If we don't have enough students of color to create a critical mass in each section, then we should admit it and explain what we're doing to create a good environment in our school for people of color anyway. This is what authenticity means: owning up to your shortcomings and working, in the long term, to fix them.

I didn't apologize *to* anyone in the meeting itself because I didn't do anything wrong. But I have told my students of color on a number of occasions that I am sorry about the way the demographics of our school affect their experience and I told the other people in the meeting that I felt that we *owed* the students of color an apology.

I was frustrated at the end of the meeting to the point that it was actually hard to concentrate on work the rest of the day. It was frustrating to hear inexpert white people not only opine uninformedly on my area of scholarly expertise, but also speak to an experience of racial isolation that they haven't lived—particularly when I've lived that experience my entire life. In such situations, it's often easier to disengage. I could have tuned out and surfed the Internet at the meeting, kept my mouth shut, and been exponentially happier when I left. But I viewed it as part of my responsibility, as someone with a degree of racial privilege who has benefited from good mentors and a lot of luck, to try to make the institutions around me better.

In this interaction, I also saw the reflection of my university's history of identity capitalism toward me. It was a big deal when I was the first Asian woman at the law school where I teach to hold the rank of full professor. My face has been on plenty of the school's promotional materials over the years. Yet when an actual issue relating to race comes up—an issue that I've studied for nearly two decades and lived for four—my scholarly expertise and personal experience were dismissed. This is the problem with identity capitalism. It's all show and no substance.

This interaction embodies everything that concerns me about identity capitalism. I feel pessimistic about eliminating identity capitalism in our society when I see it in action at a supposedly progressive law school where the faculty and administration profess attention to issues of racial equity. I feel worried when white people with power refuse to listen to people of color with knowledge and experience. I feel disappointed when my white colleagues don't back me up, even the ones who I know agree with me. And I feel sad when I know that our school could help our students by engaging in real, substantive reform, and that instead they choose identity capitalism.

But these psychic costs are the costs of calling out and trying to subvert identity capitalism and the deeper racial wounds it incompletely masks. Progress can be painfully slow, but in those moments, the victory often lies in the struggle. As pathbreaking sexual harassment plaintiff Michelle Vinson once said, "If I fight, someday some woman will win."[2]

Identity Entrepreneurship and Me

"Am I an identity entrepreneur?" I asked a friend while I was writing this book. My friend looked uneasy. Was this a trap? Friendship with a lawyer is hard. Friendship with a law professor is harder. Friendship with a law professor who writes about identity? A minefield, figuratively speaking—but at least Asian people can't call my friend a racist! (I kid!)

Perhaps I *am* an identity entrepreneur. Could a white man have written this book? Maybe. White men have written successfully about race, diversity, and even the specific problems with tokenism. People often seem to take white men more seriously on these issues—add this to the growing list of topics for another book entirely.

I am not a white man. When I pitched this book idea to publishers, I pointed out that I am an Asian American woman, a member of an underrepresented group in academia, and to my knowledge the first to hold the rank of full professor at the law school where I teach. This is all true and I am proud of it. But I also told publishers about it because I thought my biography and perspective might help pique interest in the book. You might say I leveraged my identity as an Asian American woman, one who managed to accomplish a milestone at a university that has been around for over a century.

You could also argue that identity entrepreneurship is woven into the book itself. When I told you at the beginning that identity capitalism was personal to me, when I told you about my friend's wedding, you could say I leveraged my outgroup identity for my own benefit. It gave me credibility to say that I *myself* had been pulled into the photos and added to the panels. It is probably easier and less socially costly for me to criticize other women, especially other women of color and most of all Asian American women, than it would have been for a white man. No one will ever accuse me (fairly or unfairly) of mansplaining. No one will tweet sarcastically that they can't wait for a book about race by a white guy to get all the credit and reviews. Maybe my book will sell better because an Asian American woman wrote it. If it does, will it be because people would like to be seen reading a book about race by a woman of color? Will this book be used as a prop, casually displayed on a coffee table or extracted from a handbag on the subway, a sort of literary stand-in for an Asian female friend? And if it is, wouldn't that be just what an identity entrepreneur would want?

Then again, maybe I'm not an identity entrepreneur. Maybe I'm the opposite. Identity entrepreneurs are outgroup members who perform a version of identity that benefits ingroup members. Ingroup identity capitalists have to value an outgroup member's version of identity for the outgroup member to be a successful identity entrepreneur.

In my case, I do not expect most ingroup members—white people, men—to receive this book with open arms. I anticipate that Donald Trump and Brett Kavanaugh would not exactly be thrilled to have been prominently featured. Nor will some of my (possibly now former) friends. I hope very much that some ingroup members will be interested and self-reflective about this book. I expect, though, that many will react with anger, defensiveness, and denial. Deliberately provoking that reaction from people wealthier and more powerful than I am is exactly the opposite of what an identity entrepreneur would try to do.

I'm likely not the best person to pass judgment on when and how I, personally, have been an identity entrepreneur. It's always hard to be objective about ourselves. What I can say with certainty is that identity entrepreneurship has touched my life. I have felt the pull of the incentives. If I were an Asian American woman willing to defend hard-right policies, certain powerful people would embrace me in today's political climate. Maybe I'd have a show on Fox News. Maybe I'd be a federal judge.

We'll never know for sure, because I'm not willing to do those things. I'm unwilling to defend comments that white supremacists are very fine people. I'm very willing to say that *Brown v. Board of Education* was correctly decided.[3] Perhaps these tendencies mean that I'm not a very good identity entrepreneur after all. Or, as my friend responded, "If you were really an identity entrepreneur, you definitely wouldn't be writing that book."

What About You?

So that's me. What about you? If you're honest with yourself, I bet you saw yourself somewhere in this book. Maybe a lot of places in this book. Maybe one time when someone said that you were rude to a person of color, you got defensive and pointed out that you have a friend of color. Maybe when someone told you that something you said was sexist you talked about your daughter. Maybe you brought up your gay employee when someone called you out on using a word that you kind of forgot was a slur. I bet you felt indignant or outraged or defensive or hurt at the time. Maybe reading this book brought up those memories and you felt that way again.

Or maybe you looked at the beta version of the website for the small business you built with your own hands from the ground up. You realized that almost everyone in the photos was white. You felt bad about that. You felt it didn't accurately reflect your company's values, even though, when you thought about it, you had to admit that almost everyone in the company *is* white. Obviously you hadn't done that on purpose. It just kind of worked out that way. You asked the web designer to put a photo of your one Mexican-American employee on the homepage. Maybe you felt kind of bad about that too. Maybe you did it anyway.

The way you felt is universal and the way you responded is understandable. Society teaches all of us that identity capitalism is the right way to respond to an accusation of racism, or the right way to design a website for a predominantly white company. Responding a different way is difficult and painful. Honesty is painful. Messing up is painful. But that discomfort is necessary to dismantle identity capitalism and have better, truer more substantive conversations about race in our country.

Virtually all of us are either identity capitalists or identity entrepreneurs. And because we all inhabit multiple identities, a lot of us are both. As a white person, maybe you find yourself turning to people of color for validation in some settings—making sure your social events are diverse, making sure your website isn't too monochromatic. As a woman, maybe you find yourself emphasizing your own identity in other settings—reminding your boss that your company has been criticized for a lack of women in management positions, and politely suggesting that you'd be willing to take on the work.

Whether we like it or not, we're all part of the system of identity capitalism. As with capitalism itself, opting out is almost impossible. Ingroups leverage outgroup identity for personal gain, and while in the long term that might change, in the short term we're all just stuck with it.

What are the options? In principle we could go live off the grid, farm our own food, stitch our own clothing, and build our own furniture. We'd have to be socially isolated, not just economically independent. We'd have to stop spending time with anyone, or anything, that triggers the deeply ingrained impulses of identity capitalism.

We could do that, but we probably won't. And the only alternative is to get better at recognizing and rejecting identity capitalism.

The way we think about identity in America is profoundly broken. We feel anxious and resentful around people who are different from us. But instead of talking about it, too often we point to our diverse friend group with satisfaction and pat ourselves on the back because the one employee of color at our company seems to be doing well, or at least he hasn't said he's *not* doing well. And then we settle in for some *Queer Eye*.

Ending identity capitalism is part of the process of repair. We need to develop genuine relationships with people who are not like us. We need to work to include people who are not like us in our ingroup institutions, whether at work, at school, around our neighborhoods, or in our places of worship. We need to support substantive policy solutions to ongoing inequality and to demand that our political leaders do the same.

In this book I've outlined how we can push back against identity capitalism as a society. We *also* have to push back ourselves, as individuals. We have to fight identity capitalism in our own lives, and we have to do it even when we're uncomfortable or when it makes other people uncomfortable. We have to be honest with each other. More important, we have to be honest with ourselves. Only then can we hope to move past the false promise of identity capitalism.

NOTES

INTRODUCTION: GETTING USED

1. Throughout this book, I refer to ingroups to mean identity groups that disproportionately exercise power and control resources within society, and outgroups to mean identity groups that are not part of those groups. The social science concepts are actually a little more complicated: an "ingroup" is a group with which a person identifies, and an "outgroup" is one with which that person doesn't. So ingroups and outgroups are relative: that is, a social outsider—say, a lesbian—would view other lesbians as an "ingroup" and heterosexual people as an "outgroup." For purposes of the identity capitalist frame, though, I take the relevant person as a constant, and more specifically as an insider—someone who is white, male, straight, wealthy, and so forth. The "ingroup," then, refers to people who share these identity characteristics. The outgroup is anyone who does not.

2. *Plessy v. Ferguson*, 163 U.S. 537 (1896); Brief for Plaintiff in Error at 9, Plessy (No. 210). Legal scholar Cheryl Harris has argued that whiteness is a form of property that confers both social status and more tangible forms of wealth on white people. See Cheryl Harris, "Whiteness as Property," *Harvard Law Review* 106 (1993): 1707–91.

3. Frank Newport, "Amazing Black Support for President Trump," Gallup, November 20, 2019, https://news.gallup.com/opinion/polling-matters/268517 /analyzing-black-support-president-trump.aspx.

4. Bob Kinzel and VPR News, "He's in for 2020: Bernie Sanders Is Running for President Again," VPR, February 19, 2019, https://www.vpr.org/post/hes-2020 -bernie-sanders-running-president-again#stream/o.

5. Victoria M. Massie, "Why Did Bernie Sanders Do Better with Black Voters in the Midwest? We Asked 4 Experts," March 21, 2016, https://www.vox. com/2016/3/21/11265114/black-voters-midwest-south-sanders.

6. Rebecca Aviel, "Rights as a Zero-Sum Game," *Arizona Law Review* 61 (2019): 352–54.

7. People sometimes ask whether an outgroup member could also be an identity capitalist. For example, is a black woman an identity capitalist if she emphasizes her friendship with a white person to make herself seem more palatable to other white people? While the black woman is using identity in a way that benefits her, she is not an identity *capitalist* because power and resources are distributed unequally between white people and black people in society. That the black woman has to seek status by affiliating with a white person is a result of this inequality.

8. For Diamond and Silk novices, this "little routine" provides a condensed glimpse into a typical Diamond and Silk presentation and demonstrates Trump's reaction to it. "Donald Trump Meets the Notorious Diamond and Silk, Self Described 'Black Trump Supporters,'" *Fox 10 Phoenix*, December 4, 2015, https://www.youtube.com/watch?v=oIXGpScZoCg.

9. Quoted in Liam Stack, "Who Are Diamond and Silk? A Look at 2 Pro-Trump Social Media Stars," *New York Times*, April 14, 2018, https://www.nytimes.com/2018/04/14/us/politics/diamond-silk-facebook.html.

10. Vanessa Williams, "Black Women—Hillary Clinton's Most Reliable Voting Bloc—Look Beyond Defeat," *Washington Post*, November 12, 2016, https://www.washingtonpost.com/politics/black-women—hillary-clintons-most-reliable-voting-bloc—look-beyond-defeat/2016/11/12/86d9182a-a845-11e6-ba59-a7d93165c6d4_story.html

11. Quoted in Stack, "Who Are Diamond and Silk?"

12. Asha DuMonthier et al., "The Status of Black Women in the United States," Institute for Women's Policy Research, 2017, https://iwpr.org/publications/status-black-women-united-states-report.

13. 438 U.S. 265 (1978).

14. Ibid., at 311–12. While only Justice Powell's opinion concurring in the judgment adopted diversity as an acceptable rationale for affirmative action, his opinion was viewed as the controlling one because there was no majority.

15. David Wilkins, "From 'Separate Is Inherently Unequal' to 'Diversity Is Good for Business': The Rise of Market-Based Diversity Arguments and the Fate of the Black Corporate Bar," *Harvard Law Review* 117 (2004).

16. Both Credit Suisse and Gallup are quoted in Rocío Lorenzo et al., "How Diverse Teams Boost Innovation," *Boston Consulting Group*, January 23, 2018, https://www.bcg.com/en-us/publications/2018/how-diverse-leadership-teams-boost-innovation.aspx.

17. Katherine W. Phillips, "How Diversity Makes Us Smarter," *Scientific American*, October 1, 2014, https://www.scientificamerican.com/article/how-diversity-makes-us-smarter.

18. Expert Witness Report of Patricia Y. Gurin at 12, *Gratz v. Bollinger*, 135 F. Supp. 2d 790 (E.D. Mich. 2001) (No. 97-75321), 1998 WL 35140040, reprinted in 5 *Michigan Journal of Race & Law* 363 (1999) (appendices for the report are available at http://www.vpcomm.umich.edu/admissions/legal/ expert/gurinapd.html).

CHAPTER 1: FAKE DIVERSITY

1. Deena Prichep, "A Campus More Colorful Than Reality: Beware That

College Brochure," *National Public Radio*, December 29, 2013, http:// www .npr.org/2013/12/29/257765543/a-campus-more-colorful-than-reality-beware-that -college-brochure.

2. David Roediger, "What's Wrong with These Pictures? Race, Narratives of Admission, and the Liberal Self-Representations of Historically White College and Universities," *Washington University Journal of Law and Policy* 18 (2005): 206–7.

3. "VP Pick Palin Makes Appeal to Women Voters," *NBC News*, August 29, 2008, http://www.nbcnews.com/id/25970882/ns/politics-decision_08/t/vp-pick -palin-makes-appeal-womenvoters/#.VPZwy955nzI.

4. Jim Geraghty, "First Thoughts on the 'Wow' Pick That Is Sarah Palin," *National Review*, August 29, 2008, http://www.nationalreview.com/campaign -spot/8939/first-thoughts-wow-pick-sarah-palin-jim-geraghty.

5. Matt Bai, "Retro Identity Politics," *New York Times*, September 12, 2008, http://www.nytimes .com/2008/09/14/magazine/14wwln-lede-t.html.

6. Eugene Robinson, "Donald Trump as GOP Hopeful: Take Him Seriously," *Washington Post*, April 18, 2011, https://www.washingtonpost.com/opinions /donald-trump-as-gop-hopeful-take-him-seriously/2011/04/18/AFD1ejoD_story .html?utm_term=.4732cb3e20c0.

7. Sheryl Gay Stolberg, "In Speech to N.A.A.C.P., Bush Offers Reconciliation," *New York Times*, July 21, 2006, http://www.nytimes.com/2006/07/21/washington/21bush .html; "Transcript of Bush's Address to N.A.A.C.P.," *New York Times*, July 20, 2006, https://www.nytimes.com/2006/07/20/washington/20text-bush.html.

8. Pat Jordan, "The Duke of Deception," *Southern Magazine*, October 1987, reprinted as "David Duke: The Most Charming Bigot You Ever Met," *The Daily Beast*, January 10, 2015, https://www.thedailybeast.com/david-duke-the-most -charming-bigot-you-ever-met.

9. Matthew Day, "Adolf Hitler Protected His Jewish Former Commanding Officer," *Telegraph*, July 5, 2012, https://www.telegraph.co.uk/history/world-war -two/9379575/Adolf-Hitler-protected-his-Jewish-former-commanding-officer.html.

10. "Kavanaugh Hearing: Transcript," *Washington Post*, September 27, 2018, https://www.washingtonpost.com/news/national/wp/2018/09/27/kavanaugh -hearing-transcript/?utm_term=.42e5853235b.

11. Quotes from Sarah Nechamkin, "Kavanaugh's Treatment of Renate Schroeder in High School Was Worse Than We Thought," *The Cut*, (October 4, 2018, https://www.thecut.com/2018/10/former-classmate-details-kavanaughs -cruel-mocking-of-renate.html.

12. UPS, "Diversity & Inclusion," https://sustainability.ups.com/committed -to-more/diversity-and-inclusion.

13. Walmart, "Diversity & Inclusion," https://corporate.walmart.com/global -responsibility/opportunity/diversity-and-inclusion.

14. Nike, "Championing Diversity," https://jobs.nike.com/inclusion.

15. "Black Workers at UPS Hub Say They Were Targets of Racism," *Associated Press*, March 14, 2019; Jordyn Holman, "Wal-Mart Female Employees Try Again for Sex-Bias Class Action," *Bloomberg*, November 7, 2017, https://www.bloomberg .com/news/articles/2017-11-07/wal-mart-female-employees-try-again-for-sex-bias-class

-action; Tiffany Hsu, "Ex-Employees Sue Nike, Alleging Gender Discrimination," *New York Times*, August 10, 2018), https://www.nytimes.com/2018/08/10/business /nike-discrimination-class-action-lawsuit.html.

16. Hsu, "Ex-Employees Sue Nike."

17. Daniel S. Wittenberg, "Corporate Clients Demand More Diversity from Law Firms," *American Bar Association*, January 20, 2017, https://www.americanbar .org/groups/litigation/publications/litigation-news/business-litigation/corporate -clients-demand-more-diversity-law-firms.

18. Debra Cassens Weiss, "HP Counsel Tells Law Firms to Meet Diversity Mandate or Forfeit Up to 10% Fees," *ABAJournal*, February 15, 2017, https://www .abajournal.com/news/article/hp_general_counsel_tells_law_firms_to_meet _diversity_mandate_or_forfeit_up.

19. "Deadline for Diversity Issued by Top MetLife Lawyer," *Bloomberg Law*, April 3, 2017, https://news.bloomberglaw.com/business-and-practice/deadline-for -diversity-issued-by-top-metlife-lawyer.

20. Mitu Gulati and Patrick S. Shin, "Showcasing Diversity," *North Carolina Law Review* 89 (2011).

21. Matthew Hartley and Christopher C. Morphew, "What's Being Sold and to What End? A Content Analysis of College Viewbooks," *Journal of Higher Education* 79 (2008), 671, 686–87; see also Scott Jaschik, "Viewbook Diversity vs. Real Diversity," *Inside Higher Ed*, July 2, 2008, http://www .insidehighered.com /news/2008/07/02/viewbooks.

22. Jaime Fuller, "New Campaign Insists 'Republicans Are People Too,'" *Washington Post*, September 24, 2014, https://www.washingtonpost.com/news /the-fix/wp/2014/09/24/new-ad-campaign-insists-republicans-are-people-too/?utm _term=.ca1231358880.

23. Pew Research Center, "Party Affiliation Among Voters: 1992–2016," September 13, 2016, http://www.people-press.org/2016/09/13/2-party-affiliation -among-voters-1992-2016.

24. Individual Contributions for Philip Knight, *Federal Election Commission*, 2017–2018, https://www.fec.gov/data/receipts/individual-contributions/?two _year_transaction_period=2018&contributor_name=knight%2C+phil&min _date=01%2F01%2F2017&max_date=09%2F26%2F2018&contributor_state=OR.

25. Dan MacGuill, "Did Nike Donate Vastly More to Republicans Than Democrats in the 2018 Election Cycle?" *Snopes*, September 27, 2018, https://www .snopes.com/fact-check/nike-donations-republicans.

26. Will Doran, "Was 2016 'One of the Deadliest Years Ever' for Police Officers in the US?" *Politifact*, May 23, 2017, https://www.politifact.com/north -carolina/statements/2017/may/23/thom-tillis/was-2016-one-deadliest-years-ever -police-officers-/.

27. Lauren Duca, "The 'Gay Best Friend' Effect: A Friendly Takedown of Benevolent Stereotyping," *Huffington Post*, July 31, 2013, https://www.huffingtonpost. com/lauren-duca/the-gay-best-friend-effect-a-friendly-takedown-of-benevolent -stereotyping_b_3677329.html. Consider also Heven's song "Gay Best Friend,"

which includes the lyrics, "My gay best friend / is so popular / you should get you one / ain't not stopping us." Heven, "Gay Best Friend," Ultra Records, 2013, https://www.youtube.com/watch?v=vg3borJ2CCs.

28. Bravo is owned by NBCUniversal Cable Entertainment, which in turn is owned by Comcast Corporation. Most of the executives are white, male, and heterosexual. For example, the chairman and CEO, Brian L. Roberts; the senior executive vice president and chief financial officer, Michael J. Cavanaugh; and the senior executive vice president and chief diversity officer, David L. Cohen, are all white men married to women. "Brian L. Roberts, Chairman & Chief Executive Officer," *Comcast*, https://corporate.comcast.com/news-information/leadership -overview/brian-l-roberts; "Mike Cavanagh," *Irish America*, https://irishamerica. com/2012/09/mike-cavanagh/; "David L. Cohen, Senior Executive Vice President & Chief Diversity Officer," https://corporate.comcast.com/news-information /leadership-overview/david-l-cohen.

29. For example, the CEO of Target, Brian Cornell, is a white man married to a woman. Aine Cain, "Inside the Career of Brian Cornell, Who Ran Sam's Club Before Becoming Target's First Ever Outsider CEO," *Business Insider*, January 29, 2019, https://www.businessinsider.com/target-ceo-brian-cornell -profile-2019-1.

30. damali ayo, *How to Rent a Negro* (Chicago: Chicago Review Press, 2005).

31. See, e.g., Marianne Bertrand and Sendhil Mullainathan, "Are Emily and Greg More Employable Than Lakisha and Jamal? A Field Experiment on Labor Market Discrimination," American Economic Review 94 (2004): 991, 992.

32. Robin DiAngelo, *White Fragility: Why It's So Hard for White People to Talk About Racism* (Boston: Beacon Press, 2018).

33. Greg Tate, ed., *Everything But the Burden: What White People Are Taking from Black Culture* (New York: Broadway Books, 2003).

34. Eduardo Bonilla-Silva, *Racism Without Racists: Color-Blind Racism and the Persistence of Racial Inequality in America*, 5th ed. (Lanham, MD: Rowman & Littlefield, 2017).

35. Ibid., 90–91.

36. Justin Pidot, "Intuition or Proof: The Social Science Justification for the Diversity Rationale in *Grutter v. Bollinger* and *Gratz v. Bollinger*," *Stanford Law Review* 59 (2006), 761. Pidot assumed—perhaps charitably to white people—that all the reported close friendships were with other students, and that every cross-racial friendship included one white student and one student of color.

37. See, for example, *Tademy v. Union Pacific Corporation*, in which a supervisor responded to a black employee's complaint about racist graffiti by stating that his daughter dated an African American man. 614 F.3d 1132 (10th Cir. 2008).

38. RENT-A-MINORITY, website, http://rentaminority.com.

39. Elizabeth Olson, "'A Bleak Picture' for Women Trying to Rise at Law Firms," *New York Times*, July 24, 2017, https://www.nytimes.com/2017/07/24 /business/dealbook/women-law-firm-partners.html.

CHAPTER 2: ALL-AMERICAN EXPLOITATION

1. While identity capitalism is not *uniquely* American, the version that has happened in America is influenced by our particular history and culture and is the version I examine here.

2. Leander Ker, *Slavery Consistent with Christianity* (n.c.: Sherwood & Co., 1840).

3. George Fitzhugh, "The Universal Law of Slavery," 1850.

4. George Fitzhugh, "Slavery Justified," 1854. Here Fitzhugh also advanced a remarkable argument that slavery was essentially communism: "We provide for each slave, in old age and in infancy, in sickness and in health, not according to his labor, but according to his wants. . . . A Southern farm is the beau ideal of Communism; it is a joint concern, in which the slave consumes more than the master, of the coarse products, and is far happier, because although the concern may fail, he is always sure of a support."

5. George Fitzhugh, *Cannibals All! Or, Slaves Without Masters* (Carlisle, MA: Applewood, 2008 [1857]).

6. John C. Calhoun, "Remarks in the United States Senate," February 6, 1837.

7. Remarks of Joel H. Berry, "In Convention, January 24th, on the Proposition to Lay a Special Additional Tax on Negroes," *Proceedings of the Mississippi State Convention, Held January 7–26, A.D. 1861*, 87–89, https://docsouth.unc.edu/imls/missconv/missconv.html.

8. "A Declaration of the Causes Which Impel the State of Texas to Secede from the Federal Union," February 2, 1861, https://www.tsl.texas.gov/ref/abouttx/secession/2feb1861.html.

9. Frederick Douglass, "To My Old Master," *The North Star*, September 8, 1848.

10. William W. Brown, *Narrative of William W. Brown, A Fugitive Slave, Written by Himself*, Chapter XIII, p. 96 (Boston: Published at the Anti-Slavery Office, 1847).

11. Lynda G. Dodd, "The Rhetoric of Gender Upheaval During the Campaign for the Nineteenth Amendment," *Boston University Law Review* 93 (2013), 712–13.

12. Susan Goodier, *No Votes for Women: The New York State Anti-Suffrage Movement* (Champaign: University of Illinois Press, 2013), 121.

13. William Croswell Doane, "Why Women Do Not Want the Ballot," *The North American Review* 161 (1895), 257–67.

14. Ibid., 267.

15. Goodier, *No Votes for Women*, 70.

16. Eleanor Flexner and Ellen Fitzpatrick, *Century of Struggle* (Cambridge, MA: Harvard University Press, 1996), 288–89. Flexner and Fitzpatrick also note that the suffragists saw many or most of the anti-suffragist women as relatively ineffective, and perhaps even as a front for liquor interests who opposed the vote for women.

17. Ernest Bernbaum, ed., *Anti-Suffrage Essays, Introduction* (Boston, MA: Forum Publications, 1916).

18. Quoted in Susan E. Marshall, *Splintered Sisterhood: Gender and Class in the Campaign Against Woman Suffrage* (Madison: University of Wisconsin Press, 1997), 84.

19. Ibid., 67; Lynda G. Dodd, "The Rhetoric of Gender Upheaval During the Campaign for the Nineteenth Amendment," *Boston University Law Review* 93 (2013), 709, 713.

20. Marshall, *Splintered Sisterhood*, 90.

21. Ibid., 72. Marshall notes "the proclivity of male elites to adopt covert methods of wielding power."

22. Priya Parmar, Anthony J. Nocella II, and David Stovall, eds., *From Education to Incarceration: Dismantling the School-to-Prison Pipeline* (New York: Peter Lang, 2014); Gary Orfield et al., "Brown at 60: Great Progress, a Long Retreat and an Uncertain Future," *UCLA Civil Rights Project*, May 15, 2014, https://www.civilrightsproject.ucla.edu/research/k-12-education/integration-and-diversity/brown-at-60-great-progress-a-long-retreat-and-an-uncertain-future/Brown-at-60-051814.pdf.

23. Zora Neal Hurston, untitled letter, *Orlando Sentinel*, 1955.

24. Anders Walker, *The Burning House: Jim Crow and the Making of Modern America* (New Haven, CT: Yale University Press, 2018).

25. *Ibid.*, 8.

26. Robert Penn Warren, *Segregation: The Inner Conflict* (New York: Random House, 1956), 63.

27. Walker, *The Burning House*, 50.

28. Warren, *Segregation*.

29. Walker, *The Burning House*, 52.

30. As sociologist John David Skrentny summarizes, equality was consistently being understood as both an equality of treatment and an equality of economic results, both in conversations about policy and in early case law. John David Skrentny, *The Ironies of Affirmative Action: Politics, Culture, and Justice in America* (Chicago: University of Chicago Press, 1996), 151, 161–66. I include a small sample of such cases here. *Quarles v. Philip Morris, Inc.*, 279 F. Supp. 505, 507, 516 (E.D. Va. 1968) (invalidating existing seniority system on ground that "Congress did not intend to freeze an entire generation of Negro employees into discriminatory patterns"); *Weiner v. Cuyahoga Community College District*, 238 N.E.2d 839, 844 (Ohio Ct. Com. Pl. 1968) ("The [Civil Rights Act of 1964] provides a remedy for a long-continued denial of vital rights of minorities and of every American—the right to equality before the law.").

31. For example, *Carter v. Gallagher*, 452 F.2d 315, 331 (8th Cir. 1971) (en banc) (upholding affirmative action program as "a method of presently eliminating the effects of past racial discriminatory practices and . . . making meaningful in the immediate future the constitutional guarantees against racial discrimination"). See also Paul Frymer and John D. Skrentny, "The Rise of Instrumental Affirmative Action: Law and the New Significance of Race in America," *Connecticut Law Review* 36 (2004): 677, 683–85.

32. Bakke v. Regents of the University of California, 438 U.S. 265 (1978), 313.

33. Under other Supreme Court decisions such as *Adarand v. Pena* and *Seattle School District No. 1 v. Parents Involved in Community Schools*, an institution might also implement an affirmative action program to compensate for its own past acts

of discrimination—but this justification requires institutions to engage in the unappealing act of confessing past wrongdoing.

34. For example, *Grutter v. Bollinger*, 539 U.S. 331 (2003); see also *Gratz v. Bollinger, 539 U.S. 244 (2003)*; *Seattle School District No. 1 v. Parents Involved in Community Schools* (2009); *University of Texas v. Fisher* (2016).

35. Camille Gear Rich, "Decline to State: Diversity Talk and the American Law Student," *University of Southern California Journal of Law and Social Justice* 18 (2012).

36. Robin DiAngelo, *White Fragility: Why It's So Hard for White People to Talk About Racism* (Boston: Beacon Press, 2018), 40–41.

37. Ashley Parker and Steve Eder, "Inside the Six Weeks Donald Trump Was a Nonstop 'Birther,'" *New York Times*, July 2, 2016, https://www.nytimes.com/2016/07/03/us/politics/donald-trump-birther-obama.html?module=inline.

38. Federal Bureau of Investigations, "Latest Hate Crime Statistics Released," November 14, 2016, https://www.fbi.gov/news/stories/2015-hate-crime-statistics-released.

39. The Anti-Defamation League documented 319 incidents of white supremacist propaganda on campuses in 2018, a modest increase from 2017, while the number of off-campus propaganda distributions "skyrocketed" from 129 in 2017 to 868 in 2019. Anti-Defamation League, "White Supremacists Step Up Off-Campus Propaganda Efforts in 2018," https://www.adl.org/resources/reports/white-supremacists-step-up-off-campus-propaganda-efforts-in-2018. Similarly, the Southern Poverty Law Center reported a nearly 50 percent increase in the number of white nationalist groups, from 100 in 2017 to 148 in 2018. Heidi Beirich, "White Supremacy Flourishes Amid Fears of Immigration and Nation's Shifting Demographics," *Intelligence Report, Southern Poverty Law Center*, February 20, 2019, https://www.splcenter.org/fighting-hate/intelligence-report/2019/year-hate-rage-against-change.

40. Danielle Citron, *Hate Crimes in Cyberspace* (Cambridge, MA: Harvard University Press, 2016).

41. Laura M. Holson, "Hacker of Nude Photos of Jennifer Lawrence Gets 8 Months in Prison," *New York Times*, August 30, 2018, https://www.nytimes.com/2018/08/30/arts/hack-jennifer-lawrence-guilty.html.

42. John Koblin, "Fox News Holds Its Lead in a Year of Growth for Cable News," *New York Times*, December 30, 2015, https://www.nytimes.com/2015/12/31/business/media/fox-news-holds-its-lead-in-a-year-of-growth-for-cable-news.html.

43. Tina Nguyen, "'The America We Know Doesn't Exist Anymore': Fox's Dog Whistle Becomes an Air Horn," *Vanity Fair*, August 10, 2018, https://www.vanityfair.com/news/2018/08/laura-ingraham-white-nationalist-rhetoric.

44. Justin McCarthy, "In U.S., Socialist Presidential Candidates Least Appealing," *Gallup*, June 22, 2015, https://news.gallup.com/poll/183713/socialist-presidential-candidates-least-appealing.aspx.

45. Alex Vandermaas-Peeler et al., "Diversity, Division, Discrimination: The State of Young America," MTV/PRRI Report, January 10, 2018, https://www.prri.org/research/mtv-culture-and-religion.

46. Ta-Nehisi Coates, "The First White President," *The Atlantic*, October 2017, https://www.theatlantic.com/magazine/archive/2017/10/the-first-white-president-ta-nehisi-coates/537909.

47. Eugene Scott, "Why Republicans Are Never Going to Be Successful Playing the Race Card to Win Black Voters," *Washington Post*, October 19, 2018, https://www.washingtonpost.com/politics/2018/10/19/french-hill-ad-why-republicans-are-never-going-be-successful-playing-race-card-win-black-voters/?utm_term=.911d40bd2ab5.

CHAPTER 3: ANXIETY AND ABSOLUTION

1. Mia Mercado, "White Friend Confessional," *McSweeney's*, March 23, 2017, https://www.mcsweeneys.net/articles/white-friend-confessional.

2. Alain de Botton, *Status Anxiety*, (New York: Pantheon, 2004), vii–viii.

3. Ibid., 179.

4. Rachel Godsil and Song Richardson, "Racial Anxiety," *Iowa Law Review* 102 (2017): 2235, 2240.

5. Isaac Stanley-Becker, "White Liberals Dumb Themselves Down When They Speak to Black People, a New Study Contends," *Washington Post*, November 30, 2018), https://www.washingtonpost.com/nation/2018/11/30/white-liberals-dumb-themselves-down-when-they-speak-black-people-new-study-contends/?utm_term=.c5b8de895929.

6. Robin DiAngelo, *White Fragility: Why It's So Hard for White People to Talk About Racism* (Boston: Beacon Press, 2018).

7. Robyn K. Mallett and Dana E. Wagner, "The Unexpectedly Positive Consequences of Confronting Sexism," *Journal of Experimental Social Psychology* 47 (2011): 215.

8. Corinne Moss-Racusin et al., "'I'm Not Prejudiced, but . . . ': Compensatory Egalitarianism in the 2008 Democratic Presidential Primary," *Political Psychology* 31 (2010): 543.

9. *Seinfeld*, "The Diplomat's Club," NBC, May 4, 1995, written by Larry David, Jerry Seinfeld, Tom Gammill, and Max Pross.

10. Nan Lin, *Social Capital* (Cambridge, UK: Cambridge University Press, 2001), 9.

11. Pierre Bourdieu and Loic J. D. Wacquant, *An Invitation to Reflexive Sociology* (Chicago: University of Chicago Press, 1992), 119.

12. David Knoke, "Organizational Networks and Corporate Social Capital," in *Corporate Social Capital and Liability*, ed. Roger Th. A. J. Leenders and Shaul M. Gabba (New York: Springer, 1999), 17–46.

13. Candida Brush and Robert D. Hisrich, "Antecedent Influences on Women-Owned Businesses," *Journal of Management Psychology* 6 (1991): 9–16.

14. Mary Pattillo-McCoy, *Black Picket Fences: Privilege and Peril Among the Black Middle Class*, 2nd ed. (Chicago: University of Chicago Press, 1999); James R. Elliott, "Social Isolation and Labor Market Insulation: Network and Neighborhood Effects on Less-Educated Urban Workers," *Sociological Quarterly* 40 (1999): 199–216.

15. Rochelle Parks-Yancy, "The Impact of Downsizing on the Social Capital Resources and Career Prospects of African American Survivors," *Journal of African American Studies* (2010).

16. Joel M. Podolny, *Status Signals: A Sociological Study of Market Competition* (Princeton, NJ: Princeton University Press, 2005), 7–9.

17. Groucho Marx, *Groucho and Me*, 4th ed. (New York: B. Geiss Associates, 1995 [1959]), 321.

18. Spears' affiliation with Federline tarnished her reputation and continues to prompt dire headlines: more than a decade later *E* ran a retrospective titled, "A Look Back at the Romance that Nearly Undid Pop's Princess for Good." Billy Niles, "When Britney Spears Met Kevin Federline: A Look Back at the Romance That Nearly Undid Pop's Princess for Good," *E News*, September 25, 2018, https://www.eonline.com/news/969658/when-britney-spears-met-kevin-federline-a-look-back-at-the-romance-that-nearly-undid-pop-s-princess-for-good.

19. Randall Kennedy, *Sellout: The Politics of Racial Betrayal* (New York: Pantheon, 2008), 58–69. Kennedy does not couch his analysis in market terms, but the notion of exchange—the idea that a nonwhite individual has lost a measure of racial credibility in the process of gaining entry to elite, predominantly white circles—figures prominently in his work.

20. KRS-One, "Build and Destroy," *Sex and Violence* (Boogie Down Productions, 1992).

21. Jesse J. Holland, "Black Americans Aren't Buying Omarosa's Turn Against Trump," Associated Press, August 15, 2018, https://apnews.com/8f6c754ff7344 3c5b539adf76c4cf25d/Black-Americans-aren't-buying-Omarosa's-turn-against -Trump.

22. Chris Mills Rodrigo, "Donna Brazile: 'Kanye West Has Set Us Back 155 Years,'" *The Hill*, October 11, 2018, https://thehill.com/blogs/blog-briefing-room /news/411040-donna-brazile-kanye-west-has-set-us-back-155-years.

23. Julie O'Brien, "I Don't Know Kavanaugh the Judge. But Kavanaugh the Carpool Dad Is One Great Guy," *Washington Post*, July 10, 2018, https://www.washingtonpost.com/opinions/i-dont-know-kavanaugh-the-judge-but -kavanaugh-the-carpool-dad-is-one-great-guy/2018/07/10/a1866a2c-8446-11e8 -9e80-403a221946a7_story.html?utm_term=.f48c131b2506.

24. Lisa Blatt, "I'm a Liberal Feminist Lawyer. Here's Why Democrats Should Support Judge Kavanaugh," *Politico*, August 2, 2018, https://www.politico.com /magazine/story/2018/08/02/im-a-liberal-feminist-heres-why-i-support-judge -kavanaugh-219081.

25. NARAL Pro-Choice America, "Anti-Choice SCOTUS Nominee Kavanaugh Will Gut *Roe v. Wade*, Criminalize Abortion," July 9, 2018; Planned Parenthood, "Senate Must Reject Supreme Court Nominee Brett Kavanaugh," July 9, 2018.

26. Mark Joseph Stern, "Why Is Lisa Blatt Endorsing Brett Kavanaugh?" *Slate*, September 4, 2018, https://slate.com/news-and-politics/2018/09/why-is-lisa-blatt -endorsing-brett-kavanaugh.html.

27. Podolny, *Status Signals*, 106.

28. Leslie H. Picca and Joe R. Feagin, *Two-Faced Racism: Whites in the Backstage and Frontstage* (New York: Routledge, 2007).

29. I recently spent an interesting few hours examining the political contributions of some of my well-off colleagues in the academy: they write long screeds on social media yet have no record of donating to any political candidate who might make their professed values a reality. Several white men who are self-described progressives have never actually donated money to any progressive candidate who was not also a white man.

30. Julia Reinstein and David Mack, "Trump's Lawyer Just Tweeted Pics with His Black Friends to Prove He's Not Racist," *Buzzfeed*, August 16, 2017, https://www.buzzfeednews.com/article/juliareinstein/cohen-collage.

31. Lauren Kascak with Sayantani DasGupta, "#InstagrammingAfrica: The Narcissism of Global Voluntourism," *Pacific Standard*, June 14, 2017, https://psmag.com/economics/instagrammingafrica-narcissism-global-voluntourism-83838; Malaka Gharib, "Volunteering Abroad? Read This Before You Post That Selfie," *National Public Radio*, November 26, 2017, https://www.npr.org/sections/goatsandsoda/2017/11/26/565694874/volunteering-abroad-read-this-before-you-post-that-selfie.

32. Teju Cole, "The White-Savior Industrial Complex," *The Atlantic*, March 21, 2012, https://www.theatlantic.com/international/archive/2012/03/the-white-savior-industrial-complex/254843.

33. Rafia Zakaria, "Poverty as a Tourist Attraction," *New York Times*, May 1, 2014, https://www.nytimes.com/roomfordebate/2014/04/29/can-voluntourism-make-a-difference/poverty-as-a-tourist-attraction.

34. "6-Day Visit to Rural African Village Completely Changes Woman's Facebook Profile Picture," *The Onion*, January 28, 2014, https://www.theonion.com/6-day-visit-to-rural-african-village-completely-changes-1819576037.

35. OkCupid, "Race and Attraction, 2009–2014," September 9, 2014, https://theblog.okcupid.com/race-and-attraction-2009-2014-107dcbb4f060.

36. Emily Steel and Michael S. Schmidt, "Bill O'Reilly Settled New Harassment Claim, Then Fox Renewed His Contract," *New York Times*, October 21, 2017, https://www.nytimes.com/2017/10/21/business/media/bill-oreilly-sexual-harassment.html?action=click&module=RelatedCoverage&pgtype=Article&region=Footer.

37. Lachlan Murdoch, "Lachlan Murdoch Pays Tribute to Fox News' First Female CEO, Suzanne Scott," *Variety*, October 2, 2018, https://variety.com/2018/tv/news/lachlan-murdoch-suzanne-scott-fox-news-1202963294.

38. Susanne Bruckmuller and Nyla R. Branscombe, "How Women End Up on the 'Glass Cliff'", *Harvard Business Review* (January-February, 2001), https://hbr.org/2011/01/how-women-end-up-on-the-glass-cliff; D. G. McCullough, *Women CEOs: Why Companies in Crisis Hire Minorities—and Then Fire Them*, *The Guardian*, August 8, 2014, https://www.theguardian.com/sustainable-business/2014/aug/05/fortune-500-companies-crisis-woman-ceo-yahoo-xerox-jc-penny-economy.

39. Michelle K. Ryan and S. Alexander Haslam, "The Glass Cliff: Exploring the Dynamics Surrounding the Appointment of Women to Precarious Leadership Positions," *Academy of Management* 32 (2007): 549.

40. Mitu Gulati and Patrick S. Shin, "Showcasing Diversity," *North Carolina Law Review* 89 (2011): 1033.

41. Judith Butler, *Gender Trouble: Feminism and the Subversion of Identity*, 2nd ed. (New York: Routledge, 1999); Kenji Yoshino, "Covering," *Yale Law Journal* 111 (2002): 769, 865–75; Camille Gear Rich, "Performing Racial and Ethnic Identity: Discrimination by Proxy and the Future of Title VII," *New York University Law Review* 79 (2004): 1134, 1145.

42. Yoshino, "Covering."

43. Margaret Jane Radin, "Market-Inalienability," *Harvard Law Review* 100 (1987): 1907.

44. Mitu Gulati and Devon W. Carbado, "Working Identity," *Cornell Law Review* 85 (2000): 1288–1293.

45. Ibid.; Devon W. Carbado and Mitu Gulati, *Acting White* (New York: Oxford University Press 2015).

46. Matt Thompson, "Five Reasons Why People Code-Switch," *Code Switch*, National Public Radio, April 13, 2013), https://www.npr.org/sections /codeswitch/2013/04/13/177126294/five-reasons-why-people-code-switch.

47. "Dave Chappelle," *Inside the Actors Studio*, Bravo, February 12, 2006, hosted by James Lipton.

48. *Sorry to Bother You* (Significant Productions, 2018).

49. *Price Waterhouse v. Hopkins*, 490 U.S. 228 (1989).

50. Emily Tan, "At Women's March, Asian-American Demonstrators Work to Channel Anger into Action," *NBC News*, January 23, 2017, https://www.nbcnews. com/news/asian-america/women-s-march-asian-american-demonstrators-work -channel-anger-action-n710736.

51. e. christi cunningham, "Identity Markets," *Howard Law Journal* 45 (2002): 526–27.

CHAPTER 4: IDENTITY ENTREPRENEURS

1. Sarah Palin, *Going Rogue: An American Life* (New York: HarperCollins, 2009), 23.

2. Larry Rohter, "Palin Criticizes Obama as Faux Feminist," *New York Times*, October 21, 2008, http://thecaucus.blogs.nytimes.com/2008/10/21/palin-criticizes -obama-as-faux-feminist.

3. Nico Pitney, "Palin Misquotes Albright," *Huffington Post*, May 25, 2011, http://www.huffingtonpost.com/2008/10/05/palin-misquotes-albright_n_131967 .html. Albright actually said, "There's a place in Hell for women who don't *help* other women." Albright quickly distanced herself from Palin's speech, issuing a statement: "Thought I am flattered that Governor Palin has chosen to cite me as a source of wisdom, what I said has nothing to do with politics."

4. Nancy Leong, "Identity Entrepreneurs," *California Law Review* 104 (2016): 1333.

5. Sarah Palin, *America by Heart: Reflections on Family, Faith, and Flag* (New York: HarperCollins, 2010), 132.

6. Sarah Kendzior, "The Princess Effect," *Politico*, July 14, 2014, http://

www.politico.com/magazine/story/2014/07/glass-ceilings-glass-mirrors-108516
.html#ixzz36Mw34oXg; Andrew Prokop, "More 'Feminine' Women Are More
Likely to Win Elections in Red States," *Vox*, May 15, 2014, http://www.vox
.com/2014/5/15/5720280/do- female-politicians-perceived-as-less-feminine-do
-worse-in-elections.

7. Kate Manne, *Down Girl: The Logic of Misogyny* (Oxford, UK: Oxford
University Press, 2017).

8. The economic system of capitalism, according to the critique advanced
by Karl Marx, involved capitalists exploiting the labor of others and extracting
"surplus value" for their own gain. Identity capitalists, as I define them, are often
complicated figures, but, parallel to labor market capitalists, they, too, extract value
from others—specifically, from outgroup members. Although I am not arguing for
a close analogy to Marxian analysis, his terminology provides a useful heuristic for
the way ingroup members benefit from outgroup members in a system of identity
capitalism.

9. Randall Kennedy, *Sellout: The Politics of Racial Betrayal* (New York:
Pantheon, 2008).

10. Ibid., 140.

11. I am focusing here on situations in which an individual's status as an outgroup
member is basically uncontested—that is, those who do have a colorable entitlement
to outgroup identity, and who affirmatively choose to assert or make salient that
identity to gain a social or economic benefit. An individual who simply lies about
outgroup status for personal gain might also be considered an identity entrepreneur,
but the concerns associated with such identity entrepreneurship are quite different. I
am referring here to individuals such as Rachel Dolezal, a woman whose parents are
white and who identified as white into adulthood, whose decision to reinvent herself
out as a black woman provoked strong and mostly negative reactions. Kirk Johnson et
al., "Rachel Dolezal, in Center of Storm, Is Defiant: 'I Identify as Black,'" *New York
Times*, June 17, 2015, https://www.nytimes.com/2015/06/17/us/rachel-dolezal-nbc-today
-show.html. Perhaps Rachel Dolezal is an identity entrepreneur of sorts, but claims
of identity widely viewed as fraudulent present different concerns that for the most
part I will not engage here.

12. Walter Johnson, *Soul by Soul: Life in the Antebellum Slave Market* (Cambridge,
MA: Harvard University Press, 2001).

13. Ibid.

14. Ibid.

15. Corrine M. McConnaughey, *The Women Suffrage Movement in America:
A Reassessment* (New York: Cambridge University Press, 2013). I discuss the men
of the anti-suffrage movement at greater length in Chapter 2.

16. Susan Goodier, *No Votes for Women: The New York State Anti-Suffrage
Movement* (Champaign: University of Illinois Press, 2013).

17. Page Gardner, "Ann Coulter's Disastrous Political Strategy: Take Away
Women's Right to Vote," *ThinkProgress*, October 5, 2007, https://thinkprogress.
org/ann-coulters-disastrous-political-strategy-take-away-women-s-right-to-vote

-29dfdc6775c1.

18. Emily Peck, "Peter Thiel Once Wrote That Women Getting the Vote Was Bad for Democracy," *Huffington Post*, May 26, 2016, https://www.huffingtonpost .com/entry/peter-thiel-women-democracy_us_5747079be4b03ede4413f6f5.

19. Frank H. Wu, *Yellow: Race in America Beyond Black and White* (New York: Basic Books, 2002), 278.

20. Asia Carrera, personal website, http://www.asiacarrera.com/faqs.html#13.

21. Asa Akira, *Insatiable: Porn—A Love Story* (New York: Grove Press, 2015).

22. Omarosa Manigault Newman, *Unhinged: An Insider's Account of the Trump White House* (New York: Gallery, 2018), 236.

23. Manigualt-Newman, *Unhinged*.

24. Ibid.

25. Omarosa says she was ambushed by John Kelly. The White House describes misconduct. For present purposes it doesn't really matter.

26. Jesse J. Holland, "Black Americans Aren't Buying Omarosa's Turn Against Trump," *Associated Press*, August 15, 2018, https://www.apnews.com/8f6c754ff73443 c5b539adf76c4cf25d/Black-Americans-aren't-buying-Omarosa's-turn-against-Trump.

27. See, e.g., Edward L. Deci and Richard M. Ryan, "The Support of Autonomy and the Control of Behavior," *Journal of Personality and Social Psychology* 53 (1987): 1024; Miron Zuckerman et al., "On the Importance of Self-Determination for Intrinsically-Motivated Behavior," *Personality and Social Psychology Bulletin* 4 (1978): 443.

28. *Lawrence v. Texas*, 539 U.S. 558 (2003).

29. *Queer Eye*, Netflix, Season 2, Episode 2.

30. Emily Steel and Michael S. Schmidt, "Bill O'Reilly Settled Sexual Harassment Claim, Then Fox Renewed His Contract, *New York Times*, October 21, 2017, https://www.nytimes.com/2017/10/21/business/media/bill-oreilly-sexual -harassment.html.

31. See, e.g., Tricia Rose, *Black Noise: Rap Music and Black Culture in Contemporary America* (Middletown, CT: Wesleyan University Press, 1994); Tricia Rose, *The Hip Hop Wars: What We Talk About When We Talk About Hip Hop and Why It Matters* (New York: Civitas Books, 2008); Paul Butler, *Let's Get Free: A Hip Hop Theory of Justice* (New York: New Press, 2010); Jeff Chang, *Can't Stop Won't Stop: A History of the Hip-Hop Generation* (New York: Picador, 2005); Shea Serrano, *The Rap Year Book: The Most Important Rap Song from Every Year Since 1979, Discussed, Debated, and Deconstructed* (New York: Abrams Image, 2015).

32. Karl Smith, "Choice—The Big Payback," The Hip Hop Foundation, March 22, 2014, http://www.thehiphop-foundation.com/choice-the-big-payback.

33. "Nicki Minaj Is Hip Hop's Killer Diva," *Rolling Stone*, December 30, 2014, http://www.rollingstone.com/music/news/nicki-minaj-is-hip-hops-killer-diva-inside -rolling-stones-new-issue-20141230; Jon Caramanica, "A Singular Influence," *New York Times*, March 30, 2012, http://www.nytimes.com/2012 /04/01/arts/music /nicki-minaj-is-the-influential-leader-of-hip-hop.html.

34. Patrik Sandberg, "The Full Revolution of Nicki Minaj," *Dazed*, September

19, 2017, http://www.dazeddigital.com/music/article/37367/1/nicki-minaj-new
-album-steven-klein-interview.

35. "Extra, Extra: Lost Nicki Minaj Quotes," *Vibe*, July 6, 2010, https://www
.vibe.com/2010/07/extra-extra-lost-nicki-minaj-quotes.

36. Caramanica, "A Singular Influence."

37. Madhavi Sunder, "Cultural Dissent," *Stanford Law Review* 54 (2001): 495.

38. Rich Juzwiak, "Rapper Leif's Letterman Terrific Performance Was Also
Important," *Gawker*, March 14, 2014, http://gawker.com/rapper-leifs-letterman
-terrific-performance-was-also-i-1543798565.

39. #BeyGOOD, https://www.beyonce.com/beygood.

40. Tyler Lauletta, "Colin Kaepernick Has Already Donated More Than
$1 Million of His NFL Earnings to Social Justice Charities," *Business Insider*,
September 5, 2018, https://www.businessinsider.com/colin-kaepernick-donations
-social-justice-charities-2018-9.

41. Katherine Bartlett, "Showcasing: The Positive Spin," *North Carolina Law
Review* 89, (2011): 1059.

42. Sandberg, "The Full Revolution of Nicki Minaj."

43. Chris Rock, "Chris Rock Pens Blistering Essay on Hollywood's Race
Problem: "It's a White Industry," *Hollywood Reporter*, December 3, 2014, https
://www.hollywoodreporter.com/news/top-five-filmmaker-chris-rock-753223

44. David Marx, Sei Jin Ko, and Ray Friedman, "The 'Obama Effect': How a
Salient Racial Role Model Reduces Race-Based Performance Differences," *Journal
of Experimental Social Psychology* 45 (2009): 953.

45. Gillian Flynn, *Gone Girl* (New York: Broadway, 2013), 222–23.

46. Leah Fessler, "A Lot of Women Don't Enjoy Hookup Culture—So Why
Do We Force Ourselves to Participate?" *Quartz*, May 17, 2016, https://qz.com/685852
/hookup-culture.

47. Kathleen A. Bogle, *Hooking Up: Sex, Dating, and Relationships on Campus*
(New York: New York University Press, 2008), 117.

48. Shankar Vedantam, "Hookup Culture: The Unspoken Rules of Sex on
College Campuses," *Hidden Brain*, NPR, February. 14, 2017, https://www.npr
.org/templates/transcript/transcript.php?storyId=514578429.

49. Lisa Wade, *American Hookup* (New York: Norton 2017): ("About 15 percent
of students really, really, truly enjoy hookup culture. . . . ").

50. Bogle, *Hooking Up*, 102–15.

51. Vedantam, "Hookup Culture."

52. Nancy Jo Sales, "Tinder and the Dawn of the 'Dating Apocalypse,'" *Vanity
Fair*, September 2015, https://www.vanityfair.com/culture/2015/08/tinder-hook
-up-culture-end-of-dating.

53. Post by u/quaintrelle, "Have You Ever Been 'Prude-Shamed'? As In, Been
or Felt Belittled for Not Being Sexually Liberal Enough?" *Reddit*, May 14, 2015,
https://www.reddit.com/r/AskWomen/comments/36023p/have_you_ever_been
_prudeshamed_as_in_been_or_felt.

54. Jillian Kramer, "How to Avoid the Clingy Label," *Glamour*, October 16,

2014, https://www.glamour.com/story/how-to-avoid-the-clingy-label.

55. Elizabeth Armstrong and Laura Hamilton, *Paying for the Party: How College Maintains Inequality* (Boston: Harvard University Press, 2013), 88.

56. Bogle, *Hooking Up*, 100.

57. Ibid., 101.

58. Sales, "Tinder and the Dawn."

59. Michael Eric Dyson, *Know What I Mean?: Reflections on Hip-Hop* (New York: Civitas Books, 2010).

60. Rose, *Black Noise.*

61. Paul Butler, "Much Respect: Toward a Hip-Hop Theory of Punishment," *Stanford Law Review* 56 (2004): 983.

62. Dyson, *Know What I Mean?*

63. Riché Richardson, *Black Masculinity and the U.S. South: From Uncle Tom to Gangsta* (Athens: University of Georgia Press, 2007).

64. Jonathan Capehart interviewing Wynton Marsalis, *Cape Up*, podcast audio, May 2018, https://soundcloud.com/washington-post/jazz-artist-wynton-marsalis-says-rap-and-hip-hop-are-more-damaging-than-a-statue-of-robert-e-lee/s-TRkFv.

65. Adelle Platon, "Trump Spokesperson Pins Rape Culture on Hip-Hop," *Billboard*, October 14, 2016, https://www.billboard.com/articles/columns/hip-hop/7541909/donald-trump-spokesperson-rape-culture-hip-hop.

66. Brent Griffiths, "CNN Host Shuts Down Interview with Trump Spokeswoman," *Politico*, October 11, 2016, https://www.politico.com/story/2016/10/katrina-pierson-cnn-carol-costello-fight-229602.

67. Mari Matsuda, "Beside My Sister, Facing the Enemy: Legal Theory Out of Coalition," *Stanford Law Review* 43 (1991): 1183, 1189.

CHAPTER 5: UNEQUAL PROTECTION

1. This account is drawn from the federal district court opinion in the case. *Soto v. John Morrell & Co.*, 285 F. Supp. 2d 1146 (N.D. Iowa 2003). Because the case came before the court on the defendant employer's motion for summary judgment, the court construed the facts in the light most favorable to Teresa Soto, the party not moving for judgment. That is the version of facts I adopt here, with the important caveat that some of the facts are contested while others are undisputed. I am not claiming that any specific fact is correct, although the court appears to have been substantially persuaded by Teresa Soto's account.

2. Frank Bruni, "The Worst (and Best) Places to Be Gay in America," *New York Times*, August 25, 2017, https://www.nytimes.com/interactive/2017/08/25/opinion/sunday/worst-and-best-places-to-be-gay.html.

3. Human Rights Commission, City and County of San Francisco, "How to File a Discrimination Complaint in Employment, Housing, or Public Accommodation," https://sf-hrc.org/how-file-discrimination-complaint-employment-housing-or-public-accommodation#What%20are%20protected%20classes%20in%20employment?

4. *Young v. Lehman*, 748 F.2d 194, 197 (4th Cir. 1984).

5. *Moulds v. Wal-Mart Stores, Inc.*, 935 F.2d 252, 256 (11th Cir. 1991).

6. *Dudley v. Wal-Mart Stores, Inc.*, 931 F. Supp. 773 (M.D. Ala. 1996).

7. *Smith v. Alabama Department of Public Safety*, 64 F. Supp. 2d (M.D. Ala. 1999).

8. *Velez v. Brown*, 1997 WL 394895 (M.D. Fla. July 8, 1997).

9. *Johnson v. Disney Destinations LLC*, 2010 WL 3259713 (M.D. Fla. August 16, 2010).

10. *Dawson v. Bumble & Bumble*, 246 F. Supp. 2d 301 (S.D.N.Y. 2003).

11. Allison S. Gabriel et al., "Further Understanding Incivility in the Workplace: The Effects of Gender, Agency, and Communion," *Journal of Applied Psychology* 304 (2018): 362.

12. *Bryant v. Begin Manage Program* provides one example of intraracial tension sparked by identity performance. In *Bryant*, a black woman was called a "wannabe" by her supervisor—also a black woman. According to the facts recounted by the court, Bryant dyed her hair blond, wore suits rather than "Afrocentric" attire like her supervisor, and reportedly had a lighter complexion than both her supervisor and the person who replaced Bryant after she was fired. *Bryant v. Begin Manage Program*, 281 F. Supp. 2d 561, 564–68 (2003).

13. Susan Moffat, "Splintered Society: U.S. Asians: The L.A. Riots Highlighted Tension Among Asian-American Groups, Split by Longstanding Enmities and Generational Conflict. A Search Is Underway for a Common Voice," *Los Angeles Times*, July 13, 1992, https://www.latimes.com/archives/la-xpm-1992-07-13-mn -3719-story.html. These intraracial tensions are invisible to non–Asian American racial groups.

14. Kimberlé Crenshaw, "Mapping the Margins: Intersectionality, Identity Politics, and Violence Against Women of Color," *Stanford Law Review* 42 (1991), 1241.

15. I am not weighing in as to whether members of outgroups discriminate as much as members of ingroups. My point is that in any given case an outgroup member *could* have discriminated against another member of their group.

16. Devon Carbado and Mitu Gulati, "The Fifth Black Woman," *Journal of Contemporary Legal Issues* 11 (2001): 701.

17. Kimberlé Crenshaw, "Demarginalizing the Intersection of Race and Sex: A Black Feminist Critique of Antidiscrimination Doctrine, Feminist Theory, and Antiracist Politics," *University of Chicago Legal Forum* 1989 (1989): 139–67. See also *Jeffries v. Harris County Community Action Association*, 425 F. Supp. 1208 (S.D. Tex. 1977) (denying a black woman's race discrimination claim because a black man had previously held the position she sought, and her gender discrimination claim because a white woman had previously held the position she sought).

18. Paulette M. Caldwell, "A Hair Piece: Perspectives on the Intersection of Race and Gender," *Duke Law Journal* 1991 (1991): 365–72; D. Wendy Greene, "Title VII: What's Hair (and Other Race-Based Characteristics) Got to Do with It?" *University of Colorado Law Review* 79 (2008): 1355, 1384–89.

19. Bridgett Davis, "Everything You Need to Know About Quitting Relaxing," *Oprah.com*, n.d., http://www.oprah.com/style/going-natural-hair-how-to-stop -relaxing/all.

20. Dana Oliver, "Halle Berry on How She Went Short, Advice for Her Daughter Nahla, and Owning a Whole Lot of Flip Flops," *Huffington Post*, May 29, 2012, https://www.huffingtonpost.com/2012/05/29/halle-berry-hair_n_1543462.html.

21. *Rogers v. American Airlines*, 527 F. Supp. 299 (S.D.N.Y. 1981).

22. Jena McGregor, "More States Are Trying to Protect Black Employees Who Want to Wear Natural Hairstyles at Work," *Washington Post*, September 19, 2019, https://www.washingtonpost.com/business/2019/09/19/more-states-are-trying-protect-black-employees-who-want-wear-natural-hairstyles-work.

23. Donnie Mangrum's story is drawn from *Mangrum v. Republic Industries*, 260 F. Supp. 2d 1229 (N.D. Ga. 2003). Because the case was decided on cross-motions for summary judgment, the court viewed the facts in the light most favorable to Donnie Mangrum, the plaintiff. I describe that version of the facts here. Readers, however, should bear in mind that the narrative contains some allegations contested by the parties, and I am not weighing in on the truth of any particular fact.

24. *Meritor Savings Bank v. Vinson*, 477 U.S. 57, 69 (1986).

25. Susan Estrich, "Sex at Work," *Stanford Law Review* 43 (1991): 813.

26. Margaret Moore Jackson, "Confronting Unwelcomeness from the Outside: Using Case Theory to Tell the Stories of Sexually-Harassed Women," *Cardozo Journal of Law and Gender* 14 (2007): 61, 66.

27. *Price Waterhouse v. Hopkins*, 490 U.S. 228 (1989).

28. Estrich, "Sex at Work," 828.

29. *Moulds v. Wal-Mart Stores, Inc.*, 935 F.2d 252 (11th Cir. 1991).

30. *Garrett v. Southwestern Medical Clinic*, 631 Fed. Appx. 351 (6th Cir. November 5, 2015).

31. *Garmon v. National Railroad Passenger Corporation*, 844 F.3d 307, 316–17 (1st Cir. 2016); *Johnson v. Walgreen*, 1992 WL 357828 (1st Cir. 1992) ("[T]he fact that the defendants had hired other black pharmacists suggests that the failure to interview or hire Johnson was for objective reasons").

32. The 2015 Carlton Fields Jorden Burt Class Action Survey: Best Practices in Reducing Cost and Managing Risk in Class Action Litigation (2015), 26, http://classactionsurvey.com/pdf/2015-class-action-survey.pdf; see also Cynthia L. Estlund, "The Black Hole of Mandatory Arbitration," *North Carolina Law Review* 96 (2018): 679; Jean R. Sternlight, "Disarming Employees: How American Employers Are Using Mandatory Arbitration to Deprive Workers of Legal Protection," *Brooklyn Law Review* 80 (2015): 1309.

33. *Owens v. Jackson County Board of Education*, 561 Fed. Appx. 846 (11th Cir. March 31, 2014).

34. Munger, Reinschmidt & Denne, L.L.P., "Experience," http://www.mrdlaw.net/Experience; Email from Jay Denne to Nancy Leong, April 16, 2019, on file with author.

35. Ellen Berrey, Robert L. Nelson, and Laura Beth Nielsen, *Rights on Trial: How Workplace Discrimination Law Perpetuates Inequality* (Chicago: University of Chicago Press 2017), 54–76.

CHAPTER 6: THE LAW OF IDENTITY CAPITALISM

1. Miranda July, "A Very Revealing Conversation with Rihanna," *New York Times*, October 12, 2015, https://www.nytimes.com/2015/10/12/t-magazine/rihanna -miranda-july-interview.html.

2. Ibid.

3. Jess Cartner-Morley, "Rihanna: Evolution of a Style Icon," *The Guardian*, July 17, 2012, https://www.theguardian.com/music/2012/jul/17/rihanna-evolution -style-icon.

4. July, "A Very Revealing Conversation with Rihanna."

5. For example, a 2019 NBC News/*Wall Street Journal* poll found that 88 percent of African Americans, 64 percent of Latinos, and 57 percent of voters aged eighteen to thirty-four disapprove of Trump. Mark Murray, "NBC News/WSJ Poll: 2020 Race Will Be Uphill for Trump, But He Has Strong Party Loyalty," *NBC News*, March 3, 2019, https://www.nbcnews.com/politics/meet-the-press /nbc-news-wsj-poll-2020-race-will-be-uphill-trump-n978331. Similarly, a 2019 Gallup Poll found Trump's approval rating at 18 percent among all nonwhite people and 28 percent among voters aged eighteen to twenty-nine. Jeffrey M. Jones, "Subgroup Differences in Trump Approval Mostly Party-Based," *Gallup*, March 29, 2019, https://news.gallup.com/poll/248135/subgroup-differences-trump -approval-mostly-party-based.aspx.

6. Anjali Vats, *The Color of Creatorship* (Stanford, CA: Stanford University Press, 2020); Kevin Greene, "Copyright, Culture, & Black Music: A Legacy of Unequal Protection," *Hastings Communication and Entertainment Law Journal* 21 (1999): 339, 343.

7. Kira Chochrane, "Interview: Rihanna: 'That's a Part of My Life I Want to Throw Away,'" *The Guardian*, November 20, 2009, https://www.theguardian. com/music/2009/nov/21/rihanna-interview.

8. Anemona Hartocollis, "He Took on the Voting Rights Act and Won. Now He's Taking on Harvard," *New York Times*, November 19, 2017, https://www .nytimes.com/2017/11/19/us/affirmative-action-lawsuits.html.

9. Plaintiff's Statement of Undisputed Material Facts at 6, *Students for Fair Admissions v. Harvard College*, No. 1:14-cv-14176-ADB (D. Ma. June 15, 2018).

10. Plaintiff's Memorandum of Reasons in Support of Its Motion for Summary Judgment at 1, *Students for Fair Admissions v. Harvard College*, No. 1:14-cv-14176 -ADB (D. Ma. June 15, 2018).

11. Karthick Ramakrishnan and Janelle Wong, "Survey Roundup: Asian American Attitudes on Affirmative Action," *Data Bits*, June 18, 2018, http://aapidata .com/blog/asianam-affirmative-action-surveys/.

12. Nancy Leong, "The Misuse of Asian Americans in the Affirmative Action Debate," *UCLA Law Review Discourse* 64 (2016): 90.

13. T. H. Rawls, "College Legacy Admissions: Affirmative Action for Whites," *New York Times*, August 6, 2017, https://www.nytimes.com/2017/08/06/opinion /college-legacy-admissions-affirmative-action-for-whites.html.

14. A few commentators of color have noted that the pool of legacies is also becoming more diverse. Ashton Lattimore, a black alumna of Harvard College, writes, "It's frustrating but not entirely surprising that legacy admissions stands to be eliminated just as people of color might begin to reap the benefits." But Lattimore still opposes legacy admissions: "Much more than I want my son to walk an easier path to the Ivy League, I want a higher-education system that welcomes new and diverse families. Instead of him gaining an advantage on a college application, I'd rather see him inherit a fairer world." Ashton Lattimore, "Ending Legacy Admissions Is the Right Thing to Do. But for Black Alums, It Stings," *Washington Post*, August 6, 2018, https://www.washingtonpost.com/outlook/2018/08/06/aaa7db6e-968d -11e8-80e1-00e80e1fdf43_story.html?utm_term=.f40c53706b02.

15. Emanuella Grinberg, "One Crime, Six Trials, and a 30-Minute Guilty Verdict," *CNN*, June 18, 2010, http://www.cnn.com/2010/CRIME/06/18/mississippi .curtis.flowers/index.html.

16. *Flowers v. Mississippi*, 139 S. Ct. 2228 (2019).

17. *Batson v. Kentucky*, 476 U.S. 79 (1986). The Court later extended the holding to gender in a child support case in which lawyers used peremptory challenges to target male potential jurors and seat an all-female jury. *J.E.B. v. Alabama* ex rel. T.B., 511 U.S. 127 (1994). *Edmonson v. Leesville Concrete Company* further extended the holding of *Batson* to civil cases, not just criminal ones. 500 U.S. 614 (1991).

18. Equal Justice Initiative, "Illegal Racial Discrimination in Jury Selection: A Continuing Legacy," August 2010, 14, https://eji.org/sites/default/files/illegal -racial-discrimination-in-jury-selection.pdf.

19. *Flowers v. Mississippi*, 947 So.2d 910, 937 (2007).

20. Quotes from *People v. Randall*, 283 Ill. App. 3d 1019, 1025–26 (1996).

21. Gilad Edelman, "Why Is It So Easy for Prosecutors to Strike Black Jurors?" *The New Yorker*, June 5, 2015, https://www.newyorker.com/news/news-desk/why -is-it-so-easy-for-prosecutors-to-strike-black-jurors.

22. Note, "Discriminatory Use of Peremptory Challenges: *Edmonson v. Leesville Concrete Co.* and *Powers v. Ohio*," *Harvard Law Review* 105 (1991): 255, 264.

23. *United States v. David*, 662 F. Supp. 244, 246 N.D. Ga. 1987).

24. *United States v. Montgomery*, 819 F.2d 847, 851 (8th Cir. 1987).

25. In *Powers v. Ohio*, the Supreme Court made clear that there is no precise number or percentage of a racial group that will damn or insulate the jury selection process. *Powers v. Ohio*, 499 U.S. 400 (1991). But, as one court explained, "the state's failure to use all of its strikes against venirepersons of a racial minority and the presence of a racial minority on the defendant's jury" may still be relevant factors "to the extent that they indicate that race was not the prosecutor's motive for the challenged strikes." *State v. Aziz*, 844 S.W.2d 531, 534 (Mo. Ct. App. 1992).

26. Ronald J. Sievert, "Capital Murder: A Prosecutor's Personal Observations on the Prosecution of Capital Cases," *American Journal of Criminal Law* 27 (1999): 105.

27. Ibid., 110.

28. Edelman, "Why Is It So Easy for Prosecutors to Strike Black Jurors?"

29. "Timeline: The Furor Over the Redskins' Name," *Washington Post*, n.d.,

https://www.washingtonpost.com/apps/g/page/local/timeline-the-furor-over
-the-redskins-name/2035. The first legal challenge was filed by a group of Native
Americans, led by Suzan Shown Harjo, in 1992. The Trademark Trial and Appeal
Board ruled in Harjo's favor in 1999, determining that the name was disparaging
to Native Americans. 1999 WL 375907, Trademark Tr. & App. Bd. (April 2, 1999).
But after a long series of appeals, a federal appellate court ultimately overturned
the ruling in 2009: the court did not address the issue of the team's name, but
instead focused on a legal principle called the "defense of laches," which allows
defendants to seek dismissal of a claim if plaintiffs wait too long to file suit. The
court agreed that Harjo and her fellow plaintiffs had waited too long after becoming
legal adults to challenge the trademark. *Pro-Football, Inc. v. Harjo*, 565 F.3d 880,
883–85 (D.C. Cir. 2009).

 30. 15 U.S.C. § 1052 (2006).

 31. *Pro-Football, Inc. v. Blackhorse*, 112 F. Supp. 3d 439 (E.D. Va. 2015).

 32. Robert L. Tsai and Christine Haight Farley, "Racial Slurs Shouldn't Be
Trademarked," *Slate*, April 20, 2015, https://slate.com/news-and-politics/2015/04
/washington-football-teams-name-is-a-racial-slur-doj-and-patent-and-trademark
-office-are-right.html.

 33. Matal v. Tam, 582 U.S. ___ (2017).

 34. Ailsa Chang, "After Supreme Court Decision, People Race to Trademark
Racially Offensive Words," *National Public Radio*, July 21, 2017, https://www.npr
.org/2017/07/21/538608404/after-supreme-court-decision-people-race-to-trademark
-racially-offensive-words.

 35. John Woodrow Cox, Scott Clement, and Theresa Varga, "New Poll Finds
9 in 10 Native Americans Aren't Offended by Redskins Name," *Washington Post*,
May 19, 2016, https://www.washingtonpost.com/local/new-poll-finds-9-in-10
-native-americans-arent-offended-by-redskins-name/2016/05/18/3ea11cfa-161a-11e6
-924d-838753295f9a_story.html?utm_term=.c6e2e9614e13.

 36. Jacqueline Keeler, "On the Shameful and Skewed 'Redskins' Poll," *The
Nation*, May 25, 2016, https://www.thenation.com/article/on-the-shameful-and
-skewed-redskins-poll.

 37. John E. Hoover, "Gray: Redskins Is a Slur, but Other Nicknames Objectify
Native Americans," *Tulsa World*, October 19, 2013, https://www.tulsaworld.com
/blogs/sports/johnehoover/gray-redskins-is-a-slur-but-other-nicknames-objectify
-native/article_b8559bf2-38c3-11e3-bb7a-0019bb30f31a.html.

 38. Stephanie A. Fryberg et al., "Of Warrior Chiefs and Indian Princesses: The
Psychological Consequences of American Indian Mascots on American Indians,"
Basic and Applied Social Psychology 30 (2008): 208–18.

 39. Stephanie Ann Fryberg, "Really? You Don't Look Like an American Indian:
Social Representations and Social Group Identities," PhD diss., Stanford University,
December 2002, http://www.indianmascots.com/ex-17—-fryberg-final_disse.pdf.

 40. Fryberg et al., "Of Warrior Chiefs and Indian Princesses," quotes on 215
and 216.

 41. *Casey v. Planned Parenthood*, 505 U.S. 833, 846 (1992).

42. Pew Research Center, "Public Opinion on Abortion," October 15, 2018, http://www.pewforum.org/fact-sheet/public-opinion-on-abortion.

43. *Gonzales v. Carhart*, 550 U.S. 124, 159 (2007).

44. Ibid., 159–60.

45. Ibid., at 159.

46. *Gonzales v. Carhart*, Brief of Sandra Cano, the Former "Mary Doe" of *Doe v. Bolton*, and 180 Women Injured by Abortion as Amici Curiae in Support of Petitioner, May 22, 2006.

47. Corinne H. Rocca et al., "Decision Rightness and Emotional Responses to Abortion in the United States: A Longitudinal Study," *PLOS-ONE* (July 8, 2015).

48. One study of 58 women found that most women did not experience any emotional distress post-abortion and almost all the women reported that they were doing well at the one-year mark. More than half reported only positive experiences such as mental growth and increased maturity. A. Kero et al., "Wellbeing and Mental Growth—Long-Term Effects of Legal Abortion," *Social Science Medicine* (2004). Another study of 442 women found that two years post-abortion, 72 percent were satisfied with their decision, 69 percent would have the abortion again, 72 percent reported more benefit than harm from their abortion, and 80 percent were not depressed; women with a prior history of depression were more likely to be depressed. The finding is particularly noteworthy because most subjects expressed positive views about their reproductive decisions even though the research was conducted in 1993 and thus did not account for the subsequent twenty-five years of destigmatization of abortion. Brenda Major et al., "Psychological Responses of Women After First-Trimester Abortion," *Archives of General Psychology* (2000).

49. *Gonzales v. Carhart*, Brief of the National Women's Law Center and 31 Other Organizations Committed to the Safest Health Care for Women as Amici Curiae in Support of Respondent. The brief describes several women who would likely have died without access to certain abortion procedures for medical reasons and lists other benefits to a woman that flow from abortion access, including preserving her health, maintaining her ability to earning a living wage and support herself economically, and respecting her dignitary interest in making the right decision for herself.

50. *Texas Medical Providers Performing Abortion Services v. Lakey*, 667 F.3d 570, 576–77 (5th Cir. 2012).

51. The "regret" language in *Carhart* has spread to other cases. See, e.g., *Planned Parenthood v. Rounds*, 530 F.3d 724, 734–35 (8th Cir. 2008) (using the "regret" language from *Carhart* to bolster a conclusion that the government could require a doctor to provide information relevant to the abortion procedure).

52. Louisiana Department of Health, "Women's Right to Know," http://ldh.la.gov/index.cfm/page/915.

53. Amanda Marcotte, "The Year Anti-Choicers Found Success by Arguing Abortion Is Too Dangerous to Allow Women Access," *Slate*, December 23, 2013, https://slate.com/human-interest/2013/12/less-fetus-more-feigned-concern-for-women-anti-choicers-shifted-strategies-in-2013-to-great-success.html.

54. Ramesh Ponnuru, "Kennedy's Replacement Should Be Judge Amy Coney Barrett," *Bloomberg*, June 28, 2018, https://www.bloomberg.com/opinion/articles/2018-06-28/amy-coney-barrett-should-replace-kennedy-on-supreme-court.

55. Liz Mair, "Even If You're Pro-Kavanaugh, Admit It: Trump Should Have Nominated Amy Coney Barrett," *The Daily Beast*, September 21, 2018, https://www.thedailybeast.com/even-if-youre-pro-kavanaugh-admit-it-trump-should-have-nominated-amy-coney-barrett.

56. Brian Leiter, "Penn Law Student, Anthony Ciolli, Admits to Running Prelaw Discussion Board Awash in Racist, Anti-Semitic, Sexist Abuse, *Leiter Reports: A Philosophy Blog*, March 11, 2005, https://leiterreports.typepad.com/blog/2005/03/penn_law_studen.html.

57. *Virginia v. Black*, 538 U.S. 343 (2003).

58. Mari J. Matsuda, Charles R. Lawrence III, Richard Delgado, and Kimberlé Williams Crenshaw, *Words That Wound: Critical Race Theory, Assaultive Speech, and the First Amendment* (Boulder, CO: Westview Press, 1993).

59. *R.A.V. v. City of St. Paul*, 505 U.S. 377, 392 (1992).

60. Jay Stanley, "Civil Rights Movement Is a Reminder That Free Speech Is There to Protect the Weak," ACLU, May 26, 2017, https://www.aclu.org/blog/free-speech/civil-rights-movement-reminder-free-speech-there-protect-weak.

61. John Samples, "'Hate Speech Laws' Undermine Free Speech and Equality," *Cato Institute Blog*, June 8, 2018, https://www.cato.org/blog/hate-speech-laws-undermine-free-speech-equality.

62. "Remarks by the President to the UN General Assembly," The White House, September 25, 2012, https://obamawhitehouse.archives.gov/the-press-office/2012/09/25/remarks-president-un-general-assembly.

63. Mari J. Matsuda, "Public Response to Racist Speech: Considering the Victim's Story," *Michigan Law Review* 87 (1989): 2320, 2323.

64. Despite the overwhelming amount of abuse to which Heller and Iravani were subjected, many people chose to sympathize with their abusers. Many commentators angrily upbraided Heller and Iravani for interfering with the free speech of posters. In one blog post, law professor Eric Goldman expressed no sympathy at all for Heller and Iravani but said of the defendants, "I suspect the law students whose aliases were named in the complaint had that sickening stomach-liquefying feeling when they realized they were being sued. Being sued is an expensive and scary process." Eric Goldman, "AutoAdmit Fiasco Turns into a Lawsuit—*Doe v. Ciolli*," *Technology and Marketing Law Blog*, June 12, 2007, https://blog.ericgoldman.org/archives/2007/06/autoadmit_fiasc.htm. Goldman's comments reveal selective empathy—what philosopher Kate Manne might call "himpathy," or "the inappropriate and disproportionate sympathy powerful men often enjoy in cases of sexual assault, intimate partner violence, homicide, and other misogynistic behavior." Kate Manne, *Down Girl* (Oxford, UK: Oxford University Press, 2017).

65. *Christian v. United States*, 46 Fed. Cl. 793 (2000).

66. In surveying the frequent judicial use and misuse of Martin Luther King

Jr., I have drawn from the research of Jeremiah Goulka as summarized in a blog post. Jeremiah Goulka, "How Federal Judges Use and Abuse the Words of Martin Luther King Jr. in Their Decisions," *AlterNet*, January 14, 2014).

67. *Vera v. Richards*, 861 F. Supp. 1304 (1994).

68. Ibid., 1309.

69. Justin Driver, "Recognizing Race," *Columbia Law Review* 112 (2012): 404.

CHAPTER 7: BOYCOTT

1. Devin Friedman, "Will You Be My Black Friend?" *GQ*, September 30, 2008, https://www.gq.com/story/devin-friedman-craigslist-oprah-black-white-friends-obama.

2. Christopher Ingraham, "Three Quarters of Whites Don't Have Any Non-White Friends," *Washington Post*, August 25, 2014, https://www.washingtonpost.com/news/wonk/wp/2014/08/25/three-quarters-of-whites-dont-have-any-non-white-friends/?utm_term=.2f3e9e524d6b.

3. *Kill the Messenger*, performed by Chris Rock, HBO, 2008.

4. Kevin M. Kruse, *White Flight: Atlanta and the Making of Modern Conservatism* (Princeton, NJ: Princeton University Press, 2007).

5. Maria Krysan et al., "Does Race Matter in Neighborhood Preference? Results from a Video Experiment," *National Institute of Health*, https://www.ncbi.nlm.nih.gov/pmc/articles/PMC3704191/pdf/nihms482504.pdf.

6. William James Jennings, *The Christian Imagination: Theology and the Origins of Race* (New Haven, CT: Yale University Press, 2010).

7. Allison Benedikt, "If You Send Your Kid to Private School, You Are a Bad Person," *Slate*, August 29, 2013, https://slate.com/human-interest/2013/08/private-school-vs-public-school-only-bad-people-send-their-kids-to-private-school.html.

8. Damon Young, "Why I Don't Have Any White Friends, Explained," *The Root*, March 13, 2018, https://verysmartbrothas.theroot.com/why-i-dont-have-any-white-friends-explained-1823737529.

9. Wulf D. Hund and Charles W. Mills, "Comparing Black People to Monkeys Has a Long, Dark, Simian History," *The Conversation*, February 28, 2016, https://theconversation.com/comparing-black-people-to-monkeys-has-a-long-dark-simian-history-55102.

10. Phillip Atiba Goff et al., "Not Yet Human: Implicit Knowledge, Historical Dehumanization and Contemporary Consequences," *Journal of Personality and Social Psychology* 94 (2008): 292–306.

11. B. Quammie, "Why I Don't Buy H&M's Apology for Their Racist Sweater," *Flare*, January 9, 2018, https://www.flare.com/news/hm-racist-sweater.

12. Chandrika Narayan, "Official Who Called Michelle Obama 'Ape in Heels' Gets Job Back," *CNN*, December 14, 2016, https://www.cnn.com/2016/12/13/us/official-racist-post-return-trnd/index.html.

13. Gregory S. Parks and Danielle C. Heard, "'Assassinate the Nigger Ape[]': Obama, Implicit Imagery, and the Dire Consequences of Racist Jokes," *Rutgers Race and Law Review* 11 (2010): 259.

14. H&M, "H&M Issues Unequivocal Apology for Poorly Judged Product and Image," January 9, 2018, https://about.hm.com/en/media/news/general -news-2018/h-m-issues-unequivocal-apology-for-poorly-judged-product-and -ima.html.

15. Leah Fessler, "H&M's Latest Apology for Its Racist Sweater Is an Actual, Honest-to-God Apology," *Quartz*, January 11, 2018, https://qz.com/1177010/hms -apology-for-its-racist-hoodie-is-an-actual-honest-to-god-apology.

16. Eric K. Yamamoto, "Race Apologies," *Journal of Gender, Race & Justice* 1 (1997): 47.

17. Some of these apologies are drawn from Yamamoto and some from the extensive archives of SorryWatch.com.

18. Bernard Weinraub, "In New Lyrics, Jackson Uses Slurs," *New York Times*, June 15, 1995, https://www.nytimes.com/1995/06/15/arts/in-new-lyrics-jackson -uses-slurs.html.

19. Stephen J. Dubner, "How to Optimize Your Apology," interview with Ben Ho, *Freakonomics*, podcast audio, October 10, 2018, http://freakonomics .com/podcast/apologies.

20. Karen A. Cerulo and Janet M. Ruane, "Apologies of the Rich and Famous: Cultural, Cognitive, and Social Explanations of Why We Care and Why We Forgive," *Social Psychology Quarterly* 77 (2014): 123.

21. Civil Liberties Act of 1988, Pub. L. 100-383, 50a U.S.C. § 1989b et seq (August 10, 1988).

22. See H.R. Res. 194, 110th Congress; S. Con. Res. 126 111th Cong. (2009).

23. Kari Wagner-Peck, *A Typical Son*, blog, https://atypicalson.com.

24. Kari Wagner-Peck, "An Open Letter to Chuck Klosterman, The New York Times, Ethicist," *A Typical Son*, November 7, 2013, https://atypicalson .com/2013/11/07/an-open-letter-to-chuck-klosterman-the-new-york-times-ethicist.

25. Kari Wagner-Peck, "Chuck Klosterman's Response to My Letter," *A Typical Son*, November 12, 2013, https://atypicalson.com/2013/11/12/chuck-klostermans -response-to-my-letter.

26. Just check out a small sampling of the apologies at SorryWatch.com.

27. Emily Yahr, Megyn Kelly Asked "What Is Racist" About Blackface on Halloween. Plenty of People Had Answers," *Washington Post*, October 23, 2018, https://www.washingtonpost.com/arts-entertainment/2018/10/23/megyn-kelly -asked-what-is-racist-about-blackface-halloween-plenty-people-had-answers.

28. Kelly McLaughlin, "Megyn Kelly's Colleagues Slammed Her Blackface Comments on the 'Today' Show," *Business Insider*, October 24, 2018, https://www .businessinsider.com/megyn-kelly-colleagues-slam-her-blackface-comments-on -the-today-show-2018-10.

29. Frederick Douglass, "The Hutchinson Family—Hunkerism," *North Star*, October 27, 1848, http://utc.iath.virginia.edu/minstrel/miar03bt.html. Researchers have examined and sometimes complicated Douglass' view. Eric Lott, for example, has suggested that "the audiences involved in early minstrelsy were not universally derisive of African Americans or their culture, and there

was a range of responses to the minstrel show which points to an instability or contradiction in the form itself." Eric Lott, *Love and Theft: Blackface Minstrelsy and the American Working Class* (New York: Oxford University Press, 2013 [1993]), 15.

30. C. Vann Woodward, *The Strange Career of Jim Crow*, Comm. ed. (New York: Oxford University Press, 2001 [1955]).

31. Philip S. S. Howard, "If You're Thinking of Doing Blackface for Halloween, Just Don't," *The Conversation*, October 25, 2018, https://theconversation.com/if -youre-thinking-of-doing-blackface-for-halloween-just-dont-105620.

32. David J. Leonard, "Just Say No to Blackface: Neo-Minstrelsy and the Power to Dehumanize," *Huffington Post*, August 8, 2012, https://www.huffpost .com/entry/just-say-no-to-blackface_b_1752139.

33. Peter Moore, "Most White Americans Think Black Face Is OK at Halloween," *YouGov*, October 30, 2015, https://today.yougov.com/topics/lifestyle /articles-reports/2015/10/30/most-white-americans-think-black-face-ok-halloween.

34. Lena Williams, "After the Roast, Fire and Smoke," *New York Times*, October 14, 1993, https://www.nytimes.com/1993/10/14/garden/after-the-roast -fire-and-smoke.html.

35. "Kansas Mayor Apologizes for Appearing in Blackface Drag," *Fox News*, January 13, 2015, https://www.foxnews.com/story/kansas-mayor-apologizes-for -appearing-in-blackface-drag.

36. Margaret Eby, "Julianne Hough Dons Blackface for 'Orange Is the New Black' Halloween Costume," *New York Daily News*, October 26, 2013, https:// www.nydailynews.com/entertainment/gossip/julianne-hough-dons-blackface -halloween-costume-article-1.1497396.

37. Andrew Theen, "UO Law Professor Put on Leave for Blackface Costume Is Former Diversity Committee Chair," *The Oregonian*, November 4, 2016, https:// www.oregonlive.com/education/index.ssf/2016/11/uo_law_professor_suspended_for .htm; Scott Jaschik, "Professor Apologizes for Blackface Costume," *Inside Higher Ed*, November 7, 2016, https://www.insidehighered.com/quicktakes/2016/11/07 /professor-apologizes-blackface-costume.

38. Linda Cook, "Iowa Teacher Under Fire for Wearing Blackface at Halloween Party," *Quad-City Times*, October 24, 2018, https://qctimes.com/news/davenport -district-investigates-teacher-who-wore-blackface-to-halloween-party/article _b6320ad1-f98d-5e01-a346-32a247c9eee01.html.

39. Amira Rasool, "Some White Influencers Are Being Accused of 'Blackfishing,' or Using Makeup to Appear Black," *Teen Vogue*, November 16, 2018, https://www .teenvogue.com/story/blackfish-niggerfish-white-influencers-using-makeup-to -appear-black; Wanna Thompson, "How White Women on Instagram Are Profiting Off Black Women," *Paper*, November 14, 2018, http://www.papermag.com/white -women-blackfishing-on-instagram1-2619714094.html?rebelltitem=10#rebelltitem10.

40. Tanya Chen, "A White Teen Is Denying She Is "Posing" as a Black Woman on Instagram After Followers Said They Felt Duped," comment from Ishena Robinson, *Buzzfeed*, November 13, 2018, https://www.buzzfeednews.com

/article/tanyachen/white-instagram-teen-emma-hallberg-accused-of-performing-as.

41. Even in the months since I began writing this book, new high-profile examples have emerged. Ralph Northam, the governor of Virginia, allegedly wore blackface in a medical school yearbook photo, and Mark Herring, the state's attorney general, acknowledged wearing blackface at a party as an undergraduate student. Jonathan Martin and Alan Blinder, "Second Virginia Democrat Says He Wore Blackface, Throwing Party into Turmoil," *New York Times*, February 6, 2019, https://www.nytimes.com/2019/02/06/us/politics/virginia-blackface-mark -herring.html. Other examples of celebrities in blackface abound. See, e.g., Reid Nakamura, "10 Stars Whose Blackface Blunders Backfired, from Ted Danson to Kylie Jenner," *The Wrap*, October 23, 2018, https://www.thewrap.com/9-blackface -star-backfire-ted-danson-julianne-hough-kylie-jenner.

42. Sam Sabin, "Many Adults Call 'Megyn Kelly Today' Cancellation 'Too Harsh,'" *Morning Consult*, October 30, 2018, https://morningconsult.com/2018/10/30 /many-adults-call-megyn-kelly-today-cancellation-too-harsh.

43. Doreen St. Félix, "NBC's Firing of Megyn Kelly Is as Cynical as Her Hiring Was," *The New Yorker*, October 26, 2018, https://www.newyorker.com /culture/culture-desk/nbcs-firing-of-megyn-kelly-is-as-cynical-as-her-hiring-was. St. Félix notes that NBC claims that Harris-Perry quit, not that her show was canceled; Harris-Perry disputes NBC's account.

44. Gabriele Magni and Andrew Reynolds, "The 2018 Blue Wave Included Quite a Few LGBT Wins—Even Though Voters Are Still Wary of Gay and Trans Candidates," *Washington Post*, November 25, 2018, https://www.washingtonpost .com/news/monkey-cage/wp/2018/11/25/the-2018-blue-wave-included-quite-a-few -lgbt-wins-even-though-voters-are-still-wary-of-gay-and-trans-candidates/?utm _term=.54bca3fd9f89.

45. P. R. Lockhart, "Georgia, 2018's Most Prominent Voting Rights Battleground, Explained," *Vox*, November 6, 2018, https://www.vox.com/policy -and-politics/2018/10/26/18024468/georgia-voter suppression-stacey-abrams-brian -kemp-voting-rights.

46. Center for American Women and Politics, "Women of Color in Elective Office 2019," https://cawp.rutgers.edu/women-color-elective-office-2019. Delegate Jennifer Gonzalez of Puerto Rico, a nonvoting member of the house, is a Republican.

47. Paul Kane, "Grassley Suggests Absence of Women on Judiciary Due to Committee's Heavy Workload," *Washington Post*, October 5, 2018, https:// www.washingtonpost.com/powerpost/grassley-suggests-absence-of-women-on -judiciary-due-to-committees-heavy-workload/2018/10/05/b289c0fe-c8e7-11e8 -bred-1d2d65b86doc_story.html?utm_term=.826e6b5362f0.

48. Caitlin Oprysko, "Hyde-Smith's Campaign Says Comment About Suppressing 'Liberal' Votes Was 'A Joke,'" *Politico*, November 16, 2018, https:// www.politico.com/story/2018/11/16/hyde-smith-joke-liberal-voting-995510.

49. Eliza Relman, "The 23 Women Who Have Accused Trump of Sexual Misconduct," *Business Insider*, May 10, 2019, https://www.businessinsider.com /women-accused-trump-sexual-misconduct-list-2017-12.

50. Julie Pace and Lisa Mascaro, "Transcript of the AP's Interview with Mitch McConnell," *Associated Press*, October 10, 2018, https://apnews.com /e27d3b8360e94ae6b512d7409ec24948.

51. Al Weaver, "Dwindling Number of Republican Women on Capitol Hill a Major Headache for GOP," *Washington Examiner*, November 20, 2018, https:// www.washingtonexaminer.com/news/congress/dwindling-number-of-republican -women-on-capitol-hill-a-major-headache-for-gop.

CONCLUSION: WE, IDENTITY CAPITALISTS

1. The social science literature regarding the importance of critical mass to avoiding racial isolation is robust, and many legal scholars have also addressed the issue. The importance of critical mass is not a closely guarded secret. Christine Chambers Goodman, "A Modest Proposal in Deference to Diversity," *National Black Law Journal* 23 (2010): 27–36; Vinay Harpalani, "Fisher's Fishing Expedition," *University of Pennsylvania Journal of Constitutional Law* 15 (2013); William C. Kidder, "The Salience of Racial Isolation: African Americans' and Latinos' Perceptions of Climate and Enrollment with and Without Proposition 209, *Civil Rights Project at UCLA* 13 (October 9, 2012), http://civilrightsproject.ucla.edu/ research/collegeaccess/affirmative-action/the-salience-of-racial-isolation-african -americans2019-andlatinos2019-perceptions-of-climate-and-enrollment-choices-with -and-without-proposition-209/Kidder_Racial-Isolation_CRP_final_Oct2012.pdf.

2. Vinson herself won. By a vote of 9-0, *Meritor v. Vinson* was the first case in which the Supreme Court recognized sexual harassment as a violation of Title VII of the Civil Rights Act of 1964. *Meritor Savings Bank v. Vinson*, 477 U.S. 57 (1986).

3. Conservative attorney and legal scholar Neomi Rao, the daughter of Indian American immigrants, was nominated for Brett Kavanaugh's former seat on the U.S. Court of Appeals for the District of Columbia Circuit. At her hearing, she refused to say whether she believed *Brown v. Board of Education* was correctly decided. Rao was ultimately confirmed by the Senate in a party-line vote of 53 to 46. Sherrilyn Ifill, "If Judicial Nominees Don't Support 'Brown v. Board,' They Don't Support the Rule of Law," *Washington Post*, May 12, 2019, https:// www.washingtonpost.com/opinions/if-judicial-nominees-dont-support-brown -v-board-they-dont-support-the-rule-of-law/2019/05/12/d12c542a-734d-11e9-8be0 -ca575670e91c_story.html?utm_term=.a8b65f5269b8.

INDEX